Home Health Nursing:
A Comprehensive Review of Practical and Professional Issues

WESTERN® SCHOOLS

By
Stephanie Mello Gaskell, MS, MBA, RN

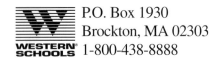

P.O. Box 1930
Brockton, MA 02303
1-800-438-8888

ABOUT THE AUTHOR

Stephanie Mello Gaskell, M.S., M.B.A., R.N. is the Vice President of Clinical Services at the Visiting Nurse Association of Southeastern Massachusetts, Inc. She is a member of the Home Healthcare Nurses Association and is currently on the editorial board of *Home Healthcare Nurse.*

ABOUT THE SUBJECT MATTER REVIEWER

Jane E. Quinn, R.N., M.S., has over 15 years experience in the nursing care of patients within the home care setting. She has held various roles including visiting staff nurse, liaison, Nurse Manager, Clinical Director and most recently Quality Assurance/Performance Improvement Manager. She has provided direct care to patients, coordinated discharge plans so as to transition patients smoothly from acute care to home, provided continual staff education and program development and directed regulatory compliance activities and performance improvement projects within a Visiting Nurse Association.

Copy Editor: Jackie Bonham, M.S.N., R.N.

Indexer: Sylvia Coates

Western Schools' courses are designed to provide nursing professionals with the educational information they need to enhance their career development. The information provided within these course materials is the result of research and consultation with prominent nursing and medical authorities and is, to the best of our knowledge, current and accurate. However, the courses and course materials are provided with the understanding that Western Schools is not engaged in offering legal, nursing, medical, or other professional advice.

Western Schools' courses and course materials are not meant to act as a substitute for seeking out professional advice or conducting individual research. When the information provided in the courses and course materials is applied to individual circumstances, all recommendations must be considered in light of the uniqueness pertaining to each situation.

Western Schools' course materials are intended solely for your use and not for the benefit of providing advice or recommendations to third parties. Western Schools devoids itself of any responsibility for adverse consequences resulting from the failure to seek nursing, medical, or other professional advice. Western Schools further devoids itself of any responsibility for updating or revising any programs or publications presented, published, distributed, or sponsored by Western Schools unless otherwise agreed to as part of an individual purchase contract.

Products (including brand names) mentioned or pictured in Western School's courses are not endorsed by Western Schools, the American Nurses Credentialing Center (ANCC) or any state board.

ISBN: 1-57801-098-5

IMPORTANT: Read these instructions *BEFORE* proceeding!

Enclosed with your course book, you will find the FasTrax® answer sheet. Use this form to answer all the final exam questions that appear in this course book. If you are completing more than one course, be sure to write your answers on the appropriate answer sheet. Full instructions and complete grading details are printed on the FasTrax instruction sheet, also enclosed with your order. Please review them before starting. *If you are mailing your answer sheet(s) to Western Schools, we recommend you make a copy as a backup.*

ABOUT THIS COURSE

A Pretest is provided with each course to test your current knowledge base regarding the subject matter contained within this course. Your Final Exam is a multiple choice examination. **You will find the exam questions at the end of each chapter.** Some smaller hour courses include the exam at the end of the book.

In the event the course has less than 100 questions, mark your answers to the questions in the course book and leave the remaining answer boxes on the FasTrax answer sheet blank. **Use a <u>black</u> pen to fill in your answer sheet.**

A PASSING SCORE

You must score 70% or better in order to pass this course and receive your Certificate of Completion. Should you fail to achieve the required score, we will send you an additional FasTrax answer sheet so that you may make a second attempt to pass the course. Western Schools will allow you three chances to pass the same course…*at no extra charge!* After three failed attempts to pass the same course, your file will be closed.

RECORDING YOUR HOURS

Please monitor the time it takes to complete this course using the handy log sheet on the other side of this page. See below for transferring study hours to the course evaluation.

COURSE EVALUATIONS

In this course book, you will find a short evaluation about the course you are soon to complete. This information is vital to providing Western Schools with feedback on this course. The course evaluation answer section is in the lower right hand corner of the FasTrax answer sheet marked "Evaluation," with answers marked 1–16. Your answers are important to us; please take a few minutes to complete the evaluation.

On the back of the FasTrax instruction sheet, there is additional space to make any comments about the course, the school, and suggested new curriculum. Please mail the FasTrax instruction sheet, with your comments, back to Western Schools in the envelope provided with your course order.

TRANSFERRING STUDY TIME

Upon completion of the course, transfer the total study time from your log sheet to question 16 in the course evaluation. The answers will be in ranges; please choose the proper hour range that best represents your study time. You **MUST** log your study time under question 16 on the course evaluation.

EXTENSIONS

You have two (2) years from the date of enrollment to complete this course. A six (6) month extension may be purchased. If after 30 months from the original enrollment date you do not complete the course, *your file will be closed and no certificate can be issued.*

CHANGE OF ADDRESS?

In the event you have moved during the completion of this course, please call our student services department at 1-800-618-1670, and we will update your file.

A GUARANTEE TO WHICH YOU'LL GIVE HIGH HONORS

If any continuing education course fails to meet your expectations or if you are not satisfied in any manner, for any reason, you may return it for an exchange or a refund (less shipping and handling) within 30 days. Software, video, and audio courses must be returned unopened.

Thank you for enrolling at Western Schools!

WESTERN SCHOOLS
P.O. Box 1930
Brockton, MA 02303
(800) 438-8888
www.westernschools.com

Home Health Nursing:
A Comprehensive Review of Practical and Professional Issues

WESTERN SCHOOLS

P.O. Box 1930
Brockton, MA 02303

Please use this log to total the number of hours you spend reading the text and taking the final examination (use 50-min hours).

Date	Hours Spent
————	————
————	————
————	————
————	————
————	————
————	————
————	————
————	————
————	————
————	————
————	————
————	————
————	————
————	————

TOTAL

Please log your study hours with submission of your final exam. To log your study time, fill in the appropriate circle under question 16 of the FasTrax® answer sheet under the Evaluation section.

Home Health Nursing: A Comprehensive Review of Practical and Professional Issues

WESTERN SCHOOLS
CONTINUING EDUCATION EVALUATION

Instructions: Mark your answers to the following questions with a black pen on the "Evaluation" section of your FasTrax® answer sheet provided with this course. You should not return this sheet. Please use the scale below to rate the following statements:

A	Agree Strongly	C	Disagree Somewhat
B	Agree Somewhat	D	Disagree Strongly

The course content met the following education objectives:

1. Identified the major events that have shaped home healthcare as it is known today.

2. Discussed the utility of the Code of Ethics for Nurses as it applies to home healthcare today.

3. Stated the six standards of practice for home healthcare nursing and applied them to patient scenarios.

4. Listed the eight standards and described their functionality in the day-to-day activities of the home healthcare nurse.

5. Stated the eight key components of an agency and described their interrelationships. In addition, described the Medicare Conditions of Participation.

6. Demonstrated the OASIS assessment and its indications for use.

7. Described how the agency can use OASIS data in its performance improvement activities.

8. Described the five major principles of the Medicare Prospective Payment System for home healthcare reimbursement.

9. Discussed the rules that govern the provision of Medicare home healthcare services.

10. The content of this course was relevant to the objectives.

11. This offering met my professional education needs.

12. The objectives met the overall purpose/goal of the course.

13. The course was generally well-written and the subject matter explained thoroughly. (If no, please explain on the back of the FasTrax instruction sheet.)

14. The content of this course was appropriate for home study.

15. The final examination was well-written and at an appropriate level for the content of the course.

16. **PLEASE LOG YOUR STUDY HOURS WITH SUBMISSION OF YOUR FINAL EXAM.**
    Please choose which best represents the total study hours it took to complete this 30-hour course.

    A. less than 25 hours

    B. 25–28 hours

    C. 29–32 hours

    D. greater than 32 hours

CONTENTS

BOXES, FIGURES, AND TABLES

PRETEST

1. Begin this course by taking the pretest. Circle the answers to the questions right on this page, or write answers on a separate sheet of paper. Do not log answers to the pretest questions on the FasTrax test sheet included with the course.

2. Compare your answers to the PRETEST KEY located in the back of the book. The pretest answer key indicates the course chapter where the content of that question will be discussed. Make note of the questions you missed, so that you can focus on those areas as you complete the course.

3. Complete the course by reading each chapter and completing the exam questions at the end of the chapter. Answers to these exam questions should be logged on the FasTrax test sheet included with the course.

1. During the earliest part of the 19th century nursing care in the United States was primarily provided by

   a. religious groups whose vocation was to alleviate the physical and spiritual suffering of man.

   b. nurses trained in the Florence Nightingale School of Nursing.

   c. middle class women who could afford the formal education and training required by law.

   d. lower and working class lay caregivers.

2. The first visiting nurse services were established by

   a. local and state departments of health to combat infectious disease.

   b. wealthy and upper class women to meet the unique needs of their communities.

   c. hospital administrators as a means to increase the capacity of inpatient beds.

   d. nurses to assure a professional practice environment.

3. A Code of Ethics

   a. is a legal document.

   b. provides a detailed explanation of the services that one can expect.

   c. applies to nurses regardless of the polices of an employer or a practice setting.

   d. is not directly applicable to day-to-day or routine activities.

4. The patient's right to confidentiality

   a. can never be violated regardless of the situation or circumstance.

   b. is an inalienable human right.

   c. does not apply to patients receiving home health care service because all of the team members have to know all of the patient related details to establish an appropriate plan of care.

   d. is only valid between a patient and their doctor or lawyer.

5. Each nurse must be accountable for their own practice and must be adequately prepared to carry out every function that they are being asked to perform. If the nurse is asked to carry out a function that they are not adequately prepared for, the nurse should

   a. complete the function as assigned.

   b. complete the function and then report dissatisfaction about the assignment to the agency's administrator.

   c. avoid attempting to carry out the function and jeopardize the patient's well-being.

   d. recognize that the home care setting is low-tech and in all likelihood the professional nurse will not ever run into this issue.

6. The term "information system" refers to

   a. the agency's computer system.

   b. information that is transmitted electronically from a referral source or physician.

   c. the patient's medical record or database.

   d. only agencies that have a complete electronic medical record.

7. According to the American Nurses' Association, advocating for the patient, teaching self care skills, and incorporating evidenced-based knowledge into practice are typically responsibilities associated with

   a. only nurses functioning in an advanced practice role.

   b. only nurses functioning in the generalist role.

   c. the licensed practical nurse's responsibilities.

   d. both the nurse generalist and the advanced practice registered nurse.

8. In home healthcare, best practice identification

   a. is not a realistic expectation due to the number of social variables.

   b. is solely the responsibility of the management team and advanced practice nurses.

   c. serves to establish standards which provide clear direction related to the provision of patient care.

   d. can only be accomplished when the agency seeks the expertise from a hospital or nursing school faculty.

9. An organization's culture

   a. is the tone set by management and the collective bargaining unit.

   b. contributes to the development of a supportive work environment and is the collective of the individual attitudes.

   c. is not the responsibility of nursing.

   d. is the responsibility of the Human Resource Department.

10. The role of the professional nurse in home care includes addressing issues of resource utilization and cost of care because

   a. patients have an inalienable right to health care.

   b. the nurse must carefully balance the cost of care with the amount of reimbursement and services provided.

   c. patients without insurance should receive less care than insured patients.

   d. patients have the right to be informed about the risks, benefits, and cost of their care.

11. The Conditions of Participation

    a. outline the basic organizational and over-sight structure for the certified home healthcare agency.

    b. are optional for agencies that were established before 1965.

    c. are optional for agencies that were established as a result of the Stagger's law suit.

    d. are only applicable to not-for-profit home healthcare agencies.

12. The collection and analysis of standardized patient data allows the Center for Medicare and Medicaid Services to

    a. penalize agencies with poor outcomes.

    b. provide financial rewards to agencies that achieve the best patient outcomes.

    c. identify agencies with best practices.

    d. eliminate agencies with poor performance from participating in the Medicare home healthcare program.

13. Regulations require agencies to incorporate the OASIS items into their comprehensive patient assessment tools. The regulations also mandate that agencies

    a. reorder the questions so that they flow within the agency assessment document.

    b. do not take liberties with the punctuation or wording of any of the questions.

    c. eliminate the MO prefix, which delineates the OASIS item as a mandatory question.

    d. read the question to the patient and ask the patient to choose the answer that best describes their status.

14. The OASIS User's Manual instructs the home healthcare nurse to answer based on the

    a. patient at their worst.

    b. patient at their best.

    c. patient's ability at least 50% of the time.

    d. patient's status most of the time on the day when the patient assessment is being conducted.

15. The implementation of OASIS has enabled agencies to measure

    a. patient satisfaction.

    b. referral source satisfaction.

    c. both aggregate and individual patient outcomes.

    d. staff efficiency.

16. The ability to benchmark an agency's performance is important because

    a. an agency can gain a competitive edge by identifying weakness in the performance of other agencies.

    b. it makes it possible to set realistic patient outcome goals.

    c. clinicians with poor performance can be identified and disciplined.

    d. the agency expects that JCAHO and the Department of Public Health surveys will be eliminated for the best performers.

17. The Medicare Prospective Payment System is based on

    a. the agency's ability to attract the patient that will result in the highest reimbursement.

    b. the agency's ability to avoid accepting patients that will result in low reimbursement or require high levels of service.

    c. agencies managing a balance of profitable and losing episodes.

    d. the number of visits provided to the patient.

18. The fee-for-service reimbursement structure

    a) always requires the completion of an OASIS.

    b) generally allows the visiting clinician to control the number of visits the patient will receive.

    c) generally requires that the number of visits provided to the patient be controlled by the insurance company or case reviewer.

    d) always results in a profitable PPS episode for the agency.

19. Which of the following would disqualify a patient from receiving Medicare home health services?

    a) the patient's ability to pay for services

    b) the patient's inability to visit the physician office at least every six months

    c) the absence of a caregiver in the home

    d) the patient requiring home health services on a daily basis with no end point in sight

20. The determination of reasonable and necessary care depends on the

    a) physician's definition.

    b) nurse's definition.

    c) individualized and unique needs of the patient.

    d) written request from the referral source.

INTRODUCTION

This course is intended to meet the needs of registered nurses who practice in home healthcare by providing a comprehensive review of both practical and professional issues. This course will provide the inexperienced home healthcare nurse with the information necessary to develop the skills associated with a successful home healthcare practitioner. The experienced home healthcare nurse will find opportunities to reflect on the professional implications of practicing in this complex setting.

As with any subject of study, it is important to start at the beginning. For that reason, Chapter 1 describes the evolution of home healthcare as it is known today. Chapters 2, 3, and 4 present issues of professional practice including ethics, practice, and standards. Illustrative case examples are provided to clarify concepts and principles.

Chapter 5 provides a description of the home healthcare agency's structure. This chapter is broken down into the eight functions that are common to agencies regardless of their size and geographic location. In addition, a review of the Medicare Conditions of Participation provide the reader with insight to the role the Federal government plays in the provision of home healthcare services.

The Outcome and Assessment Information Set (OASIS) is presented in Chapter 6. The intent of this chapter is to highlight the intricacies and details that every home healthcare nurse must consider when they are completing these documents.

No home care study course would be complete without a discussion of home healthcare reimbursement and and applications of Medicare reimbursement rules. Chapter 7 provides a discussion of the home healthcare Prospective Payment System and utilizes real-life case examples to highlight the concepts discussed. The applications of Outcome-Based Quality Improvement and Outcome-Based Quality Monitoring initiatives are presented in Chapter 8. Since Medicare is the single largest purchaser of home healthcare services, a discussion of the qualifying and coverage criteria provided in the Federal Health Insurance Manual are presented in Chapter 9.

CHAPTER 1

EVOLUTION OF HOME HEALTHCARE

CHAPTER OBJECTIVE

At the completion of this chapter, the reader will be able to identify the major events that have shaped home healthcare as it is known today.

LEARNING OBJECTIVES

After studying this chapter, the reader will be able to

1. identify Florence Nightingale's contribution and influence on the practice of Home Healthcare.

2. recall the evolution and mission of the first Visiting Nurse Services in the United States.

3. recognize the accomplishments of Lillian Wald and her impact on modern Home Healthcare.

4. state at least two pieces of Federal legislature that have impacted the Home Healthcare industry.

INTRODUCTION

The nursing profession in the United States can trace its roots back to the late 1700s. Long before there was a formal healthcare system and schools of nursing, lay nurses provided in-home care to their family, friends and neighbors.

As people immigrated from rural villages to large urban centers in the 1800s, public health nurses were providing care in many communities. The Women's Suffrage movement of the 1920s expanded the rights and opportunities for women, and the nursing profession provided them with a forum to exercise these new found freedoms. As American culture evolved from its puritan colonial past to a modern diverse society, the practice of nursing has also advanced to meet the needs of the patients, and communities in the 21st century.

For over two centuries, home healthcare has changed and remained ready to meet the needs of communities and citizens. To understand the role of home healthcare today and recognize the potential of the future, one must understand from where this profession and industry emerged.

THE 1700s

During the 1700s, care of the sick was the responsibility of religious groups whose vocation was to alleviate physical suffering and tend to the spiritual needs of the patient. Suffering and illness were believed to be the result of evil spirits or retribution from God for one's misdeeds. Due to ignorance, fear and superstitious beliefs, the infirm were ostracized and segregated from their community and family.

The Boston Dispensary, founded in 1796, was one of the earliest healthcare organizations in the United States. The Dispensary was organized around the following three principles:

- Care of the sick could be provided in the patient's home, and the pain caused by separation and segregation from one's family and community could be avoided;

- The home was the least expensive environment for care; and

- Care of those who needed charity could be provided in a confidential and respectable way (The Boston Dispensary, 1955).

The Boston Dispensary provided organization to lay caregivers who remained the primary providers of health services. In 1801, the Boston Dispensary became incorporated and formed the first Visiting Doctors Association, where many well-known physicians were trained. In 1886, the Instructive Nursing Association was established as part of the Boston Dispensary and later evolved into what is now known as the Boston Visiting Nurse Association (The Boston Dispensary, 1955).

1800-1880

The period from 1800 to 1880 is characterized by two major events in American history. The American Civil War, fought from 1860 to 1865, marked the beginning of the Industrial Revolution. These events, coupled with the teachings and publications of London's Florence Nightingale, greatly influenced the development and advancement of formalized nursing and home healthcare during this period.

Influence of Florence Nightingale

Florence Nightingale, born in 1820, was raised by an affluent British family. As a young adult, she was interested in many of the social questions and ills of British society. Consistent with the social norms of this era, her family refused to allow her to pursue her interests in nursing, since it was not a suitable profession for educated well-bred women (History of Nursing, 2002).

In an effort to distract Florence from her desire to work in nursing, her family sanctioned a tour of Europe with family friends. While in Germany, she met the superintendent of the Kaisersworth School for Nurses, who served to heighten her interest in caring for the ill and the poor.

Contrary to her family's wishes, Nightingale remained in Germany where she received three months of formal nurse training. Upon her return to Britain in 1853, she qualified for the Superintendent's position at the Institute for the Care of Sick Gentlewomen in Distressed Circumstances (History of Nursing, 2002). Florence Nightingale remained in this position until she was recruited by the British military during the Crimean War.

In 1854 Britain, France and Turkey declared war on Russia. During this time, the British military was highly criticized by the British press for the inadequate care of soldiers and military casualties. Florence Nightingale was placed in charge of introducing female nurses into military hospitals in Turkey. Initially, physicians were not responsive to the presence of nurses in military hospitals, however as they became overwhelmed with the number of casualties, the contributions of the nurses were welcomed. The work of these 38 nurses resulted in improvements in the environment and the morale in the hospitals and barracks (The Florence Nightingale Story, 1999).

In 1860, the Florence Nightingale's Training School for Nurses was established. Nurses in training (Probationers) received one year of experience on the wards of St. Thomas Hospital. Once nurses completed their formal training, they staffed hospitals in Britain, Europe and the United States.

Although Nightingale oversaw the training of the Probationers, it was during this time that she wrote *Notes on Nursing: What It Is and What It Is Not,* which outlined her observations and concepts of nursing and patient care (The Florence Nightingale Story, 1999). In this publication,

Nightingale theorized that although an important role of nurses was to care for the sick, it was more important that they care for the well in an effort to avoid sickness all together. She also wrote about the notion that nurses should not be educated and managed by hospitals and doctors. Instead, she advocated for a "matron of nurses" who would be responsible for the education and practice of nursing (History of Nursing, 2002). In addition, she published many writings about healthcare organizations and healthcare systems.

It was Nightingale's concept that organized nurses into geographic districts to provide home healthcare in Britain's neighborhoods and communities. This model was later expanded to the cities of the United States as a means to combat communicable disease and other social ills of the 19th century.

Florence Nightingale was the recipient of many "firsts." In recognition of her war time efforts, she was the first female appointed to the Royal Commission of the British Army and the first female fellow of the British Statistical Society (The Florence Nightingale Story, 1999). Her greatest accomplishment was to advance the standing of nursing from an undesirable endeavor for the well-bred and educated to a profession that continues to have the highest ethical and moral standards (The Florence Nightingale Story, 1999).

INDUSTRIAL REVOLUTION

During the earliest part of the 19th century, growth of American cities was phenomenal. People immigrated from rural towns and villages and from European countries in search of employment in American factories. These growing cities lacked hospital beds and adequate housing and were complicated by cultural and language differences. During this expansion, great strides were being made in the advancement of both the arts and sciences. Class distinction and separation was com-

mon. Women of the middle and upper class were not allowed to work outside of the home. Instead, they were expected to pursue artistic and philanthropic endeavors.

Nursing care in the early part of the 19th century was provided by working and lower class women. They were untrained and functioned as lay nurses, despite the lack of any formal healthcare system. Lay nurses were generally employed by individuals to assist them to care for a sick family member. Home care was provided by one or two lay nurses, who usually worked for a family 24 hours a day, six or seven days a week. Early public health services were provided by volunteers, or if the community was lucky, services were provided under the direction of at least one trained nurse.

This period of nursing in the United States was informal and unregulated. Organized nurse training was not available until 1872 when the first two schools of nursing were opened in Philadelphia and Boston (History of Nursing, 1996). It was not until 1873 and the opening of three additional schools, that the principles of infection control, taught and published by Florence Nightingale, were incorporated into the curricula.

The growing cities of the 1800s created environments of poverty, inadequate sanitation and food storage and poor personal hygiene. These factors, coupled with crowded conditions, accelerated the spread of infectious and communicable disease. Morbidity and mortality from these conditions was high among the very young and the very old. To combat these conditions, New York City established the Division of Child Hygiene in 1880 and hired trained nurses to reduce infant mortality (Helping and Healing People, 2002). These public health nurses made home visits and taught mothers and their families how to provide a sanitary environment for their infants.

Recognizing the benefits of having trained nurses, many communities began to support the establishment of a public health nurse service, and the demand for formally trained nurses grew. In addition to working for agencies supported by local governments, trained nurses were also employed by local visiting nurse services. During this era, wealthy and upper class members of society provided the financial resources necessary to secure and support the development of their local visiting nurse service. Each organization was structured in a manner that met the needs of the community in which it was located, and the scope of the agency's service was often dictated by the interests of the group or individuals providing the financing. The District Nurse Association of Fall River Massachusetts was incorporated for:

> "The purpose of promoting the social and physical well-being of the citizens of Fall River; supplying the needy with necessary articles; providing medical, surgical and nursing attendance and means of instruction; and, in general, doing what may be done for improving social conditions in the city of Fall River."

(Certificate of Corporation provided
by the Commonwealth of Massachusetts to the
District Nurse Association of Fall River, April 12, 1912)

1880-1929

By 1890, there were 21 Visiting Nurse Associations (VNAs) in the United States, and the number was growing rapidly. Although organizations became more sophisticated in structure, their purpose remained largely as it did in the 1800s – to care for the physically ill and the poor.

Poverty and infectious disease continued to plague citizens. By 1909, tuberculosis was responsible for hundreds of deaths on a daily basis. Metropolitan Life, a life insurance company for working families, found itself paying approximately 20% of its claims to victims of tuberculosis (Helping and Healing People, 2002). Haley Fiske, the vice president of Metropolitan Life at that time,

announced that the company's philosophy was about to change. He stated that "insurance is not merely a business proposition but a social program" and then took an aggressive two-pronged approach to combat tuberculosis (Helping and Healing People, 2002).

First, in 1909, Metropolitan Life published and distributed a pamphlet titled *A War on Consumption* as a means to teach citizens methods to reduce the spread of the infection (Helping and Healing People, 2002). The second, and most notable endeavor it undertook was to collaborate with Lillian Wald, a nurse recognized for her commitment to social reform and care of the city's poor.

Lillian Wald had already established and was directing the operations of the Henry Street Settlement House (later known as the Visiting Nurse Service of New York) and was already providing home visits to New York residents (Profiles in Caring, 1996-2003). Ms. Wald convinced Metropolitan Life executives to participate in a three-month pilot program to evaluate the effectiveness of in-home services in the reduction of deaths related to tuberculosis.

The pilot was so successful that Metropolitan Life extended its home care benefit to policyholders in many American cities. Metropolitan Life employed a nursing force of their own to deliver care in areas where there were no organized visiting nurse services. In addition to tuberculosis, these nurses treated policyholders for common ailments such as diphtheria, influenza and smallpox.

The success of these programs supported Metropolitan Life's expansion of the home healthcare benefit to over 20 million policyholders in 7000 cities (Helping and Healing People, 2002). At the height of the program, home care was provided to approximately 35 of every 1000 Metropolitan Life beneficiaries free of charge. By 1924, over 3000 communities could boast of having their own visiting nurse service. Other insurance companies, such as John Hancock in Boston, began similar programs.

As Metropolitan Life was expanding the availability of home healthcare to its policyholders, the American Red Cross also recognized the benefit of community-based nurses and began developing a national nursing service. The American Red Cross had already demonstrated their ability to train and mobilize nurses to care for the casualties of war.

Under the guidance of Clara Barton, Red Cross nurses were successful at reducing the spread of infection and alleviating pain and suffering of soldiers during the Spanish-American War. Nurses found the conditions of the soldiers and the camps deplorable. One nurse reported; "desperately sick fever patients, United States soldiers on United States soil were lying on the cots between heavy military blankets, no sheets, no pillows, no towels, no mosquito netting although they were being tormented beyond words by mosquitoes, flies and sand fleas" (American Red Cross , 2000, p. 3).

The Army officers and President McKinley recognized that without the help and contribution of the Red Cross nurses the entire military operation would have been at risk. Recognizing the success of the Nursing Corp, the Red Cross changed its focus to develop a program to assure that there would be a volunteer nurse in every American community. The administration of the Red Cross envisioned a legion of Red Cross nurses that could be mobilized in times of crisis such as flood, fire, or war.

Jane A. Delano, the Superintendent of the Army Nurse Corps, was charged with the development of a Red Cross Nursing Service. Despite the lack of trained nurses nationwide by the time the United States entered World War I, there were 18,000 nurses ready to serve their country (American Red Cross, 2000). Although many of the nurses remained in the United States, nearly 9,000 served war casualties in American field hospitals in France (American Red Cross, 2000). The

nurses who remained in the United States were responsible for assuring the health and sanitation of more than 50 American Army and Naval bases (American Red Cross, 2000).

Between October and November of 1918, the home healthcare nurses who were so successful at combating the tuberculosis epidemic in 1909 were once again put to the test. The influenza epidemic of 1918 stretched the resources of every healthcare provider in the cities, suburbs, and county. Unlike the tuberculosis epidemic, the influenza epidemic began and ended in roughly eight weeks. The cooperative efforts between the Red Cross Nurses and the Visiting Nurse Service were responsible for limiting the devastating influenza epidemic of 1918.

Permellia Murnan Doty was the Executive Secretary of the Nurses Emergency Council in 1918; she described how communities mobilized any able-bodied individual to assist in hospitals, clinics and in homes. Communities organized headquarters from which all operations were directed. Radio announcements and handbills instructed volunteers where to report for an assignment. Ms. Doty wrote: "For this work women were needed who were not only willing to take care of the sick but also to help with household affairs. It was of course, a good deal of a risk to send untrained women about whom we knew so little, into the homes to care for desperately ill people, but under the circumstances it was the only thing to do" (Doty, 1919, p. 951).

In the article *A Retrospect of the Influenza Epidemic,* Doty described the conditions that visiting nurses found patients and their families in. She stated, "Nurses were finding many households where whole families were ill, or perhaps a mother and several children, without anyone to give them even the simplest nursing care. Some patients were critically ill. Because of the prejudice against hospitals, which was doubtless accentuated during the epidemic by reports of so many deaths in institutions, it was necessary that someone be found to stay with the sick in the homes-since many people refused to allow their friends and relatives to be taken to the hospital" (Doty, 1919, p. 954). Despite the heroic efforts of the nurses during the influenza epidemic, 700,000 American lives were lost (The American Experience, 2002).

At the end of the influenza epidemic, the home healthcare nurses returned to their role as health educators and direct care providers. They continued to teach about modes of disease transmission and prevention; infant and child care and also provided direct care to the acutely ill. During this period, the model of having one nurse care for many families evolved as the most efficient means for a limited number of professional nurses to have the greatest impact on the community they served. During this time, the services of professional nurs-

---

BOX 1-1

February 19, 1915

Dear Sir:

I have your letter of February 17th, and before submitting it to the Board of Managers should like to know more definitely what your proposition covers.

We (the Fall River District Nurse Association) undertake to care for all persons in the City needing nursing attention so far as time of our nurses will allow. Various corporations pay the expense of five nurses; the Anti-Tuberculosis Society pays the expense of another; the Union Hospital contributes $1200 a year, thus obliging us to care for discharged patients requiring dressings and other service in their homes; the Metropolitan Life Insurance Company pays 50 cents a visit: and it is, of course, our first duty to see that the work which we undertake for this is satisfactorily performed. After this is done, the nurses give their attention to calls coming from individuals, making a charge of 50 cents per visit when the patients are able to pay, but otherwise rendering free service. As result of all these activities, our corps of ten nurses is already fully occupied, and we cannot see how we can undertake any further obligations without adding to our nursing force, and this we are unable to do without addition to our funds.

We recognize the importance of following up discharged patients, by inducing them to return to clinics, in accordance with instructions, and also by rendering such nursing care as may be necessary at the homes, and should be very glad to assist in this work if we had nurses available, but we cannot see how it can be accomplished unless the expense of such work is covered.

It has been our experience that patients may be discharged from the hospital, if properly cared for at the home, at an earlier date than would otherwise be possible, with resulting good to the patient and economy to the hospital; and we also believe that may be accomplished more economically and efficiently by a district nursing service than by a single nurse because of the acquaintanceship of each nurse in her district and the saving of travel. We do not know how many such cases would develop from the City Hospitals. If only a few and the Hospital were willing to take the chance of a nurse's time being available, the Board of Managers would probably be glad to authorize us to do what we could. But even a call to induce a patient to report at a clinic often requires much time for persuasion, and nursing call require even more time. Our nurses are able to make between eight and nine visits a day on the average; and the cost for each nurse, including supplies and carfare, approximates $800.00 a year.

Yours truly, L.

es were also sought to staff hospitals, to work for private businesses and to care for private individuals. The services of the visiting nurses were also frequently requested by other community-based or social service organizations that identified people in need of healthcare services. Box 1-1 contains the response of the administrator from one agency to one such request.

1930-1955

Between 1930 and 1940, there was a major shift in the provision of healthcare in the United States. This post World War II era saw the rapid advancement of science and the subsequent decline of infectious disease as the major health problem. Instead, the growth of chronic and acute illness emerged.

The shift from community-based to hospital-based healthcare was rapid. Although more costly, hospital care was available to all social classes and became the primary source of healthcare for American citizens. Advances in healthcare increased the numbers of chronically ill and the elderly in the population.

The availability of hospital care diminished the need for home-based services and, by the early 1950s, Metropolitan Life eliminated its home health benefit, and the American Red Cross closed the national nursing service. However, the local visiting nurse services that were previously established continued to receive financial support from charitable donors and local governments. The visiting nurse services carried on their tradition of infection control, healthy lifestyle education, caring for the poor and addressing the social ills in their communities.

1955-1964

Hospital costs that resulted from caring for the growing number of chronically ill and elderly had risen dramatically. By 1955, the value and cost savings associated with home healthcare services was once again sought. Like the Boston Dispensary of the 1700s, society's attitude toward home healthcare services shifted. The healthcare system once again began to recognize that the patient's own home was perhaps the most efficient place for care. This realization spawned the development of hospital-based home health agencies and community-based homemaker services, in addition to the visiting nurse services that already existed. All of these agencies continued to depend on the generosity of charitable organizations and private foundations for funding. In addition, some funding was received from town and city governments as a means to care for their citizens.

1965-1987

The demand for these programs by the growing number of patients was beyond the scope and resources of most agencies. Despite the generosity of philanthropic endeavors, agencies could not meet the needs of all who required care. In 1965, in an effort to meet patient needs while reducing costs, the Federal Government enacted Medicare legislation establishing a home health benefit for beneficiaries. The Medicare home health benefit would ignite the most significant growth of home healthcare services to date. The original benefit provided financial reimbursement for the provision of skilled nursing. Due to patient needs, coverage was later expanded to provide services of the medical social worker, physical, speech and occupational therapist, as well as home health aide.

To participate in the Medicare reimbursement system, the Center for Medicare and Medicaid Services (CMS) established a process to "certify" agencies. Initially, only not-for-profit organizations were certified to receive reimbursement for providing home healthcare services to Medicare beneficiaries.

Medicare home health benefits were primarily available only to those over 65 years of age; however, CMS required each state to provide a home health benefit to qualified elderly and the poor through their state funded Medicaid programs. Finally, the Older Americans Act of 1965 solidified the home health benefit as it required both the Federal and state governments to design programs to assist and support elders to remain in their homes and avoid costly facility-based care and institutionalization.

Initially, reimbursement was intended for home health services that were the result of at least a three-day hospital stay. For beneficiaries to be eligible, they had to be strictly homebound, and the services had to be short-term and recuperative in nature. These criteria severely limited the utilization of this benefit by Medicare beneficiaries. At this time (1965), there were approximately 1,275 organizations certified by Medicare to provide home health services to Medicare beneficiaries (Reichley, 1999).

The growth in the number of certified agencies from the inception of the Medicare certification in 1965 to the 1980s and 1990s was phenomenal. In testimony provided to the House Commerce Subcommittee on Health and Environment, Bruce Vladeck, the Administrator of the Center of Medicare and Medicaid Services, estimated that the number of agencies certified to receive Medicare reimbursement in 1982 was approximately 3,125 (On Reforming Medicare..., 1997). Many of these agencies were small local organizations that provided care to friends and neighbors.

Recognizing this growth and the expense implications associated with it, the Center for Medicare and Medicaid Services implemented new policies aimed at slowing the proliferation and cer-

tification of new home healthcare agencies. In essence, this policy would reduce the availability of rapidly expanding home health services, hence curbing the growth.

The Center for Medicare and Medicaid Services used medical record review as a mechanism to "teach" home healthcare providers to properly administer the Medicare benefit. Although CMS always conducted a limited amount of medical record review, more stringent medical review policies and procedures were implemented. Claims were reviewed from both a clinical and technical perspective.

The decision to review a claim required the home health agency to photocopy and mail a portion (usually one month's documentation) of the medical record to Medicare. Records were then evaluated for indicators such as the reasonableness and necessity of services. If a Medicare reviewer did not agree that the services provided by the agency were reasonable and necessary, the reviewer had the authority to deny payment for the claim.

1987-1997

In 1987, as a result of a public outcry related to reduced access to home care services, a Congressional Delegation led by senators Harley Staggers and Claude Pepper filed and won a lawsuit against CMS. This resulted in an easing of the restrictions used by CMS to govern and control the home health industry (Reichley, 1999). The easing of medical review policies, the elimination of the three-day hospital stay eligibility requirement and the broadening of homebound criteria and certification requirements ignited the growth in the home care industry that CMS would find problematic in the 1990s.

Until the Staggers lawsuit, all Medicare certified home healthcare providers were required to be not-for-profit organizations. One of the unanticipated effects of the easing of the certification restrictions was the entry of for-profit providers into the home healthcare field.

In addition, the easing of the restrictions and decreased medical review encouraged home health agencies to provide large numbers of visits to beneficiaries. An agency would bill Medicare for every visit it provided to the beneficiary, and Medicare would reimburse up to $120 for each nursing visit. This visit-based reimbursement system created an incentive to provide large numbers of visits to Medicare beneficiaries. Unfortunately, these circumstances led to the proliferation of less scrupulous agencies which defrauded the Medicare trust fund.

In his testimony to the Subcommittee on Health and Environment in March of 1997, Bruce Vladeck asserted that approximately 25% of all home health claims were inappropriate or outright fraudulent (On Reforming Medicare..., 1997). Vladeck provided examples of unscrupulous providers who billed for services provided to patients who were deceased and agencies that billed Medicare for services that were never provided to beneficiaries who never existed (On Reforming Medicare..., 1997). He cited examples where foreign nationals obtained Medicare certification and had Medicare payments sent to their countries of origin without ever providing any patient care.

1997-2002

By the mid 1990s, the industry peaked to over 10,000 home health providers, and CMS was once again on the move to control costs. In an effort to again curb the growth and spending on home health service, CMS introduced the concept of a prospective payment system (PPS).

Changing from a visit-based reimbursement system to a prospective payment system was not a new concept. During the 1980s, hospital systems shifted from a fee-for-service system to a diagnostic related group (DRG) reimbursement system, as did the nursing home industry in the early 1990s. Simply stated, under PPS a provider receives a fixed dollar amount to provide care for a patient based on the severity of the patient's clinical status for a finite period of time.

The Balanced Budget Act signed by President Clinton in August 1997 put the home health industry on notice that effective October 1, 1997, reimbursement would be capped. The period from October 1, 1997 to October 1, 2000 was known as the interim payment system (IPS). IPS was designed to limit the amount Medicare would pay to the agency regardless of the number of visits it provided to the patient. These limits were intended to prepare the home healthcare industry for the transition to PPS effective October 1, 2000.

Provisions mandated by the Balanced Budget Act and enforced by CMS, were based on the perception that the home health industry was fraught with fraud (On Reforming Medicare, 1997). The Balanced Budget Act provided a multitude of strategies to reduce fraud and abuse. To meet the outlined objectives, agencies had to:

- Alter billing practices;
- Secure surety bonds;
- Undergo increased scrutiny of medical records;
- Withstand increased payment denials;
- Institute the electronic transmission of clinical data to both state and federal agencies;
- Administer changing interpretations of beneficiary eligibility criteria;
- Reduce services; and
- Cut the costs of operations.

As a result, the perception of the home care industry was that it was under siege. From 1997 to 2000, over 4000 agencies closed. Those that remained open hoped that the implementation of PPS would provide both regulatory and financial relief. To survive, agencies had to change quickly to maximize efficiency. Only 6000 agencies were successful in making these rapid, wide-spread changes.

2000-2002

As of October 1, 2000, Medicare has reimbursed home healthcare agencies for service to beneficiaries via the Prospective Payment Model. In general, after the clinician completes the patient assessment, the agency receives one payment to manage all of the patient's home healthcare for the next sixty days. Although some agencies have fared well in this system and even managed to generate a

profit, the Balanced Budget Act of 1997 required another 15% cut in home health reimbursement effective October 1, 2002. (See Figure 1-1.)

WHAT IS HOME HEALTHCARE IN THE 21ST CENTURY?

Often the terms Home Healthcare Nurse, Public Health Nurse and Community Health Nurse are used interchangeably. Although the entire nursing profession's roots are community-based, home health, public health, and community health nursing are distinct areas of practice.

FIGURE 1-1: NUMBER OF MEDICARE CERTIFIED HOME HEALTHCARE AGENCIES 1925-2000

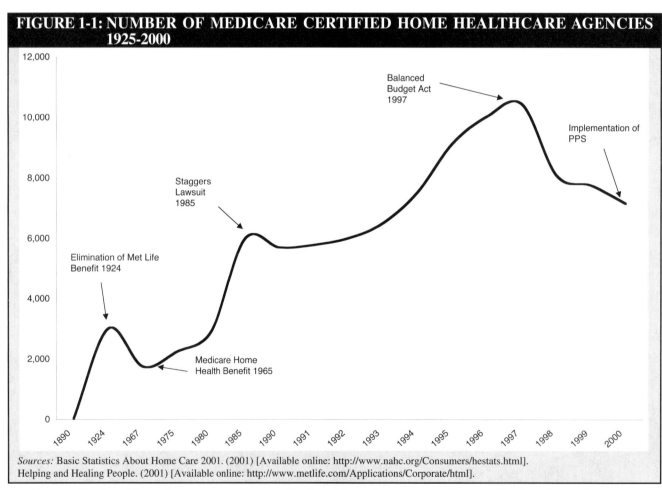

Sources: Basic Statistics About Home Care 2001. (2001) [Available online: http://www.nahc.org/Consumers/hestats.html].
Helping and Healing People. (2001) [Available online: http://www.metlife.com/Applications/Corporate/html].

Year	Number of Agencies	Year	Number of Agencies	Year	Number of Agencies
1890	21	1985	5983	1995	9120
1924	3000	1990	5695	1996	10027
1967	1753	1991	5780	1997	10444
1975	2242	1992	6004	1998	8080
1980	2924	1993	6497	1999	7747
		1994	7521	2000	7152

However, some agencies and their nurses serve the function of all within a single community or geographic area. For the purpose of this course, home healthcare is a cadre of services for patients who are disabled, chronically or terminally ill, or are recovering from an acute illness.

Home healthcare agencies typically provide skilled, nursing, home healthcare aide, social or rehabilitative services. Depending on the unique needs of the patient, any combination of these services may be provided. Regardless of which service the patient requires, the goal of home healthcare is to provide the services necessary to restore the patient to their optimal level of function within the limits of their capacity.

The home healthcare nurse achieves this through the assessment of the patient in their own environment, understanding the impact that the environment has on the patient's well-being. The nurse mobilizes and coordinates both agency and community resources that are necessary to safely maintain the patient in their own home for as long as the patient wishes.

SUMMARY

Through the efforts of nursing matriarchs like Florence Nightingale, Lillian Wald, Jane Delano and countless others, the cost effectiveness of home healthcare nursing was demonstrated. For over one hundred years, home care nurses have been able to improve the physical and social health of individual citizens and the community. This model of providing healthcare was so profound that its influence continues to shape the delivery of home healthcare services in the 21st century.

EXAM QUESTIONS

CHAPTER 1
Questions 1-6

1. Florence Nightingale's greatest accomplishment was to

    a. organize home healthcare nurses into geographic districts.

    b. publish *Notes on Nursing.*

    c. advance the standing of nursing from an undesirable endeavor to a profession that continues to have the highest ethical and moral standards.

    d. establish the Florence Nightingale Training School for Nurses.

2. Lillian Wald convinced the executives of Metropolitan Life Insurance company to participate in a 3-month pilot program to

    a. evaluate the effectiveness of in-home service in the reduction of tuberculosis-related deaths.

    b. treat common aliments such as diphtheria, influenza and small pox.

    c. teach mothers how to provide care to their newborn babies.

    d. conduct physical assessment prior to the company issuing a life insurance policy.

3. Clara Barton was most noted for mobilizing Red Cross nurses to

    a. care for victims of natural disasters.

    b. inoculate citizens of large cities against the spread of Tuberculosis.

    c. teach principles of sanitation and hygiene to people living in rural communities.

    d. care for the casualties of war.

4. After World War II, the American healthcare system experienced rapid advancement in technology and sciences which increased the

    a. number of home healthcare agencies.

    b. availability of hospital care.

    c. amount of Medicare payments for home healthcare services.

    d. number of proprietary agencies in the home healthcare industry.

5. In 1965, the Older Americans Act required both federal and state government to design programs to assist and support elders with remaining in their homes. To qualify beneficiaries were required to

    a. have experienced at least a 3-day hospital stay prior to the initiation of home healthcare services.

    b. be in need of services from at least two professional disciplines.

    c. have a primary care provider who would provide assistance to the elder.

    d. agree to a 10% copayment for all services received.

6. In August of 1997, in an effort to curb expenses and reduce fraud and abuse in the home healthcare industry, President Clinton signed the

    a. Staggers law suit.

    b. Medicare Home Health Benefit.

    c. Balanced Budget Act.

    d. DRGs into law.

13

CHAPTER 2

CODE OF ETHICS FOR NURSES

CHAPTER OBJECTIVE

At the completion of this chapter, the reader will be able to recall the utility of the Code of Ethics for Nurses as it applies to home healthcare today.

LEARNING OBJECTIVES

After studying this chapter, the reader will be able to

1. choose the purpose of the American Nurses' Association's *Code of Ethics for Nurses*.

2. recognize the patient's right to self-determination and the professional nurse's responsibility with regard to their own opinions and judgements.

3. list three examples that demonstrate the home healthcare nurse's ability to advance nursing knowledge and professional practice.

4. identify the benefits and indications for interdisciplinary and multidisciplinary collaboration.

5. identify the risks associated with delegation of patient care activities to ancillary staff.

6. recall the characteristics of a professional relationship.

INTRODUCTION

A code of ethics is a set of "imperatives formulated as statements of personal responsibility and identifies elements of such a commitment" to a profession or organization (Association for Computing Machinery [ACM], 1997, p. 1). An ethical code describes the expectations and values of an individual or organization and serves to address many, but not all, issues a professional is likely to face (ACM, 1997).

The first statement of ethics for nursing can be traced back to late 1800s when Lystra Gretter wrote *Nightingale's Pledge*. (See Box 2-1.) Between 1893 and 1950, a number of nursing organizations authored various codes of ethics for nursing; however, it was not until 1950 that the American Nurses' Association drafted the *Code of Ethics for Nurses* that is widely accepted today. The practice of nursing has significantly evolved over the last 50 years. The Code of Ethics for Nurses has also evolved and has been revised to reflect the changes in nursing practice; however, the fundamental concepts of ethical nursing practice and behavior have endured.

The American Nurses' Association's (ANA) 2001 *Code of Ethics for Nurses* consists of nine provisions that outline the conduct that is expected of every nurse. Like all ethical codes, the *Code of Ethics for Nurses* is intended to serve as a framework for decision making, conduct, and practice.

BOX 2-1

Nightingale's Pledge
Lystra Gretter 1893

"I solemnly pledge myself before God and in the presence of this assembly, to pass my life in purity and to practice my profession faithfully. I will abstain from whatever is deleterious and mischievous, and will not take or knowingly administer any harmful drug. I will do all in my power to maintain and elevate the standard of my profession, and will hold in confidence all personal matters committed to my keeping and all family affairs coming to my knowledge in the practice of my calling. With loyalty will I endeavor to aid the physician, in his work, and devote myself to the welfare of those committed to my care" (The Nightingale Pledge, 1893).

Although not a legal document, the *Code of Ethics for Nurses* represents the promise that all professional nurses make to the patients that they care for. It is similar to a contract between business partners. It succinctly outlines the services that the patient should expect and will receive.

The *Code of Ethics for Nurses* serves to remind the nurse that the privilege of caring for patients and their families is not one that should be taken lightly. These expectations apply to nurses regardless of the policies of an organization or setting of practice, and are applicable in the day-to-day activities of every nurse.

THE PROVISIONS

The American Nurses' Association's *Code of Ethics for Nurses* has nine provisions. Each general provision is further clarified by a subset of interpretative statements. The role of the nurse as it relates directly to patient care is outlined in the first three provisions. For the purposes of the *Code of Ethics for Nurses*, it is important to note that the

patient may be defined as an individual, a family, or an entire community.

Provisions Four, Five and Six outline the nurse's obligation to cultivate and develop their own practice. These provisions address issues of clinical competence, professional growth and the individual's responsibility to exert influence on healthcare systems and organizations in an effort to maximize the quality of nursing care provided within these institutions.

Finally, Provisions Seven, Eight and Nine outline the obligations that each nurse has to support and advance the agenda of the nursing profession. In essence, these provisions delineate the obligation that each individual nurse has to the entire body of professional nurses. While Provision Seven requires the nurse to develop and advance nursing knowledge, Provisions Eight and Nine describe the nurse's role in initiatives to influence and improve health on a local, national, and international level.

Society holds the profession of nursing to the highest ethical standards; therefore, nurses must also hold themselves and their nurse colleagues to the standards outlined in Table 2-1. It is adherence to these provisions and standards that has allowed nurses to remain the most respected and trusted healthcare providers today.

CASE STUDY

The case study of Mrs. Smith will demonstrate the application of the first three provisions outlined in the *Code of Ethics for Nurses*.

Mrs. Smith is an 80-year-old patient with congestive heart failure (CHF). She was referred to your home care agency after experiencing three hospitalizations for CHF in the last two months. Your clinical manager has assigned her case to you.

As you approach her address, you note that she lives in a residential suburban neighborhood, and

TABLE 2-1: ANA CODE OF ETHICS FOR NURSES

Provision One

The nurse, in all professional relationships, practices with compassion and respect for the inherent dignity, worth, and uniqueness of every individual, unrestricted by considerations of social or economic status, personal attributes, or the nature of health problems.

Provision Two

The nurse's primary commitment is to the patient, whether an individual, family, group or community.

Provision Three

The Nurse promotes, advocates for, and strives to protect the health, safety, and rights of the patient.

Provision Four

The nurse is responsible and accountable for individual nursing practice and determines the appropriate delegation of tasks consistent with the nurse's obligation to provide optimum patient care.

Provision Five

The nurse owes the same duties to self as to others, including the responsibility to preserve integrity and safety, to maintain competence, and to continue personal and professional growth.

Provision Six

The nurse participates in establishing, maintaining and improving health care environments and conditions of employment conducive to the provision of quality health care and consistent with the values of the profession through individual and collective action.

Provision Seven

The nurse participates in the advancement of the profession through contributions to practice, education, administration and knowledge development.

Provision Eight

The nurse collaborates with other health professionals and the public in promoting community, national and international efforts to meet health needs.

Provision Nine

The profession of nursing, as represented by associations and their members, is responsible for articulating nursing values, for maintaining the integrity of the profession and its practice, and for shaping social policy.

Reprinted with permission from American Nurses' Association, Code of Ethics for Nurses with Interpretative Statements, © 2001 American Nurses Publishing, American Nurses' Association, Washington DC.

her home appears to be reasonably well kept. As you go up the six stairs to her front door you note that although the stairs seem safe, there is no hand railing. When you knock on the door you hear a distant, "Come in."

As you enter the home, a number of cats scamper out of the way and disappear into other rooms blending in among a large volume of clutter. The patient calls once again, "Who's there? Come on in so I can see you."

Once you enter the room, you see Mrs. Smith. She is lying in a hospital bed with her head elevated. You note the bed itself is in a raised position. Placed all around her on various tables and in the bed are her medication bottles, various foodstuffs, reading material, bottles of water, bottles of what appear to be alcoholic beverages and personal hygiene products.

Mrs. Smith appears to be angry and states, "I have been sitting on this bed pan since the ambulance brought me home." You recall that your referral documents state that Mrs. Smith left the hospital yesterday afternoon.

Once you find a reasonably clean place to set your nursing bag down, you use your waterless soap to wash your hands and put on gloves so you can assist Mrs. Smith off of the bedpan. As you do, you notice that her bed linens are soiled and recognize the odor as urine. She remains in a hospital gown, and it appears that she has not had any personal care for at least 24 hours. You note that it is remarkable that she has not suffered any breakdown in her skin on her back or buttocks.

When you enter the bathroom to empty the bedpan, you realize that what first appeared to be only clutter now appears to be hazardous. The facilities are not clean, and there appears to be cat excrement on the floor in various places.

When you return to her bedroom, you begin your assessment of Mrs. Smith and her environment realizing that none of this information is on your hospital referral. She readily tells you that she lives alone and has an "aide" who usually helps her out, but she has not shown up since Mrs. Smith got back from the hospital.

When you query her about additional help, she gets angry once again and states, "Yeah, I got kids and not one of them is good for anything." Quickly you realize that this line of questioning is upsetting to Mrs. Smith, and before you can move on to another topic, she asks, "Are you just like the rest of them, all you want to do is come in here and know my business?"

You now change the subject to something that you hope is less upsetting to Mrs. Smith and begin to explain to her that your agency received a request from the hospital to evaluate how she is managing at home. You explain to her that you are a Registered Nurse and that her doctor has requested an assessment of her cardiac condition.

PROVISION ONE

When evaluating the case of Mrs. Smith, it is clear to see how the provisions of the *Code of Ethics for Nurses* can be applied to the day-to-day practice of the home healthcare nurse. Provision One requires that, "The nurse provides services with respect for human dignity and the uniqueness of the client unrestricted by considerations of social or economic status, personal attributes, or the nature of health problems" (ANA, 2001, p. 7). Provision One also dictates that the need for healthcare is universal, and nursing care must be delivered without prejudice. When planning a patient's care, the nurse must consider the lifestyle and value system of the patient and customize care to meet that individual patient's need.

Although Mrs. Smith's current lifestyle and value system may not be conducive to what is considered a healthy environment, it is clearly her choice. The *Code of Ethics for Nurses* does not require the nurse to condone or agree with a patient's choice, it does however require the nurse to provide care to the patient regardless of the patient's choices (ANA, 2001). If Mrs. Smith chooses to keep 20, 30 or even 100 cats in her home and allow them to roam freely across all surfaces it is her right to do so.

As the nurse standing in her bedroom, you can identify a number of interventions to "improve" the condition of Mrs. Smith and her home. Unless declared incompetent, it is up to Mrs. Smith to dictate what type and how much help or care she is willing to receive. It is your obligation to provide her with information to help exercise her right to self-determination and choose the care and interventions that she feels are appropriate for her needs.

Self-determination is a phrase that is frequently used in clinical settings. Self-determination is defined as the patient's "moral and legal right to determine what will be done with their own person; and

- to be given accurate, complete, and understandable information in a manner that facilitates an informed judgement;

- to be assisted in weighing the benefits, burdens, and available options in their treatment including the choice of no treatment;

- to accept, refuse, or terminate treatment without deceit, undue influence, duress, coercion, or penalty; and

- to be given necessary support throughout the decision-making and treatment process" (ANA, 2001, p. 8).

Unlike providing nursing care in a clinic, physician's office, hospital or long-term care facility, home healthcare is provided to a patient in their home, and the locus of control changes from the organization to the individual patient. The patient determines how they will live, what they will have for dinner – whether or not the selection is within their dietary restrictions. It is not uncommon for a home healthcare nurse to characterize the choices that the patient has made as right, wrong, good, or bad. However, the experienced home healthcare nurse realizes that characterization of patient choices is fruitless. The competent home healthcare nurse realizes that patients make these choices despite receiving the "best" care, information, and instruction, and it is the nurse's obligation to work within these choices.

Mrs. Smith is clear in her decision to remain in her current environment stating, "I have lived in this house all my life. I was born here, I had my children here and I will die here. These cats keep me company all day and night they are all I have left." At first blush, these choices may seem "bad" or "poor;" however, when you take the time to hear Mrs. Smith's words, you realize that her home and her cats are her personal treasures.

Provision One of the *Code of Ethics for Nurses* requires the nurses "respect for the worth and dignity of the individual applies irrespective of the nature of the health problem" (ANA, 2001, p.7). In the case of Mrs. Smith, this creates an immediate difficulty for you. Through your education and experience, you know that Mrs. Smith's condition will continue to deteriorate if she remains in her current situation. At the very least, you anticipate pressure sores due to poor nutrition and immobility; exacerbations of CHF, as well as potential complications related to her alcohol intake. The question here is what intervention if any, can be implemented in caring for Mrs. Smith?

Provision One requires that you provide appropriate care to Mrs. Smith even if her home environment is distasteful. You must assure, to the best of your ability, that decisions you make related to Mrs. Smith's care safeguard her well-being and safety. This becomes a critical moment in the home visit of Mrs. Smith, what are you going to do?

- Leave Mrs. Smith's home and call your supervisor and discuss the concerns that you have about Mrs. Smith's living situation.

- Apologize to Mrs. Smith since she seems upset with the questions you have asked her and attempt to continue the visit by beginning her physical assessment.

- Inform Mrs. Smith that her unwillingness to be more cooperative and her obvious displeasure with you makes her inappropriate for home care services and move on to your next patient.

Both options one and two are reasonable and would not conflict Provision One of the code. Depending on the experience of the home healthcare nurse and agency policy, the nurse may choose one or both of these strategies to complete the visit with Mrs. Smith. The third option, deciding that Mrs. Smith is not appropriate for services because of the nurse's discomfort with the patient and environment, would violate Provision One.

PROVISION TWO

Provision Two requires that the nurse collaborate with other members of the healthcare delivery team and defines collaboration as the "concerted effort of individuals and groups to attain a shared goal" (ANA, 2001, p. 10). In the case of Mrs. Smith, there are a number of opportunities for collaborative care.

In all likelihood, Mrs. Smith would benefit from a physical therapy evaluation to address safety issues and improve her ability to get out of bed. Perhaps if she could tolerate aggressive therapy, she might eventually be able to maneuver around her home with a walker or a cane.

A referral to a medical social worker would be appropriate to help identify additional community-based services such as adult day care or adult foster care that might be mobilized to reduce Mrs. Smith's isolation. You must consider whether or not Mrs. Smith would benefit from a visit by a registered dietician to evaluate her eating habits, to make suggestions to improve her nutrition, and to minimize complications like fluid retention. As the nurse assigned to Mrs. Smith's case, it is your obligation to make the appropriate referrals and coordinate her care so that the goals established for her are met.

PROVISION THREE

The third provision outlined in the *Code of Ethics for Nurses* obligates nurses to "safeguard the client's right to privacy by judiciously protecting information of a confidential nature" (ANA, 2001, p. 10). The right to privacy is described as an inalienable human right. You now have to determine if Mrs. Smith's situation places her in such jeopardy that it should be reported to the local Bureau of Elder Services for a formalized "elder at risk" assessment or to the Board of Public Health to evaluate the conditions inside her home.

Although it is clear that Mrs. Smith has made some poor lifestyle choices, you have to consider that it is her right to make them. Mrs. Smith has already stated that she is not interested in allowing "outsiders" to "know her business." Although involving the elder services seems like the "right" thing to do, you must consider your rationale for making or not making the decision to report Mrs. Smith's living situation. From your conversation with Mrs. Smith, she has been able to answer all questions appropriately (even if she is a little angry and upset), and she has demonstrated her ability to understand and follow directions. Her competence to make decisions does not appear to be an issue.

Is Mrs. Smith's home environment so hazardous that it should be reported to the local Board of Health or health agent? The decision to disclose protected health information to those not directly involved in Mrs. Smith's case is a serious one. It is not likely that Mrs. Smith would give you permission to contact either the Bureau of Elder Services or the Board of Health; therefore, doing so would certainly be against her wishes.

If you make the decision to report Mrs. Smith's situation, Provision Three requires that you disclose only the information necessary for her treatment and well-being. If you decide to report the conditions inside Mrs. Smith's home to the Board of Health, only the information related to home environment should be disclosed and not her apparent alcohol use and estrangement from her family. In Mrs. Smith's case, would you:

- Report Mrs. Smith's home environment to local authorities?

- Report Mrs. Smith's condition to the Bureau of Elder Services?

- Do neither and continue to assess her and build a therapeutic relationship?

If you decide that Mrs. Smith is appropriate for the home healthcare services provided by your agency, you must also consider how much of your assessment, observation, and interaction with Mrs. Smith is necessary to document in her medical record. How much should be discussed with the other members of the home health team? How much should you report to Mrs. Smith's physician?

Provision Three also requires you to consider the state of Mrs. Smith's home in light of the "aide" that should be assisting her with her personal care and homemaking. Could the house be in such disarray because of the few days Mrs. Smith was hospitalized? Is the disarray the result of Mrs. Smith's refusal to allow the aide to perform the necessary homemaking duties?

You decide to continue your assessment of Mrs. Smith. You ask her which agency her aide is from and whether this agency has been notified about her return from the hospital. Mrs. Smith states, "I have the number right here. They told me my girl would be here today but she hasn't come yet."

Mrs. Smith continues, "She is supposed to be here from 9 to 11 in the morning and then she comes back at night. Sometimes she can't come back at night so I sign her papers and stay in bed all day. If she is coming back, she gets me up into the wheelchair and I can go sit in the living room for the day. Once she said she was coming back and never showed up. I had to spend the night in the wheel chair. Boy, that was a tough night."

Your experience tells you that there is something questionable about the services being provided to Mrs. Smith. At the very least, you recognize that she is at the mercy of this aide and her inconsistent service. As a result of this brief assessment and conversation, you begin to formulate your plan of care and decide:

- Mrs. Smith is appropriate for admission to the services of your agency;
- Social work services are necessary to sort out the issues around the lack of community-based support for Mrs. Smith; and

- You are obligated to inform the agency that employs the aide about what appears to be substandard performance and uncertain attendance.

Once you have decided to admit Mrs. Smith to the agency's caseload, you explain the services that your agency provides and the services requested by the hospital. You explain to her which services she is eligible for and what her insurance will pay. You explain that as part of the admission process you will have to ask her a few more questions and complete a physical assessment. You provide her with a copy of the agency's Patient's Rights and Responsibilities form and tell her that once you get through all of this paperwork you will leave copies of it for her for future reference. Once she agrees, you explain that she has to sign a Consent for Treatment form and other agency paperwork required by home healthcare regulations.

You make a note to contact the agency that provides the aide to inform them of the lack of attendance of their worker. Past experience reminds you that many aides are paid when visit documentation includes a patient's signature. Clearly, if Mrs. Smith is signing the forms in advance of receiving service, the agency is potentially paying the aide for services that were not provided. You are also aware that that this accusation has serious consequences for the aide and the agency that employs her; however, the *Code of Ethics for Nurses* requires you to act on questionable or uncertain practices. Your options are:

- Call the agency that provides the aide to Mrs. Smith and inform them that your agency will now be involved in Mrs. Smith's care;
- Plan your next visit to coincide with the visit of the aide to conduct your own assessment of the care she is providing Mrs. Smith; or
- Plan to discuss the situation with your Clinical Manager when you return to the agency.

At this point, you realize that you have made significant progress in the planning of Mrs. Smith's care. You have identified several problems but have not yet conducted a physical assessment.

You explain to Mrs. Smith that her physician has ordered a cardiopulmonary assessment, medication compliance assessment and has also requested that you perform a generalized home safety assessment. You explain that you would like to complete her physical assessment, and she agrees.

You have already noted that Mrs. Smith is alert and oriented. She is able to communicate her needs and follow directions. She has gross and fine motor control of her upper extremities as evidenced by her ability to hand and receive items to and from you along with her ability to sign her name. You know that she can move both of her legs, since she used them to roll in the bed and lift her buttocks off of the bedpan. She denies any numbness, tingling or weakness in any of her extremities.

Her pupils are equal and reactive to light. You note that she has two pairs of glasses, one she has worn the entire time you were in the house except when she changed to another pair to read and sign her name.

Mrs. Smith is able to move her head and neck from side to side, and as you palpate these areas, you do not feel any lumps or masses. You noticed a denture cup on the bedside table and question her about her teeth and her ability to swallow both liquids and solids. She informs you she has a full set of dentures and has never had any trouble swallowing a thing as long as she has a good "swig of water."

You assist Mrs. Smith in sitting upright. You listen to her lungs and note that there are diminished breath sounds at the bases. Mrs. Smith also has a slight expiratory wheeze, but denies shortness of breath or a cough.

You observe that Mrs. Smith's mucous membranes are moist. It is during this assessment that you smell a faint odor of alcohol. You decide that you will ask her about this later. Mrs. Smith's apical pulse is 58 and regular as is her radial pulse. You are not able to identify any abnormal heart sound. Her blood pressure is 158/94 on her right arm and 162/92 on her left.

Mrs. Smith's bowel sounds are present in all four quadrants. You question her about a scar on her right upper abdominal quadrant, and she states, "They took something out a long time ago, probably before you were born." You measure her abdominal girth explaining that since she will not be able to stand on the scale, this measurement might help to identify early signs of congestive heart failure.

You assess Mrs. Smith's lower extremities. You note that her skin is very dry and scaly. You are unable to palpate her pedal pulses, and you notice bilateral pitting edema with a 10 to 15 second capillary refill time. Although the color of her feet is good, they are cool to touch.

You note the presence of nickel size blackened areas on both of Mrs. Smith's heels. You ask her how long she has had them, and she states, "I never knew I did, are you pulling my leg?" You ask her for a mirror and show them to her. She denies any pain in either heel.

You ask to look at Mrs. Smith's prescriptions. She begins to hand you the prescription bottles that are on the left side of her. As she hands you the bottles she explains, "This one is my heart medication, I take it once a day. This little one is for my pressure, they say I got high blood pressure you know. I take it in the morning. I have bad cholesterol. I am supposed to take this one three times a day but I don't. It is very expensive so I cut it in half and take one in the morning and one at night."

Mrs. Smith continues to hand you five additional bottles which include Tylenol®, Colace® and other over–the-counter drugs. As she hands them to you, you compare them to the list provided on your hospital referral. You ask Mrs. Smith, "Do you take a fluid pill?"

She states, "Oh that one. That one is a devil, I have it here somewhere." Mrs. Smith looks on the table next to her bed and retrieves two additional prescription bottles. One you recognize as sublingual Nitroglycerin, and the other is Lasix®.

"Here they are. Doctor Jones wants me to take them everyday, but how can I? As soon as I take them I have to use the pan (bedpan). I have to use it and use it. It's not easy for me you know, and if my girl doesn't come or comes late… well I am in big trouble." You now realize that you are beginning to see the source of Mrs. Smith's recidivism.

PROVISION FOUR

As a professional nurse you understand that you are entirely responsible for your actions and judgements. Due to the complexities of Mrs. Smith's case you will request a case conference to assist in the development of an appropriate plan of care. Provision Four of the *Code of Ethics for Nurses* requires that when the patient's needs are "beyond the qualifications and competencies of the nurse, consultation and collaboration must be sought from qualified nurses, other health professionals, or other appropriate sources" (ANA, 2001, p. 17).

As part of your plan of care you consider utilizing the following services:

- A certified wound-ostomy continence nurse (CWOCN) to address Mrs. Smith's skin integrity;

- A cardiac nurse to evaluate the medication plan and increase Mrs. Smith's overall compliance; and

- The services of a psychiatric nurse to help you address Mrs. Smith's feelings of anger and her lack of trust.

Every nurse "is responsible and accountable for individual nursing practice and determines the appropriate delegation of tasks consistent with the nurse's obligation to provide optimum patient care" (ANA, 2001, p.16). As noted earlier, society's trust of professional nurses is the result of the standards that nurses established for themselves in day-to-day practice. Provision Four requires that every nurse accept accountability for their own practice. For the home healthcare nurse, there are many obvious examples of being accountable for one's own practice.

In the case of Mrs. Smith, you have to make a judgement about whether or not to make a report to the Bureau of Elder Services. Although that decision seems benign, consider the potential results. A report to the Bureau of Elder Services might require you to:

- Violate the trusting relationship that has begun between you and Mrs. Smith. If the Bureau does not substantiate the concerns and thereby does not intervene, will you be able to rebuild the trust that is necessary for a therapeutic relationship?

- Disclose not only protected health information but also very personal and intimate details about Mrs. Smith's current living situation and personal life, i.e. her estrangement from her children.

- Witness Bureau intervention, which could result in Mrs. Smith being unwillingly removed from her home and being placed in a long-term care facility.

Although any of the three scenarios listed are a possibility, you as the home healthcare nurse initiating the process must also be accountable for the outcome.

Accountability as defined by the American Nurse Association "refers to being answerable to someone for something one has done, it means providing an explanation or rationale to oneself, to clients, to peers, to the nursing profession and to society" (ANA, 2001, p. 16). The decision to report Mrs. Smith to the Bureau of Elder Services, due to her unsafe or "at risk" situation, may be easily rationalized to your peers, the profession and even society, but how do you rationalize it to Mrs. Smith, and will your rationale matter to her?

A decision not to report Mrs. Smith's situation to the Bureau of Elder Services may be easily rationalized regarding Mrs. Smith, but what about your accountability to your peers, profession, and society? It is important to understand that the *Code of Ethics for Nurses* may or may not exceed the requirements of law. You, as a professional nurse, must be familiar with the *Code of Ethics for Nurses*, agency policy, and the laws and regulations governing nursing practice in your state.

Would you report Mrs. Smith to the Bureau of Elder Services? Would your agency require you to? What guidance or direction does your licensing board or state laws provide?

Provision Four also offers guidance to the nurse related to issues of delegation. It is a phenomenon that affects nurses in virtually every practice setting, including home healthcare. Delegation is a reality that has resulted from the changes in the healthcare delivery system due to financial pressures to reduce costs. The delegation of nursing care by the professional nurse does not diminish the nurse's accountability for the care actually provided to the patient. Further, the professional nurse is responsible for the competence of the healthcare worker to whom they are delegating and must be sure that the individual is competent to carry out the assigned patient care. The *Code of Ethics for Nurses* points out that "employer policies or directives do not relieve the nurse of accountability for making judgements about the delegation of nursing care activities" (ANA, 1985, p. 17).

When considering issues of delegation, nurses commonly think of hospitals and other facility-based care environments. Another important issue of delegation relates directly to the area of home healthcare aides (HCA). In some states HCAs are allowed to insert Foley catheters, perform venipuncture, give medications and change dressings. Identification of tasks that can be delegated is governed and regulated by each state and every home healthcare nurse should have a thorough understanding of these regulations.

Consider the case of Mrs. Smith. At this point, there are a number of tasks that have been identified, and they may or may not be delegated to the HCA. As the nurse in Mrs. Smith's home, consider which task or tasks you would delegate.

- Due to Mrs. Smith's inability to remove the wrapper, you ask the home healthcare aide to change Mrs. Smith's Nitropatch after she bathes her.

- Mrs. Smith has a treatment ordered to debride the necrotic areas on her heels. As part of the home healthcare aide's plan of care, you instruct the home healthcare aide to change the outer dressing on both heels every day and to report any drainage that has come through the dressing.

- Mrs. Smith's care requires the level of peripheral edema to be measured every other day. As part of the home healthcare aide's plan of care, you instruct the home healthcare aide to measure the edema and notify you if an increase occurs.

The issues related to Mrs. Smith's case are not uncommon in home healthcare. Any seasoned home care nurse can readily provide examples of similar cases and scenarios. What is important to understand is that in every case the provisions of the *Code of Ethics for Nurses* are applicable and can provide guidance to every nurse in their daily practice.

The first four provisions above describe the values and commitment required of all professional nurses. The situation and circumstances of Mrs. Smith are fairly common and each nurse should explore their decision making and rationale when faced with similar scenarios.

PROVISION FIVE

As noted earlier, Provisions Five, Six and Seven address "boundaries of duty and loyalty" (ANA, 2001, p. 6). Provision Five outlines the nurse's obligation to cultivate and develop their own practice and knowledge base.

As a professional nurse, it is not likely that you have forgotten the rigors of nursing school. You must also acknowledge that learning is a lifelong endeavor, and if learning stopped when you graduated from nursing school, you would not be able to function as a professional nurse today. Remember, what you learned in nursing school was the very minimum required to take state licensing exams. Provision Five requires nurses to maintain competence in nursing and states: "Nurses are required to have knowledge relevant to the current scope and standards of nursing practice, changing issues, concerns, controversies, and ethics" (ANA, 2001, p. 18). This provision outlines the obligation that each nurse has to actively seek new knowledge and incorporate that knowledge into the delivery of patient care.

Many individual states require professional nurses to continue formalized education through completion of contact hours or continuing education units; however, there are many states that have no requirement at all. The absence of a state regulation does not relinquish the professional nurse from their obligation to continue to expand their knowledge.

The practice of nursing is dynamic and evolving. The scope of nursing is shaped by advancement of nursing knowledge and by influences of the healthcare delivery system. This ever-changing environment is not without risk for the professional nurse. As already stated, each nurse is accountable for their own practice – regardless of the setting or circumstance. Each nurse must be adequately prepared to carry out every function that they are being asked to perform. If the nurse is inadequately prepared to complete a function, they must not attempt to carry out the function and jeopardize the patient's well-being.

The most obvious examples of this in home care are usually related to specific tasks, i.e. changing of an Unna Boot dressing or maintenance of an epidural catheter for pain management. In the case of Mrs. Smith, there are clearly issues that are better addressed by other disciplines or by nursing specialists.

Provision Five also introduces the concept of "wholeness" of character and preservation of integrity as crucial to the nurse's ability to demonstrate ethical decision making. In the earliest days of formalized nursing, only the "right" or "good" people were allowed into the profession. The "rightness" and "goodness" of individuals was judged by nursing leaders who were primarily educators or administrators. Nursing leaders were revered and occasionally used their authority to exert influence on personal and professional lives of the nurses they encountered. For example, when nurses were trained in hospital based schools of nursing, the students were required to live on campus, they could not be married and were even subjected to weekly weigh-ins (personal conversation, Cynthia Cardoza).

In the 21st century, nurses are as diverse as the patients and communities they serve. Nurses have both personal and professional identities, and the process of becoming a nurse requires the individual to accept and integrate the values of nursing as outlined in the *Code of Ethics for Nurses* into their existing value structure. Achieving this and understanding integration is especially important in the nurse/patient interaction.

To illustrate this point, consider the patient who requests your personal opinion about their health or personal issue. Almost every nurse has been asked:

- "Do you think my doctor is doing the right thing?"
- "What would you do if you were in my place?"

- "Do you think I should get a second opinion?"

- "Do you think I did the right thing?"

Although you are likely to have a personal opinion about each of these questions, in answering them you must recognize that your role as a nurse represents a "knowing" opinion and may exert unintentional influence on the patient or their decision. When you, as the nurse, are placed in this position, it is always better to assist the patient to clarify their own expectations and guide them to make an informed decision.

PROVISION SIX

The privilege of autonomous practice and self-regulation increases the nurse's responsibility to assure that the practice setting is "conducive to high quality nursing care" (ANA, 2001, p. 20). In fact, Provision Six specifically states: "All nurses have a responsibility to create, maintain, and contribute to environments that support the growth of virtues and excellences and enable nurses to fulfill their ethical obligations" (ANA, 2001, p. 20). For the purpose of this passage, virtues are defined as the nurse's actions which promote well-being, health, and independence of the patient. Working in home healthcare, nurses will find unique professional opportunities to participate in initiatives to enhance the practice of nursing.

Although most home healthcare agencies work within the medical/disease model, nursing is the primary service provided. Unlike many other practice settings, home healthcare is organized to provide and support the provision of nursing care. There are often many opportunities for the nurse to participate in committees and task forces that are organized to improve the conditions of the work setting and improve the quality of patient care. Participation on committees that address issues such as safety and infection control fulfills the nurse's obligation to contribute to an environment conducive to high quality nursing service and patient care.

Provision Six puts the responsibility for maintaining and improving healthcare environments squarely on the nurse's shoulders. It requires the nurse to participate in collaborative relationships with colleagues and peers that work to identify and solve issues related to the practice setting and working conditions. Provision Six states: "Acquiescing and accepting unsafe or inappropriate practices, even if the individual does not participate in the specific practice, is equivalent to condoning unsafe practice. Nurses should not remain employed in a facility that routinely violates patient rights or requires nurses to severely and repeatedly compromise standards of practice of personal morality" (ANA, 2001, p. 21).

Although these statements may initially seem severe, consider them from the patient's perspective. The trusting relationship that exists between society and the nursing profession should never be compromised. If a professional nurse participates in or is employed by an unscrupulous provider, they are directly responsible for undermining the trusting relationship that has developed between society and the nursing profession over the last two hundred years.

In home healthcare, an example of unsafe or inappropriate practice might include:

- The discharge of a patient because the care they require is too costly;

- Performing a task for which the nurse does not have the clinical skill or there is no clinical procedure i.e. blood transfusions; or

- Performing duties that are beyond those outlined in the scope of practice of the nurse or limited by the state Board of Professional Licensure, i.e. sharp debridement of wounds.

Clearly, no nursing professional wants to be associated with an organization that routinely denies a patient's right to participate in the care planning process, self-determination, or informed consent.

The *Code of Ethics for Nurses* acknowledges that, for some nurses, collective bargaining may be a mechanism to change organizational practice. If collective bargaining is used, the collective bargaining agreement must "be consistent with the profession's standards of practice, the state law regulating practice and the Code of Ethics for Nurses" and "balance the interest of patients and nurses" (ANA, 2001, p. 22).

PROVISION SEVEN

Provision Seven outlines the professional nurse's responsibility to participate in activities that advance nursing knowledge and professional practice. Reading this provision might make you, as a nurse, question how this can possibly be an individual responsibility. Is not the advancement of knowledge best left to nursing educators and researchers?

Unfortunately, many nurses are so consumed by the activities of daily practice that they do not often realize how often they participate in knowledge development and professional advancement. In an effort to improve patient outcomes, home healthcare agencies have instituted specialty or disease management teams. Participation on these teams enables nurses to share the latest research and then utilize and apply it to patient care.

For example, the *Clinical Practice Guidelines* published by the Agency for Health Care Research and Quality (formerly known as the Agency for Health Care Policy and Research) discourages the use of solutions such as Dakin's or acetic acid for wound packing. Although these treatments were commonly used in the past for treatment of infect-ed wounds, the home healthcare nurse now recognizes that this treatment is a detriment to wound healing and therefore seeks treatment alternatives.

On occasion, a home healthcare nurse has the opportunity to participate in or conduct nursing research. Given this opportunity, the nurse is obligated to assure that the participant's rights are protected and that all of the necessary approvals are received.

In the advancement of nursing knowledge and professional practice, nurse educators must also adhere to the *Code of Ethics for Nurses* by assuring that individuals eligible to take licensing exams have "demonstrated the knowledge, skills and commitment considered essential to professional practice" (ANA, 2001, p.2).

Many home health agencies are privileged to provide a clinical experience for nursing students. Whether the experience is observational or one in which the student conducts independent home visits, it is the home care nurse's obligation to give honest and constructive feedback to the student and the instructor.

In home healthcare, the nurse might think that providing a clinical experience for a student nurse seems burdensome. However, at the end of the day, week, or semester, many nurses find the experience rewarding and one way to meet their obligation to participate in the development and advancement of the profession. In some home healthcare agencies, nurses may have the opportunity to participate in a preceptor or mentoring program for new employees. Participating in these programs also provides nurses with an avenue to fulfill their professional obligations.

PROVISION EIGHT

The longstanding relationship between the public and the nursing profession is highly valued. Each nurse bears the responsibility to be aware of and knowledgeable about the major threats to health and wellness in their community. Nurses who support and participate in civic and political initiatives have the unique opportunity to educate the public to make informed choices about health and health-related issues such as poverty, homelessness, domestic abuse and violence.

In Chapter 1, the efficiency of a district nurse included having knowledge of the issues that families, neighborhoods and entire communities were facing. The modern home healthcare nurse continues to have the same level of knowledge; however, they are also aware of the services available to address these issues.

Do you know:

- Which churches in your community have an active Parish Nurse program?

- If there is a woman's shelter in your city or town?

- Are there homeless people sleeping in your parks and alleys? If so, are there places where they can seek shelter from inclement weather?

- Does the nurse at the local high school distribute condoms?

- Where members of your community can get a flu or pneumonia vaccine?

- Is there an individual or group who provides holiday meals to homebound elders and shut-ins?

- Are the children in your town at risk for asbestos or lead poisoning?

PROVISION NINE

Provision Nine acknowledges that nursing has a long-standing commitment to social reform and requires nurses to work through professional associations and affiliations to identify political solutions to local, national and international health and social problems. While working with these groups, individual nurses should seize the opportu-

nity to meet with and educate their local, state or federal representatives and senators about the issues that affect the health and welfare of the community. Participating at this level empowers nurses and nursing organizations to shape the healthcare delivery system, healthcare reimbursement mechanisms and health-related social issues.

ADDITIONAL CONSIDERATIONS

Professional Boundaries

The *Code of Ethics for Nurses* establishes expectations with regard to professional boundaries and impaired practice. Although these issues are not unique to home healthcare, nurses who practice in this setting face challenges in maintaining these standards. The American Nurses' Association defines a professional relationship as one that "has as a foundation, the purpose of preventing illness, alleviating suffering, and protecting, promoting and restoring the health of patients" (ANA, 2001, p. 11).

Like all practice settings, home healthcare provides the professional nurse with pros and cons. The concept of one patient and one nurse is probably the most appealing characteristic of home health nursing. For some nurses, it is this same appeal that can jeopardize the ability to maintain professional boundaries and limits.

Many agencies are organized in a way that one nurse is assigned to a group/caseload of patients for whom they are responsible. In addition to providing the direct/hands-on care, the nurse is also responsible for the coordination of agency and community-based services for their caseload. This case management role fosters the development of intimate and long-term relationships between the nurse and the patient. Nurses in home healthcare often report that this level of involvement leads to job satisfaction and professional fulfillment.

However, for some nurses it also lends itself to the compromise of professional boundaries and limits.

Most agencies have policies and procedures designed to minimize the blurring of professional boundaries and limits. Nurses who violate these policies may be subject to progressive discipline or termination from the agency. Depending on the severity of the violation, nurses may also be subject to a report being filed with their state Board of Nursing Licensure.

The failure to maintain professional boundaries and establish limits is usually an insidious process. Home healthcare nurses who have difficulties with professional boundaries do not necessarily realize that a problem has developed until it is too late. By the time the problem is recognized, the nurse has great difficulty changing the behavior especially with a "favorite" patient or family. After all, once the nurse has exceeded the limits of professional boundaries how do they tell the patient that the behavior cannot continue?

It is true, that on occasion, a patient will tug at your heartstrings; however, as the professional nurse, you are expected to provide care that is compassionate while remaining within the professional boundaries outlined in the *Code of Ethics for Nurses*. It is not uncommon for you, the nurse, to be the only person a patient sees in a day or even a week. As the home healthcare nurse, you may be the only person who knows that one, two, or three of your patients will spend an entire holiday alone, without the company of family or friends. In all likelihood. you will encounter a patient or two who will challenge your ability to maintain these boundaries.

The *Code of Ethics for Nurses* is clear that the nurse is solely responsible to maintain the professional relationship, and if they are in jeopardy "the nurse should seek assistance from peers or supervisors or take appropriate steps to remove him/herself from the situation" (ANA, 2001, p. 11). Table 2-2 provides a list of warning signs that, individually or in combination, could signal to the home healthcare nurse that they are at risk for compromising professional standards.

The following scenarios are intended to highlight potential violations of the standards of professional boundaries. If you were the nurse in Mr. Donovan or Mrs. Smith's case as they are outlined below, what would you do?

Mr. Donovan

Mr. Donovan is an elderly patient who has a history of cardiac disease and diabetes. He is also deaf and mute. Until recently, he was independent and able to get around the city using public transportation. The home health plan of care requires

TABLE 2-2: BREECH OF PROFESSIONAL BOUNDARIES WARNING SIGNS

- Checking voice mail or email on days off.
- Calling the agency to "check on things" while on vacation.
- Forgetting that the patients that you are assigned to case manage do not "belong" to you.
- Expecting that if you change jobs, you will be allowed to transfer patients to the new agency with you.
- Thinking that none of your colleagues can do the job as well as you can.
- Visiting your patient on your day off or after your regular working hours.
- Introducing your family members or children to your patients.
- Purchasing groceries, prescriptions or other items for your patients.
- Taking a patient to your home.
- Representing yourself as the patient's friend or caregiver.
- Providing services beyond those that are reasonable or necessary.

the nurse to assess his cardiac status twice each week. Mr. Donovan communicates to you that he would like you to stop at a local candy store to pick up some diabetic chocolates before your next visit and hands you a ten-dollar bill.

How would you respond to this simple request from a patient who has no other means of obtaining this very small pleasure? After all, he has lost his independence and you will be going right by the store. In fact, that store is right in your district and you must go by it two or three times a day. What harm could possibly come from granting this request?

Mrs. Smith

Consider the case of Mrs. Smith who was discussed in depth earlier in this chapter. You may recall she had multiple readmissions to the hospital for management of congestive heart failure exacerbations. On one of your visits, you identify that she is beginning to retain fluid again. She states that she has been following the diet and fluid restriction that the Registered Dietician planned for her. She also tells you that she has no money to refill her prescriptions and will not have any money until her check comes late next week. She ran out of her diuretic three days ago.

What will you do? Will you call her pharmacy and ask them to send her a few pills until her check comes? Will you call her physician and ask him if he has any free samples in his office that you could go and pick up for her? Perhaps you could pay to have her prescription refilled just this once.

In both of these cases the "correct" answer can be found by considering the role of the professional nurse in home health and the definition of a professional boundary. Would your decision meet the objectives of these directives?

IMPAIRED PRACTICE

Addressing a colleague whose practice is impaired as a result of drug and alcohol use is the most difficult professional experience that a nurse will encounter. It is estimated that 6% to 7% of all nurses are chemically dependent (Nurses Learning Network, 2001). Historically, the highest incidence of chemically dependent nurses is found in the emergency room or in critical care. The *Code of Ethics for Nurses* outlines the responsibility of every nurse "to protect the patient, the public and the profession from potential harm when a colleague's practice, in any setting, appears to be impaired" (ANA, 2001, p. 15). Every nurse is bound by duty to act when they identify a colleague who is practicing while impaired.

Although the incidence of chemical dependence and impaired practice is not readily documented in home healthcare, it does not mean that this is not an issue. Home healthcare is one of the fastest growing practice settings for nurses. The autonomy and independence of home healthcare creates an environment where a chemically dependent nurse could function with a low risk of being detected.

Outlined below is the case study of Nancy Nurse. Consider this scenario and identify at which point your professional duty would require you to intervene.

Nancy Nurse

Nancy has 20 years of nursing experience, and many of the nurses in your agency know her from working with her in previous settings. She has been assigned to the same district of the city that you work in. During her orientation, you have an opportunity to talk with her everyday, and your Clinical Nurse Manager tells you that she expects the two of you to cover each other's patients for days off and vacations.

After a couple of months of working with Nancy, you realize that she has fallen asleep during a staff meeting. You ask her if she is "okay." She tells you that she is having marital and other personal problems that have diminished her ability to get enough sleep, but other than that she is "fine."

The nurses who work in your district customarily meet one day a week to have lunch at a local diner. You arrive just after Nancy, but before she gets out of her car, you notice she has a couple of sips of what appears to be mouthwash and places a fresh piece of gum in her mouth. Come to think of it, she is always chewing gum, or eating candy or mints.

When Nancy comes into the office early one morning, you note a faint odor of alcohol on her breath. Although you do not mention it to her, she later tells you that she had a few drinks last night to relax after fighting with her husband. She tells you she is worried that someone might notice and asks if you can still smell alcohol on her breath. You minimize the issue and tell her, "not really."

After a few months of working with Nancy, you notice one day that her speech is slurred, and she appears to be having difficulty concentrating. When you ask her about her behavior, she informs you that she has a number of newly diagnosed medical problems; her physician is currently adjusting her medication regimen; and she must be experiencing side effects.

While conducting a routine home visit, you mistakenly lock your keys in your car. You call the agency to inform your Clinical Nurse Manager and ask if someone could bring you the spare key that you keep in your desk. Your Clinical Nurse Manager tells you that someone will bring it out shortly. Unbeknown to you, Nancy was in the office at the time of your call and arrives with your spare key. When she opens the door of her car to get out, two beer cans fall to the sidewalk. She explains that her husband was returning them to the recycling center. She says he must have dropped them in the car, and they rolled under her seat.

Nancy has completed the probationary period just in time for her to cover some of your patients while you are on vacation. When you get back, you get report from Nancy, and she tells you that nothing unusual happened while you were away. When you begin to see your patients, they tell a different story and make subtle comments about Nancy. Mr. Ellis is one of your patients who tells you, "I am glad your back, my medications were all messed up when you were gone. I even ran out of my pain medication. Good thing that other nurse called the pharmacy, picked them up and straightened them out for me."

Later in the week, you visit Mrs. Flannigan. Her plan of care includes the prefilling of liquid Morphine into individual spill-proof cups. She tells you that since you left for vacation her back pain had gotten much worse. Nancy had to call the physician and arrange for her to begin taking twice the amount of medication to get the same relief. She reports that today she feels much better and thinks that she could go back to the previous dose.

Finally, Mrs. Gagnon tells you, "I think that other nurse looked in my medicine cabinet in the bathroom. She was taking a long time in there. You never take that long, and you never close the door when you go in to wash your hands. When my daughter knocked on the door to see if she was all right, she thought she heard a pill bottle hit the floor. When that Nancy came out, she said she was taking one of her own medications because she has high blood pressure. My daughter and I felt very funny about her, please don't send her back."

When considering these examples, it is clear that there was definitely something questionable about Nancy's behavior. However, it is unlikely that the behavior of the chemically dependent nurse will be as obvious. It is more realistic to expect the behavior to be subtle and insidious. Recognizing that the *Code of Ethics for Nurses* requires nurses to protect patients, the public and the profession, what would you do when faced with a nurse who may be practicing while impaired? Most practice settings have policies and procedures that will provide guidance in the reporting of this sensitive issue. These policies should be stringent enough to protect all parties, while providing an environment that is conducive to the professional nurse's treatment, recovery and return to work.

In the area of home healthcare, some additional issues must be considered. When Mr. Ellis reported that Nancy called the pharmacy, picked up and delivered his medications, you must question if she returned all pills that were dispensed by the pharmacy. What if the correct number of pills was delivered, but plain Tylenol was switched for the Tylenol with Codeine that the patient usually receives?

Is it a coincidence that Mrs. Flannigan experienced an exacerbation of her back pain while you were on vacation? Would you be surprised to find out that it took twice as much Morphine to restore her comfort? Would you recognize that her remaining doses of prefilled Morphine appear to be lighter in color than you remembered and seem somewhat watery in consistency? Is it possible that Mrs. Flannigan's Morphine had been diluted with water, and half of a bottle removed from her home?

In the case of Mrs. Gagnon, is it possible that Nancy looked through the medicine cabinet and removed something? If not an entire bottle of medication, could she have removed a few tablets?

It is clear that if Nancy switched, diluted or outright stole a patient's medication for her own use, in addition to the impaired practice issues that you suspected, you also have issues of theft. Will the theft of patient's medication require that Nancy's behavior be reported to the state Board of Nursing or the local police? Will her license to practice be suspended while she receives treatment for her chemical dependency, or will she lose her license to practice nursing as a result of diverting or

stealing patient medications? Will Nancy's position at the agency be held for her while she receives treatment, or will she be forced to resign her position? Should she practice in home health once she completes her treatment, or does the autonomy and independence of home healthcare create a situation that might jeopardize her recovery? Will she be subject to criminal prosecution?

How will you feel if Nancy's behavior is only coincidental, and you falsely accused her of practicing while impaired or diverting a patient's medication? How will you rationalize your decision not to report Nancy's behavior if a patient suffers needlessly or is hurt as a result of clouded judgement?

As stated earlier, addressing a colleague's issue of impaired practice or chemical dependency is the most difficult professional decision that a nurse may face. It is important that the employer and the nurse(s) reporting these issues do so in a manner that preserves the dignity of their colleague and respects their right to confidentiality.

SUMMARY

The scope of nursing is defined as the "protection, promotion, restoration of health; prevention of illness; and alleviation of suffering in the care of clients, including individuals, families, groups and communities" (ANA, 1985, p. i). On any given day, home health care nurses find themselves caring for patients and families along this continuum. The Code of Ethics for Nurses is the yardstick by which all nurses, regardless of their area of practice, are measured. While the goal of nursing is to "support and enhance the client's responsibility and self determination to the greatest extent possible," the home environment poses challenges that are not always anticipated or easily overcome (ANA, 1985, p. i).

EXAM QUESTIONS

CHAPTER 2
Questions 7-14

Consider the case of Mrs. Rodrigues when answering questions 7 through 10.

Mrs. Rodrigues is an 87-year-old patient who lives in a poor inner city neighborhood. You are going to see Mrs. Rodrigues to administer her evening dose of antibiotics. When you turn down Mrs. Rodrigues' street, you notice many of the multifamily houses are run down. Some even have their doors and windows boarded up and look uninhabited. When you reach address 45 you slowly drive past the house because you are not sure if you have the correct address. Once you double check the address, you realize that you are at the right location and that the porch light is now on.

The street is empty and it is dark outside. Although you are uncomfortable with the neighborhood, you do not feel threatened or perceive any safety risks.

7. The *Code of Ethics for Nurses* requires you to

    a. complete the visit and suggest to Mrs. Rodrigues that she find a "better" neighborhood to live in.

    b. call your manager and refuse to complete the visit because of your discomfort.

    c. respect human dignity and the uniqueness of Mrs. Rodrigues, unrestricted by considerations of social or economic status.

    d. suggest to your manager that referrals for patients similar to Mr. Rodrigues be declined.

Mrs. Rodrigues tells you that most of the houses on the street are empty, and she suspects that sometimes the homeless people stay in them. "Sometimes," she says, "those boys even sell drugs on the corner." She tells you that she never walks the street anymore, if she needs to leave her home she calls a cab because it is "safer." She reminisces that she and her family have lived in this house for almost one hundred years and that her great-grandfather built the house for the family so she could never leave it.

8. Provision One of the *Code of Ethics for Nurses*

    a. requires the nurse to condone and agree with a patient's choices regardless if the choices may jeopardize the patient's safety.

    b. requires that the nurse not form an opinion about a patient's circumstance regardless of what it is.

    c. does not provide any guidance for the nurse when it comes to differing opinions.

    d. does not require the nurse to condone or agree with a patient's choice; it does, however, require the nurse to provide care regardless of the patient's choices.

9. By remaining in her home, Mrs. Rodrigues

    a. is exercising poor judgement.

    b. may be incompetent to make this decision.

    c. is jeopardizing her ability to receive services.

    d. is exercising her right to self-determination.

After your conversation with Mrs. Rodrigues, you get a sense that she is sad and might be somewhat depressed. Without any friends or neighbors, she is isolated at the very least. You make a note of these findings and plan to discuss this issue further with your manager and the team assigned to this district. You consider whether Mrs. Rodrigues would benefit from attending adult day care for socialization.

10. Provision Two of the *Code of Ethics for Nurses* requires you as the nurse

    a. collaborate with other team members in an effort to attain the goals of Mrs. Rodrigues care plan.

    b. notify elder-at-risk services to address the poor choices that Mrs. Rodrigues is making.

    c. discharge Mrs. Rodrigues from your agency's caseload because you are not supposed to support a plan of care that is unsafe or jeopardizes patient safety.

    d. document your findings and leave the information as to who will be conducting the morning visit.

Provision Four of the *Code of Ethics for Nurses* requires that when the patient's needs are "beyond the qualifications and competencies of the nurse, consultation and collaboration must be sought from qualified nurses, other health professionals, or other appropriate sources" (ANA, 2001, p. 17).

11. The realities of practicing in home healthcare make this

    a. impossible to uphold regardless of the practice setting.

    b. necessary, and it frequently occurs.

    c. provision outdated and not applicable.

    d. unrealistic and rarely done.

12. When a home healthcare aide is assigned to a case, the nurse is responsible to supervise them because

    a. the home health plan of care is signed by the physician, and there is an order to conduct supervision visits at least every two weeks.

    b. agency policy requires it.

    c. every nurse is responsible and accountable for individual nursing practice and determines the appropriate delegation of tasks, and it is the nurse's obligation to assure that optimum patient care is being provided.

    d. there may be a change in the patient's plan of care or condition.

13. The first four provisions outlined in the *Code of Ethics for Nurses* describe the

    a. values and commitment required of all professional nurses.

    b. nurses role in policy and procedure development.

    c. boundaries of duty and loyalty.

    d. nurse's obligation to continue to develop their practice and continued education.

14. The responsibility to create, maintain and contribute to an environment that supports growth and excellence in nursing is typically

    a. an administrative function.

    b. the responsibility of every professional nurse.

    c. results when the nursing staff is unionized.

    d. not a realistic expectation.

15. Participating in nursing research activities, acting as a preceptor to a new staff member, or participating in performance improvement teams

    a. are considered going "above and beyond" the duties typically associated with the professional nurse.

    b. are not practical for most professional nurses.

    c. require knowledge and skills only associated with the advanced practice nurse.

    d. are the responsibility of all professional nurses as outlined in Provision Seven of the ANA *Code of Ethics for Nurses.*

16. Working in districts affords the home healthcare nurse the opportunity to learn about the needs of the community and the services available to meet patient needs. Provision Eight of the *Code of Ethics for Nurses* identifies that the professional nurse bears the responsibility to

    a. support the political candidates that the agency's administration is recommending.

    b. support and participate in civic and political initiatives designed to improve the health and wellness of the community.

    c. remain apolitical.

    d. run for public office whenever possible.

17. Provision Nine of the *Code of Ethics for Nurses* requires the professional nurse to

    a. recognize that health and social problems faced by local communities are basically irreversible.

    b. recognize that, without increased economic opportunities, the nursing profession is powerless to affect meaningful change.

    c. "think globally and act locally."

    d. work through professional associations and affiliations that are committed to identifying political solutions to local, national and international health and social problems.

18. A professional relationship is one that "has a foundation, the purpose of preventing illness, alleviating suffering and protecting, promoting and restoring the health of patients" (ANA, 2001, p. 11). Home healthcare nurses

    a. are not at risk for breaching professional boundaries.

    b. are not subject to these expectations due to the uniqueness of the home healthcare practice setting.

    c. may be subject to progressive discipline, termination or action by the State Board of Licensure.

    d. respond to a higher standard and therefore cannot be held to this standard.

19. Visiting a patient on your day off or while you are on vacation or providing services beyond those that are reasonable and necessary are examples of

    a. a consciousness decision to be kind.

    b. lack of confidence in your professional skills.

    c. lack of confidence in the skills of the staff covering in your absence.

    d. potentially exceeding professional boundaries.

20. It is estimated that the number of nurses who are chemically dependent is approximately

    a. 0-3%.

    b. 6-7%.

    c. 8-10%.

    d. >15%.

CHAPTER 3

SCOPE AND STANDARDS OF HOME HEALTH NURSING PRACTICE

CHAPTER OBJECTIVE

At the completion of this chapter, the reader will be able to state the six standards of practice for home healthcare nursing and recognize how to apply them to patient scenarios.

LEARNING OBJECTIVES

After studying this chapter, the reader will be able to

1. define terms of art such as information system, data and database.

2. differentiate between an outcome and an expected outcome.

3. discriminate between a nursing plan of care and a home health plan of treatment.

4. list between three and five patient rights.

5. list between two and three patient responsibilities.

INTRODUCTION

The American Nurses' Association defines a standard as a "norm that expresses an agreed-upon level of excellence that has been developed to characterize, to measure, and to provide guidance for achieving excellence in practice" (ANA, 1986, p. 21). *Standards of Practice* represent the expectations for the personal and professional integrity of nurses. The American Nurses' Association (ANA) published the first *Standards of Home Health Nursing Practice* in 1986. This publication outlined 12 standards which, as a whole, represented the complex nature of home care nursing. These original standards included structural (agency-related), process (nurse-related) and outcome (patient-related) criteria for each of the standards.

In 1999, the standards were revised, consolidated and renamed the *Scope and Standards of Home Health Nursing Practice.* This revision eliminated the structural components of the standards and as they currently stand, define and recognize home healthcare nursing as a unique and distinct area of nursing practice. This document is organized into six patient-focused Standards of Care and eight Standards of Professional Performance. The Standards of Care will be covered in this chapter, and the Standards of Professional Performance will be covered in Chapter 4.

Regardless of the setting, the goal of nursing can be defined as the promotion of the patient's optimal level of function within the limits of their disease process. Nurses achieve this goal through the implementation of an organized nursing process.

The home healthcare nurse focuses on the patient and their interactions with family, caregivers and their community. The repertoire of home healthcare nursing skills includes assessment, intervention, teaching, counseling, managing and mobilizing resources and providing direct care all in the patient's home.

DATA COLLECTION AND INFORMATION SYSTEMS

Before moving onto the discussion of the Standards of Care, it is important to clarify some of the terminology used in this chapter. The Standards of Care frequently use the terms data and information systems, which are not commonly used by nurses to describe patients or patient-related issues. For many nurses, these terms are more easily related to computers than patients.

To provide context for these terms, consider that nursing is both an art and a science. All scientific endeavors require data and a mechanism to organize it, so that it is useful. For the purposes of this discussion, patient data refers to patient information, and information systems refer to the patient medical records.

All home healthcare nurses collect patient data and enter it into the agency's information system. Information systems found in home healthcare are rapidly evolving. Although the majority of agencies continue to utilize paper-driven patient information systems, most are actively investigating electronic medical record systems. Regardless of the type of information system the agency uses, at the very least, it must provide patient data that is easily accessible, organized and presents the most current information while protecting patient confidentiality.

STANDARDS OF CARE

Each of the six Standards of Care is simply stated and includes measurement criteria to clarify and define them. Like all professional standards, the ANA Standards of Care are organized in a manner that makes them easily applicable to the day-to-day practice of every home healthcare

nurse. Outlined below is a discussion of each of the standards. Illustrative patient examples are provided where applicable.

Standard I: Data Collection/Assessment

Standard I states that "the home health nurse collects client health data" (ANA, 1999, p. 9). Every nurse/patient relationship begins with an assessment. The nurse usually begins the day by calling all of the patients they intend to see that day. Even the simple phone conversation provides clues to the home healthcare nurse. The nurse evaluates the patient's hearing and cognition. While the nurse is waiting for the front door to be opened, the astute home healthcare nurse evaluates how long it took the patient to answer the door. Did the nurse have to knock or ring the bell more than once? If so, does the patient have a hearing deficit? Did the patient actually come to the door or just holler for the nurse to come in? Why did the patient not come to the door? Is the patient's mobility limited? If the patient did manage to get to the door, did they do it in a reasonable time? If not, would the patient be able to get out of their home in an emergency, such as a fire?

Once the patient opens the door to the home healthcare nurse, the assessment process continues. Every detail of the patient and their environment are observed and "stored" by the nurse for later use. The nurse uses many sources of information in the assessment process.

In the case of Mrs. Smith presented in Chapter 2, your first source of patient data was provided by the hospital's discharge forms and referral information. It was immediately clear to you that this information was incomplete and inadequate.

When reconsidering the case of Mrs. Smith, you remember that from the outside, her home appeared to be well-kept and orderly. However, once you actually entered the home, you realized that there was no way the hospital or any other referral source could have anticipated the condition of the inside of Mrs. Smith's home.

As data is collected, it is prioritized based on the patient's most immediate needs. In the case of Mrs. Smith, you determined that her inability to complete her activities of daily living (ADLS) and instrumental activities of daily living (IADLS) were her most urgent issues. The majority of the first visit with Mrs. Smith was spent collecting data related to the presence of a caregiver, the adequacy of the care provided and the lack of other social supports.

The ongoing collection of data is necessary for the nurse to establish a nursing diagnosis, identify expected outcomes, plan, intervene and then evaluate the patient as they react to their environment, disease process and interventions.

When conducting an assessment, the nurse collects and records data related to the patient's physical status, including current and past history. Information related to the patient's psychosocial status, economic status, environment, religion and culture are also collected. The nurse is responsible to assess the patient's ability to perform activities of daily living and instrumental activities of daily living. The Joint Commission on Accreditation of Health Care Organizations (JCAHO) defines a comprehensive home health nursing assessment as one that includes an assessment of:

- "The patient's problems, needs and strengths;
- The patient's prognosis, diagnosis, physical findings including medical history;
- Age-specific and gender-specific findings;
- Laboratory results;
- Prescribed and over-the-counter medication;
- Any identified symptoms of pain;
- The patient's nutrition status and dental function;

- Functional status, including mobility, continence, independence in activities of daily living and ability to operate and maintain equipment;
- The patient's psychosocial status, including emotional barriers to treatment, cognitive limitations, memory and orientation;
- History of chemical dependency;
- Cultural and religious practices;
- The patient's wishes regarding care, treatment and end of life decisions;
- The home environment;
- Equipment;
- Preventative and periodic health screening;
- The patient's family or support system and the care they are capable of and willing to provide;
- The patient's and family's educational needs, abilities, motivation and readiness to learn; and
- Anticipated discharge needs" (Comprehensive Accreditation Manual for Home Care, 2001, p. HH-11).

In 1999, the Center for Medicare and Medicaid Services (CMS) mandated the use of a standardized assessment tool for home healthcare. The Outcome Assessment Information Set (OASIS) is a tool that requires the home care nurse to collect data at several points in time (Conditions of Participation, 1999). This data is then used to determine the outcome of the care that was provided to the patient. Chapters 6 and 7 provide an in-depth discussion of the OASIS documents and their value in measuring outcomes and quality in home healthcare.

The usefulness of the data collected by the nurse is measured by assuring that the database (medical record) is comprehensive and accurately reflects the patient's status. In essence, the database provides a detailed picture of the patient which allows the nurse to proceed to the development of the nursing diagnosis.

Standard II: Diagnosis

The second standard of care encompasses the formulation and integration of patient data into nursing diagnoses. In home healthcare, the nurse formulates nursing diagnoses that are based on the patient's current status as derived through the data collection process. Nursing diagnoses must take into account the patient's needs while respecting their right to self-determination.

One way to validate your nursing diagnoses is to ask the patient to state what they hope to accomplish as a result of your nursing visits. Once again, consider the case of Mrs. Smith. As a result of the nursing assessment, a number of nursing diagnoses could be established. Outlined below are examples of some diagnoses that might be appropriate for her.

- Alteration in skin integrity related to decreased mobility, decreased circulation and compromised nutritional status.

- Knowledge deficit related to medication management evidenced by lack of compliance with physician ordered plan.

- Decreased ability to cope as evidenced by alcohol use and minimal social support.

- Potential for injury related to inability to safely transfer out of bed.

Once nursing diagnoses are formulated, it is important to validate the diagnoses with the patient to assure that they represent the patient's perspective of their needs. An inexperienced home healthcare nurse can easily become overwhelmed with the number of issues they perceive to be problematic. Often, from the patient's perspective, the issues identified by the nurse are not problematic at all. When these differing perspectives are not resolved, the nurse and the patient will lack the coordinated effort required to meet goals. This results in both the nurse and the patient becoming frustrated and dissatisfied. The nurse may deem the patient "non-compliant" and the patient may request another caregiver due to a personality conflict or complaints about the nurse and their skills. To illustrate this point consider the case of Mrs. King.

Mrs. King

You have been assigned to admit Mrs. King to your agency's services. Mrs. King's physician has requested skilled nursing to teach her how to prepare and administer insulin. When you approach her home you hear loud voices. It sounds like Mrs. King is arguing with someone. After you ring the doorbell the apartment becomes quiet.

An elderly lady answers the door; she is in a bathrobe and looks as if she has not combed her hair, even though it is 2:30 p.m. She states, "Are you the nurse that called, come on in." As you enter, you observe that the small apartment is spotless except for the clutter on one small end table near a reclining chair. An elderly man is sitting in the chair and appears angry and upset.

Mrs. King states, "Ignore him, he is all bark and no bite." Mr. King shoots back, "Yeah, that's right I'm all bark, all bark! If I had a bite you'd be in trouble."

"Trouble," shouts Mrs. King, "I have had nothing but trouble since I married you." Mrs. King turns to you and says, "I have had nothing but trouble since I married him in 1945. Look, look at him, he is a no good lazy slob."

At this point you interrupt Mrs. King and try to redirect her to the reason for your visit. She turns her attention to you and says, "Fifty-two years, four kids and eleven grandchildren with him. Can you believe it? Ok, let's get on with it."

During your visit the bickering between Mr. and Mrs. King continues intermittently. From the livingroom, Mr. King listens to your conversation with Mrs. King and occasionally interjects a comment, which results in an unpleasant rebuttal from Mrs. King.

As the result of your visit, it is clear that you will establish a nursing diagnosis or two related to Mrs. King's diabetes, but what about the relationship between Mr. and Mrs. King? Would you establish a nursing diagnosis to address their relationship? Does either of these individuals appear to be victims of domestic abuse or violence? Is their constant bickering a problem that requires intervention, or has their 52-year marriage always been filled with bickering and unkind words? If you establish a nursing diagnosis to address their relationship, would Mrs. King be inclined to agree or would she more likely want to focus on expecting that she will be able to administer and manage her insulin independently?

Standard III. Outcome Identification

The *Standards of Home Health Care Nursing Practice* require the nurse to identify patient-related outcomes. For the purposes of this chapter, outcomes are used to describe the change in the patient's health status between two points in time. Since the majority of home healthcare services are provided on an intermittent, short-term basis, it is imperative that the care be focused on the achievement of patient outcomes within the identified time frames.

Expected outcomes are established at the patient's start of care and are based on the patient's assessment and diagnoses. They are identified through the collaborative efforts of the nurse, patient, physician and other members of the healthcare team. Since these outcomes provide direction for all interventions, it is essential that they are measurable, realistic and attainable.

Although the identification of patient outcomes appears to be easily achieved, home healthcare provides some interesting challenges for the nurse. Achievement of an outcome may take weeks or even months of intensive intervention. The nurse

must consider who will be providing reimbursement for the home healthcare services and assist the patient in understanding the limitations or restrictions that may be placed on the level of services provided.

The home healthcare nurse can not avoid addressing issues of the cost and insurance coverage. Both the American Nurses' Association's and the Joint Commission on Accreditation of Healthcare Organizations' standards require the nurse to acknowledge the cost of patient care.

In most inpatient facilities, the reimbursement details are addressed by the Admissions or Billing Departments as part of the application or screening process. In most home healthcare agencies, some preliminary reimbursement screening occurs when the referral is taken. A more thorough evaluation of the patient's insurance and the ability to qualify for home healthcare services cannot be achieved until the nurse actually makes a visit to the patient's home. Home healthcare is one of the few practice settings where the nurse who provides the direct patient care is also responsible for evaluating and substantiating that the patient meets the criteria of their insurance plan. In addition, the nurse has the responsibility of informing the patient of what their estimated financial liability would be if the insurance company refuses to pay for the services, or if the patient is required to make a co-payment for each visit. In fact, JCAHO accredited agencies are required to provide the patient with an actual dollar amount in writing. To illustrate this point, consider the case of Mr. Highland.

Mr. Highland

Mr. Highland is a 75-year-old man who was admitted to your agency after the repair of an inguinal hernia. He developed a postoperative wound infection and now requires skilled nursing to manage his wound. Mr. Highland's primary insurance is Medicare, and he meets all the criteria necessary to receive home healthcare services.

Once his plan of care is established and certified by the physician, your agency will receive one episodic payment from Medicare to provide his services for the next 60 days. Based on his clinical needs and the physician's order, Mr. Highland will require daily nursing visits to change his dressing and assess the status of the infection and the healing of the wound. Since daily nursing visits will most likely exceed Medicare's reimbursement, you must work aggressively to promote wound healing, resolve the wound infection and reduce the frequency of nursing visits.

If Mr. Highland's insurance is provided by another insurance company, perhaps one with a limited home healthcare benefit, you will have to discuss his progress toward the outcomes with a case reviewer every week or two to obtain further authorization for visits. You will have to provide written documentation and justification as to why it would be inappropriate to delegate his care to a friend or family member or for him to do the dressing himself.

If his insurance plan only includes coverage for six or eight visits each quarter, your expected outcomes might be very different. Your primary outcome may be to teach a friend or family member the dressing technique and the signs and symptoms to report to the physician. If Mr. Highland has no one available to teach, you might have to get creative and teach him to change his own dressing while lying on his back using a mirror, or he may need to return to the physician's office for the dressing change.

Standard IV: Planning

The planning standards require the nurse to "develop a plan of care that prescribes intervention to attain expected outcomes" (ANA, 1999, p. 10). The patient's plan of care must be customized to meet their specific and unique needs. Although many home healthcare agencies use care paths or protocols, there are just as many that have aban-

doned these models of care delivery. To be effective, a care plan must be flexible enough to adapt to the unique needs of the patient while considering the effects of their home environment.

Consider the care path for a patient who is hospitalized with a primary diagnosis of heart failure (HF). The acute inpatient plan of care for HF patients will likely include routine or standing orders for the administration of diuretics, blood work to monitor the patient's electrolytes and renal function, oxygen, and a chest x-ray. The nursing plan of care might include plans for vital sign monitoring, medication administration, monitoring of the patient's response to the diuretics, dietary teaching, a referral to home healthcare, and instructions to follow up with the primary care physician. The patient's entire length of stay might be two or three days. The expectation may be that the same protocol be implemented for every patient with a primary diagnosis of HF admitted to the facility.

When a HF patient returns to their home environment, a number of factors that are not directly related to the patient's diagnosis may impact the plan of care, as were seen with the case of Mrs. Smith. The nurse must be able to identify and plan for simple barriers such as:

- Affordability of medications;

- Ability of the patient to obtain medications and adhere to the prescribed schedule;

- Ability of the patient to adhere to dietary restrictions; and

- The patient's willingness to comply with the prescribed plan of care.

From an inpatient perspective, these barriers are absurd. After all, the patient's medications are dispensed from the pharmacy and administered by the nursing staff at the frequency prescribed by the physician. Adherence to dietary restrictions is easily achieved. The patient's no added salt dinner arrives from dietary promptly at 7:30 a.m., 12 noon and 5:30 p.m. In addition, the nurse's aide makes rounds every hour to monitor and record the patient's intake and output. Can this structure be achieved in the patient's home as well?

At first blush, one might think the four barriers discussed above are not barriers at all, they are merely excuses and examples of the patient sabotaging the plan of care through noncompliance. In actuality, the reality for this patient in their home might be something very different. The home healthcare nurse must first ascertain whether or not the patient can afford to purchase the medications that have been prescribed. It is important to remember that many home healthcare recipients have a fixed income and that a significant portion of it may be spent on medications. Frequent changes in medication regimes result in wasted medicine and increased burden on the patient's limited financial resources.

For homebound elders, obtaining medications might pose a serious and real barrier to following the plan of care. If the patient cannot drive or use public transportation how will they obtain the medications? Does a pharmacy in the neighborhood make home deliveries? What if the patient uses a mail order system to obtain medications? Customarily, the patient has to order a three-month supply to achieve a discount and wait up to two or three weeks for the medication to arrive. With a brittle HF patient, a two-week wait could result in at least one additional hospitalization, another change in the medication regime and the cycle continuing again and again and again.

Diuretic therapy can pose an additional challenge to the homebound elder, and the astute home healthcare nurse will recognize this immediately. It is not uncommon for a patient to manipulate their medication schedule due to frequent urination. Consider what 40, 60 or 80mg of Lasix might do to the patient with limited mobility or severe joint pain. The case of Mr. Indeglia highlights this point.

Mr. Indeglia

Mr. Indeglia is a 74-year-old widower. He has no children and currently lives in an apartment complex that is restricted to elderly residents. In addition to his complex underlying medical problems, he has a history of degenerative joint disease and underwent a total hip replacement six months ago. He now uses a rolling walker at all times.

Mr. Indeglia was admitted to your agency after he suffered a myocardial infarction (MI) resulting in right-sided heart failure. When you first visit him, you find that, although he appears medically stable, he also appears somewhat depressed. He tells you that he used to go to the Community Room every morning, to have coffee and play cards with his "buddies." He then reveals that he now has problems with "holding his water," and one time he even had an "embarrassing accident." He states, "When I have to go, I better be close to the bathroom or look out, it's a terrible thing."

Since Mr. Indeglia had a Foley catheter in the hospital, you further inquire about whether he has pain or burning when urinating to rule out any signs or symptoms of a urinary tract infection. He denies any symptoms.

You ask him to describe his daily routine before he went to the hospital and uncover that he was usually in the Community Room from 8:30 a.m. to 11:30 a.m., then returned to his apartment for lunch and remained there until dinner. He tells you that after the evening news he always returned to the Community Room to watch evening television with his friends.

Recognizing that the effects of Lasix peak in one to two hours, you suggest to Mr. Indeglia that he alter the schedule of his medication and take his "fluid pill" with lunch instead of breakfast. You explain that this change will allow him to return to his old routine and join his friends in the Community Room without the risk of an "embarrassing accident."

Clearly, the discharge plan established for Mr. Indeglia by the hospital was medically appropriate. Typically, patients on diuretic therapy take their medications every morning. There is no way the nurse in the hospital setting could take into consideration the impact that one pill would have on this patient when he returned home. Would the nurse in the hospital be surprised to realize that the diuretic therapy could result in Mr. Indeglia's feelings of social isolation and depression?

Finally, it is important to discuss the documentation of the plan of care. Whether the agency uses care paths or protocols, a traditional nursing plan of care, or physician certified plan of treatment, the nurse who establishes the plan of care is responsible to document in the medical record system regardless if the record is computerized or on paper. The documentation must "provide for continuity of patient" care and can be altered with the changing needs of the patient (ANA, 1999, p.10).

Home healthcare regulations and reimbursement require that the plan of care be physician driven. All home health plans of care require a physician signature to verify/certify that the care is appropriate for the patient. These requirements force the nurse to organize the patient care based on the medical diagnoses. Home healthcare regulations provide little room for nursing interventions that are not sanctioned by the physician.

Standard II requires that "diagnoses are documented in a manner that facilitates the determination of expected outcomes and plan of care" (ANA, 1999, p. 9). Since the plan of care is physician driven and developed in the medical/disease model of care, there is a general trend to move away from a separate list of nursing diagnoses or a nursing care plan. Nursing care that is not ordered by a physician can result in survey deficiencies from accrediting and regulatory bodies.

Once again, it will be useful to consider the case of Mrs. Smith to highlight this point. As a result of your assessment of Mrs. Smith and her environment, you identified that she would benefit from the skilled nursing visits twice a week to evaluate her cardiac and environmental status. You include this on the plan of care that is sent to the physician for certification and signature.

On your third visit, Mrs. Smith appears short of breath and also has an increase in peripheral edema. Your previous patient required you to measure her oxygen saturation with a portable pulse oximeter. Since you have the equipment in the car, you decide to test Mrs. Smith's oxygenation as part of your assessment and document the results in her medical record. Although this seems like a reasonable nursing intervention, you would be cited by JCAHO for providing care without physician orders.

From this example, it becomes easy to understand why it is risky to establish both a nursing and medical plan of care in home health. Providing services that are not physician ordered or not providing services that are ordered will result in a quality of care citation from regulatory and accrediting agencies.

The organizing and documenting of patient care is complex in any setting. In home healthcare, this is further complicated because, as discussed previously, the plan of care must be approved/certified by the physician. The way nurses plan, intervene and document patient care is primarily the result of having to demonstrate the provision of skilled nursing care to the payer.

Information systems/medical records tend to be organized in a way that the reimbursable skills are easily identified. In addition, the presence of a nursing plan of care separate from a physician certified plan of treatment increases the potential for clinicians failing to obtain physician orders for every treatment. For this reason, many agencies have eliminated the traditional nursing plan of care and work off of a physician certified plan of treatment.

The physician certified plan of treatment is commonly known as the 485. The 485 is a Medicare form that has been adopted by virtually all home healthcare payers. (See Appendix A, CMS form 485.) When evaluating many home health medical records, you will see a plan of treatment that is a dynamic document that incorporates the changing needs of the patient. The plan of treatment includes goals and an outline of the interventions necessary to achieve them.

When planning care, it is imperative that the patient right to self-determination is respected. The patient, physician, family, and other members of the healthcare team must be considered (and sometimes consulted) when the nurse is establishing the patient's plan. Home care agencies require the patient to acknowledge in writing that they are aware of the plan of care and agree to participate in the planning process. As part of the process, the nurse is responsible for establishing and informing the patient of the services that will be provided and the frequency that they will occur. In addition, the patient has the right to be informed when the plan of care changes, including changes in visit frequency or additional services or disciplines that may be participating in the plan.

Although patients have the right to self-determination, the agency also has rights. When a home health plan of care is established, it is essentially an agreement between the patient and the agency. Requirements of patient rights vary from state to state. Tables 3-1 and 3-2 provide a list of patient rights and their responsibilities.

Standard V: Implementation

Although home healthcare is an extremely autonomous practice setting, Standard V requires "the home health nurse to implement the interventions identified in the plan of care" (ANA,

TABLE 3-1: PATIENT RIGHTS

Patients have the right to:

- Be treated with dignity, respect and consideration;

- Receive services regardless of race, color, sex, religion, disability, sexual preference or ability to pay;

- Have their home healthcare provider communicate with them in a language that they can understand;

- Be free from physical and mental abuse and or neglect, as well as have their property treated with respect;

- Be given complete and accurate information concerning their diagnosis, treatment, alternatives, risks and prognosis;

- Refuse treatment or medication without reprisal or discrimination, as well as be informed of the consequence of such actions;

- Receive effective coordination and continuity of services;

- Expect that their reports of pain will be believed, receive information about pain and preventative measures, and have concerned staff who respond quickly to reports of pain;

- Confidentiality;

- Access to their medical records and bills; and

- Information about the agency and its ownership.

Conditions of Participation. Chapter IV-Health Care Financing Administration, Department of Health and Human Services. Retrieved January 15, 2003 from [http://www.access.gpo.gov/nara/cfr/waisidx_99/42cfr484_99.html].
Joint Commission on Accreditation of Health Care Organizations (JCAHO). (2001). Comprehensive accreditation manual for home care, 2001-2002. Oakbrook Terrace, Il: Author.

TABLE 3-2: PATIENT RESPONSIBILITIES

Patients have the responsibility to:

- Provide a safe environment for agency staff;

- Provide the agency with accurate, complete and timely medical and insurance information;

- Inform their physician or nurse of changes in health, reactions to medications or instruction given to them regarding treatment;

- Follow the plan of care as designed and determined by them and their care providers;

- Promptly notify the agency if they are not going to be home for a scheduled visit;

- Assume the costs for services and supplies not covered by insurance; and

- Ask their nurse what to expect regarding pain management.

Conditions of Participation. Chapter IV-Health Care Financing Administration, Department of Health and Human Services. Retrieved January 15, 2003 from [http://www.access.gpo.gov/nara/cfr/waisidx_99/42cfr484_99.html]. Joint Commission on Accreditation of Health Care Organizations (JCAHO). (2001). Comprehensive accreditation manual for home care, 2001-2002. Oakbrook Terrace, Il: Author.

1999, p. 11). Even though nurses do not require a physician to dictate the patient systems to be assessed, a nurse working in home care must be careful not to implement interventions that require a physician's order. As a rule of thumb, any time the nurse adds a new service or discipline, changes a visit frequency, or alters a treatment, a physician order is required. Failure to obtain an order means the nurse is practicing out of their scope of practice and this will result in denial of payment and will subsequently jeopardize the agency when it is surveyed. It is just as important for the nurse to recognize that failure to complete an intervention that was ordered by the physician will have the same negative consequences.

When reviewing the plan of care established for Mr. Indeglia, the expected interventions are clear. The nurse is to:

- Assess his cardiovascular status, medication compliance, nutrition, hydration and diet;

- Perform venipuncture every week to evaluate his prothrombin time, electrolytes, BUN and creatinine; and

- Teach him signs and symptoms to report, energy conservation techniques and an emergency plan.

These physician certified interventions give clear direction to every nurse visiting Mr. Indeglia. Each nursing note should include documentation of the patient assessment, tasks performed, and teaching accomplished. In addition, the visit note should include Mr. Indeglia's response to the teaching and his progress toward the anticipated outcomes.

Standard VI: Evaluation

The final standard relates to the evaluation of the patient's progress toward the anticipated outcomes. This standard is clarified by eight measurement criteria. Although an evaluation usually occurs at the completion of a task or a process, the evaluation of the patient's progress toward the outcomes is ongoing and should be documented systematically and in a timely fashion. The process of evaluation is ongoing, and it affords the nurse the opportunity to revise the diagnoses, expected outcomes, and the overall plan of care based on the changing needs of the patient and the dynamics of the patient's living situation. As a result of ongoing evaluation, the nurse might find that the diagnoses, expected outcomes, and plan of care are appropriate, and only the interventions need to be revised. Consider the case of Mrs. Jones.

Mrs. Jones

Mrs. Jones is a 68-year-old patient who experienced a stroke and has a residual right-sided hemiparesis. She is cognitively intact. Although she lives alone in her single-family home, her daughter stayed with her for the first two weeks following Mrs. Jones' return from the hospital. Her daughter has assisted Mrs. Jones with all of her activities of daily living and instrumental activities of daily living. Although Mrs. Jones has had occupational and physical therapy since her stroke, she is unable to complete her personal care independently. You are the nurse assigned to Mrs. Jones' case and are aware that she is a Medicare beneficiary, which qualifies her for home healthcare aide (HCA) services. Mrs. Jones is agreeable to this service, so you contact her physician and obtain an order and establish a plan of care for the HCA to follow.

At the time of Mrs. Jones' admission to the agency, one of her expected outcomes was to return to independence in all ADLS and IADLS within one or two months. However, the loss of her daughter as a primary caregiver represents a major change in her living situation, and a re-evaluation of the expected outcomes is warranted. As the nurse assigned to Mrs. Jones' case would you:

- Change the expected outcomes and begin planning for Mrs. Jones' permanent dependence in ADLS and IADLS?

- Extend the time frame to achieve the expected outcomes from one to two months to three to four months?

- Request a multidiscipline case conference to discuss realistic goals and establish new time frames?

Although the first option might seem like the most reasonable of all three options, Mrs. Jones' home healthcare benefits only provide for short-term intermittent home care services. Therefore, as the nurse caring for her, you realize that the home healthcare aide services will not be available to her indefinitely. The planning for permanent dependence may require Mrs. Jones to change her current living environment resulting in a transfer to an assisted living or skilled nursing facility. At the very least, altering the plan would require a discussion with Mrs. Jones to determine if this is the course of action that she would choose.

Extending the timeframes for her to achieve the expected outcomes sounds like a reasonable option; however, with the change in the caregiver situation continuing on the same course, the plan of care might be inadequate.

In this case, requesting a multidiscipline case conference to discuss realistic goals and establish new timeframes is the best course of action for Mrs. Jones' plan of care. The multidiscipline approach, which includes the nurse, home healthcare aide, occupational and physical therapist, and a medical social worker, will allow each unique discipline to discuss Mrs. Jones' progress to date and formulate reasonable expectations for additional progress toward independence. As a team, the group can establish a new plan of care that is tailored to Mrs. Jones' current needs and then confer with the physician, the patient, and the family.

SUMMARY

Every patient admitted to home healthcare represents a unique set of circumstances and health-related issues. The American Nurses' Association's Standards of Care provide some basic guidelines for the home healthcare nurse in the day-to-day performance of their duties.

In all practice settings, it is the responsibility of the professional nurse to develop a plan of care. The plan of care is based on data collected, diagnoses, and the expected outcomes. The plan of care is a dynamic document that provides a focus and direction for the implementation of the nurse's interventions as the needs of the patient change.

EXAM QUESTIONS

CHAPTER 3
Questions 21-33

21. The patient's medical record

    a. is not considered part of the agency's information system unless it is computerized.

    b. only becomes part of the information system after the patient is discharged from the agency, and the record is archived.

    c. is part of the agency's information system regardless of whether it is in an electronic or paper medium.

    d. cannot become part of the large information system due to confidentiality and HIPAA regulations.

22. The ongoing collection of patient data is

    a. not necessary due to the short home health length of stay.

    b. necessary for the nurse to establish a nursing diagnosis, identify expected outcomes, plan, intervene and evaluate the patient.

    c. only necessary if the nurse is concerned that the patient's case may be subject to litigation.

    d. only necessary in cases that require interdisciplinary collaboration.

23. A comprehensive database

    a. provides a detailed picture of the patient that allows the nurse to develop nursing diagnoses.

    b. can only be achieved when the agency uses a computerized medical record.

    c. is in jeopardy if the agency utilizes a paper/traditional medical record.

    d. not a realistic expectation due to unique issues associated with the home healthcare setting.

24. The nurse uses the information recorded during the assessment to formulate nursing diagnoses. Once nursing diagnoses are formulated, it is important to

    a. have the patient's attending physician verify them in writing.

    b. obtain approval from the agency's medical director.

    c. validate them with the clinical manager, supervisor or quality assurance department.

    d. validate them with the patient to assure that they represent the patient's perspective of their own needs.

25. The most realistic expected outcomes are identified through the collaborative efforts of the home healthcare nurse, the physician, and the

    a. patient.

    b. patient's significant other or spouse.

    c. Center for Medicare and Medicaid services medical review nurse.

    d. case reviewer.

26. Home healthcare is one of the few practice settings where the nurse who provides direct care is also responsible for

    a. evaluating and substantiating that the patient meets the criteria of the insurance plan.

    b. completing duties or services that are typically associated with ancillary services such as homemaking.

    c. achieving the expected outcomes.

    d. sharing the responsibilities for the patient's outcomes with other members of the healthcare team.

27. The patient's plan of treatment must

    a. be customized to meet the patient's specific and unique needs.

    b. follow the agency's care path.

    c. be based on a physician certified protocol.

    d. only consider the patient's physical and physiological needs.

28. Home health regulations and reimbursement require that the plan of care be driven by the

    a. physician and the medical diagnoses.

    b. nurse and the nursing diagnoses.

    c. patient and their needs.

    d. Medicare guidelines.

29. In order to reduce the potential of failing to obtain physicians' orders for every treatment, many agencies have eliminated the traditional nursing plan of care and work off of a physician certified plan on treatment commonly known as the

    a. M0080.

    b. M0245.

    c. M025.

    d. 485.

30. Patient's have the right to

    a. jeopardize the health and safety of agency staff by exercising their right to self-determination.

    b. require that the agency assign a nurse who is the same race, religion, or sex.

    c. be treated with dignity, respect, and consideration.

    d. manage the type and frequency of service that the agency will provide.

31. Patient's have the responsibility to

    a. alter their own plan of care.

    b. provide a safe environment for the agency staff.

    c. accept all treatments and services offered by the agency.

    d. protect their own personal health information by requiring the nurse to document a minimal amount of information and include only the information that the patient feels is necessary.

32. Each nursing note should include

    a. only documentation of the physician ordered treatments.

    b. documentation of the patient's current condition.

    c. a minimum amount of information to avoid the legal risks associated with poor or excessive documentation.

    d. documentation of the patient's assessment, tasks performed and teaching accomplished.

33. The process of evaluation

    a. is necessary only at discharge to evaluate if the patient's expected outcomes were met.

    b. is only necessary if the patient experiences an unanticipated change in their condition.

    c. affords the nurse the opportunity to revise the plan of care.

    d. is not necessary due to the short length of a home healthcare stay.

CHAPTER 4

STANDARDS OF PROFESSIONAL PERFORMANCE

CHAPTER OBJECTIVE

At the completion of this chapter, the reader will be able to list the eight standards and recall their functionality in the day-to-day activities of the home healthcare nurse.

LEARNING OBJECTIVES

After studying this chapter, the reader will be able to

1. differentiate between the roles of the generalist nurse and the advanced practice nurse in home healthcare.

2. recognize the role of the home healthcare nurse in the agency's performance improvement activities.

3. specify the nurse's role in the identification and development of agency "best practices."

4. recognize the value of the performance appraisal process.

5. identify the standards related to the enhancement of the professional nurse's education and competence.

INTRODUCTION

The American Nurses' Association's (ANA) *Scope and Standards of Home Health Nursing Practice* defines two levels of practice in home

healthcare. The standards describe the generalist nurse as one who is prepared at a Baccalaureate level, while the advanced practice nurse typically possesses a Master of Science degree (ANA, 1999). Despite the recommendations of the standards, many of the registered nurses practicing in home healthcare today come from a variety of educational and clinical backgrounds. Like all practice settings, home healthcare agencies employ nurses with diplomas and Associate degrees in nursing, as well as Baccalaureate and Master's degrees.

Regardless of their educational background, the generalist nurse's primary focus is on the patient and their family. In addition to the responsibilities outlined in the standards of care discussed in Chapter 3, the nurse generalist is required to demonstrate skills in:

- Advocating for the patient and their family with respect to self-determination;

- Participating in performance improvement activities;

- Educating and counseling the patient in relation to self-care activities, health promotion and maintenance; and

- Incorporating "evidenced-based multidisciplinary knowledge into their nursing practice" (ANA, 1999, p. 4).

In addition to all of the functions that the generalist nurse performs, the advanced practice nurse possesses substantial clinical experience with individuals, families and groups. The objective of this chapter is to provide a basic overview of the ANA's standards of professional performance.

STANDARD I: QUALITY OF CARE

Many regulatory and accrediting bodies require home healthcare agencies to monitor and improve the quality of the services they provide. The ANA standards specifically require home healthcare agencies to "systematically evaluate the quality and effectiveness of nursing practice" (ANA, 1999, p. 13).

There are many opportunities for the generalist nurse and the advanced practice nurse to participate in quality initiatives in their agencies. Through the application of the nursing process, nurses at both practice levels have a role and an obligation to assist the agency's management and performance improvement staff to identify "aspects of care that are important for quality monitoring" (ANA, 1999, p. 13). Although the perspective of the generalist nurse and the advanced practice nurse may differ, both are necessary for meaningful and sustained improvement in the quality of patient care.

The generalist nurse represents the patient's perspective and provides the agency with an understanding of the impact changes in policy and process might have on them; whereas the advanced practice nurse must represent the patient and organizational impact of changes. These perspectives are equally important, and both the generalist nurse and the advanced practice nurse are in a position to exert substantial influence on both patient-related and organizational processes. Consider the example of Mary, R.N. and My Town Visiting Nurse Association (VNA).

Mary, R.N. and My Town VNA

Mary, R.N. is a Baccalaureate prepared home healthcare nurse with over 20 years of experience at My Town VNA. Over the years, she has devel-

oped a strong interest in the care and management of patients who require wound or ostomy care. As a participant on many agency committees, Mary sought an opportunity to discuss with agency management her thoughts and recommendations for improving care for this cohort of patients. By collaborating with the agency's advanced practice nurse and other management staff, a proposal to the agency's administrative staff was presented. The efforts of these three nurses convinced the administration that, through the use of a wound care team, the agency could achieve improved patient and financial outcomes.

The development of a wound care team required My Town VNA to change the agency's clinical structure and processes. Clinical resources were reallocated to enhance and develop a wound care team in a cost efficient manner. The agency had to invest in the education and development of its clinical staff to meet this objective. Policies and procedures were re-evaluated and amended to give clear guidance to all clinicians. When wound team members were identified and oriented, they participated in data collection to monitor the appropriateness and quality of wound and ostomy related nursing care. As the wound team grew, physical therapy, nutrition and social work disciplines were added to the team.

Once the wound team was implemented, Mary decided to seek formal training related to the care of wound and ostomy patients and enrolled in a certification program. Again, the agency's administration supported her initiative and granted her a scholarship to defray the cost of pursuing the Wound Ostomy Continence Nurse certification (CWOCN). Mary completed her certification and continued her work at My Town VNA, actively working to improve the effectiveness of nursing care and the quality of life for wound and ostomy patients.

From the example above, it is clear that Mary was a self-motivated individual who had an understanding of her agency's structure, process and mission. Through her thoughtful recommendations, she was responsible for igniting a major restructuring of the agency's entire nursing practice.

Many agencies organize their quality improvement activities around standards and recommendations of accrediting bodies such as the Joint Commission of Healthcare Organizations (JCAHO). Typically, agencies monitor quality improvement activities that are high volume, low volume, high risk or problem prone (Joint Commission on Accreditation of Health Care Organizations [JCAHO], 2001). The home healthcare nurse has a responsibility and the ability to assist the agency in identifying the practice issues that meet these criteria. The agency may take a task-oriented or patient cohort approach to identifying the important aspects of care. Table 4-1 provides examples of tasks and patient cohorts that might be found in a home healthcare agency's quality monitoring program.

By participating in the collection and analysis of patient and agency-related data, the home healthcare nurse can influence the development of recommendations to improve the effectiveness of nursing practice. Once recommendations are made, every nurse in the organization has a responsibility to implement them, even if they have to amend their practice to do so.

In the example of My Town VNA, the organization clearly made a commitment to implement a wound care team, which significantly changed the clinical structure and operations. The change required all wound and ostomy patients to be evaluated by a wound team nurse, and if the patient met the agency's criteria, they would receive the services of the wound team on an ongoing basis. Agency policy required the wound team nurse to co-manage all wound care patients with their primary clinicians. The wound team nurse was to revisit the patient at least once every two weeks to evaluate wound healing and make treatment recommendations, if warranted.

Initially, some of the agency's staff were resistant to the concept of a wound management team. The coordinated efforts of the agency's management team and the improved patient outcomes convinced the staff of their professional obligation to change their practice to benefit the patient. Once the changes were framed from the patient perspective, the cooperation of all agency staff was achieved.

The nurse's participation in quality improvement processes has the potential to assist the agency in identifying "best practices." Through collaboration with other members of the home healthcare team, both the generalist nurse and the advanced practice nurse will find many opportunities to improve their practice and patient care.

TABLE 4-1: EXAMPLES OF TASK AND PATIENT COHORT GROUPS APPROPRIATE FOR QUALITY MONITORING		
Criteria	**Tasks/Skills**	**Patient Cohort**
High Volume	Foley catheter insertion and maintenance	COPD and CHF
Low Volume	Unna boot dressing changes	Cystic Fibrosis
High Risk	Management of Epidural and Intrathecal Catheters	Addicted or premature infants
Problem Prone	Ostomy management	Psychiatric patients

Documentation of "best practices" in agency policies, procedures and clinical guidelines serve to establish an agency standard which provides the home healthcare nurse with clear direction related to the provision of patient care. The implementation of a wound care team at My Town VNA resulted from the idea of a single nurse who recognized a weakness in the agency's process of care. By working with the agency's advanced practice nurse and clinical management, Mary was able to positively impact the care of hundreds of patients at My Town VNA. The idea of one nurse in an organization committed to the delivery of quality care elevated the clinical practice and effectiveness of the agency's nursing staff and improved both patient and financial outcomes.

STANDARD II: PERFORMANCE APPRAISALS

For most people, the term "performance appraisal" conjures thoughts of written performance evaluations that typically occur between the nurse and the nurse manager. Although documentation of performance evaluations is incorporated into this standard, it also includes the concept of peer review and self-appraisal. Standard II specifically requires the nurse to "evaluate his or her own nursing practice in relation to professional practice standards, scientific evidence, and relevant statues and regulations" (ANA, 1999, p. 14).

In reality, having one's performance evaluated by a manager or peer can be an anxiety provoking experience. However, it is important to recognize that professional growth and development cannot occur until each nurse takes the time to participate in the performance appraisal and self-evaluation process.

The process of self-appraisal allows the individual nurse to identify both strengths and weaknesses in their own practice. This process enables the nurse to develop a plan to either improve weaknesses or share strengths. In either case, this results in the overall advancement of the individual, the profession and patient care. Consider the example of Dr. Landry.

Dr. Landry

Dr. Landry is a new physician who has established a pain management practice in the same city as your agency. In addition to subcutaneous and intravenous methods, Dr. Landry also uses advanced techniques such as epidural and intrathecal delivery systems to achieve pain control for his patients.

Once your agency became aware of Dr. Landry's practice and methodology, it established an inservice education and competency assessment program related to the care and management of patients with epidural and intrathecal catheters.

Like many of the nurses in your agency, you are comfortable and competent with managing pain through common methodologies, but what about the new, more advance techniques? Through the self-appraisal process, you recognize that failure to expand your knowledge in this area could be detrimental to your patients and career. As part of the self-appraisal process you ask yourself:

- If I have a patient who might benefit from a referral to the pain management clinic, would I avoid making it because I am not comfortable with their techniques and what might be required of me? Would I deprive my patient of a referral to the pain management clinic and allow my patient to suffer?

- If I make the referral and it results in the placement of an epidural or intrathecal catheter, what will I do? Explain to my patient that I do not have the skills to manage their pain anymore and request a transfer to another more skilled clinician?

- What happens when my agency begins to have more and more patients with these devices? Will the agency have to avoid sending me to these patients? Is that reasonable? What about coverage on weekends and holidays? Will I refuse to see these patients?

- What if all of the agency's nurses demonstrated the same unwillingness to develop their knowledge and skills? Who would take care of these patients?

In home healthcare, nurses should expect regular evaluations of their clinical and case management skills in-office, as well as in the field. It is not uncommon for the nurse manager to conduct joint home visits to witness the nurse's interaction with the patient and their family. Joint home visits provide an opportunity for the nurse's manager to see them "in action." The nurse manager will take this opportunity to evaluate clinical techniques such as infection control, wound care and venipuncture. The clinical nurse manager will also have an opportunity to witness the nurse's assessment, teaching and communication skills.

In addition to the formal one-on-one performance appraisal system, the home healthcare nurse may be asked to participate in a peer review process. The intent of peer review is not to criticize or second guess one's actions. It is intended to provide nurses with insights into their performance, as it is perceived by their colleagues. Participation in the peer appraisal process should be viewed as a non-threatening and nonjudgmental opportunity for professional growth.

STANDARD III: EDUCATION

As a result of the performance appraisal process, the home healthcare nurse will be able to identify areas of their practice that may be enhanced by additional education. Regardless of the nurse's perceived need, Standard III requires each nurse to "acquire and maintain current knowl-

edge and competency in nursing practice" (ANA, 1999, p. 14). The home healthcare nurse is further expected to practice in a way "that reflects knowledge of current professional practice standards, contemporary science, clinical guidelines, laws, and regulations" (ANA, 1999, p. 8).

Although home healthcare regulations and standards require agencies to assure that patient care is delivered by competent and skillful staff, it is not the sole responsibility of the agency. As in any practice setting, the home healthcare nurse must work to acquire knowledge and maintain competency and skills that support the services of the agency and the practice of nursing (ANA, 1999). Reconsider the case of My Town VNA. Is it practical for the agency to allow a single nurse to refuse to learn a new skill?

The ANA Standards do not restrict or dictate the methods or settings that nurses use to achieve continuing education requirements. Professional education may be achieved through continuing education programs, inservices, self-learning modules, seminars, lectures or through the return to formal classroom education in the college or university setting.

STANDARD IV: COLLEGIALITY

As previously discussed, the individual home healthcare nurse bears the responsibility of assuring that their own practice and the practice of their peers is high quality and effective. Achievement of this goal can only be realized in an environment that is collegial and supportive in nature. Standard IV requires the home healthcare nurse to "interact with and contribute to the professional development of peers and other healthcare practitioners as colleagues" (ANA, 1999, p. 15).

It is important to recognize that the provision of constructive feedback and the sharing of knowledge and skills ultimately benefits patients and patient care. The complexity of the home healthcare system and the acuity of patients demand that the home healthcare nurse develop relationships with colleagues from nursing and other disciplines. Understanding and exercising these relationships contributes to the professional development of the individual nurse. To this end, Standard IV requires the nurse to "contribute to an environment that is conducive to the clinical education of nursing students, other health profession students, and other employees, as appropriate" (ANA, 1999, p. 15).

The organization's culture contributes to the development of a supportive work environment, and it is the collective of individual attitudes that results in the organization's culture. Every nurse must recognize and accept their own responsibility for achieving an effective and supportive work environment. The old saying, "if you are not part of the solution, you are part of the problem" could not be truer.

STANDARD V: ETHICS

Chapter 2 provided an in-depth discussion of the *Code of Ethics for Nurses*. It is worth mentioning that the fifth standard of professional performance describes the responsibility of the nurse to make ethical decisions and behave in a manner that is ethical in nature. Standard V requires the nurse to have a working knowledge of the ANA's *Code of Ethics for Nurses* and to incorporate the provisions outlined in the document as guidelines for practice.

STANDARD VI: COLLABORATION

Standard IV, Collegiality, requires the nurse to advocate for patients in a manner that respects the patient's right to self-determination and promotes patient autonomy, dignity and rights. It outlines the expectation for a collegial work environment.

Standard VI extends the benefits of the collegial work environment to the realm of the patient. It requires the home healthcare nurse to "collaborate with the physician, patient, family, other healthcare practitioners, and payers in formulating overall goals and the plan of care, making decisions related to care and the delivery of services, and accessing appropriate services" (ANA, 1999, p. 15).

The expectations outlined in Standard VI are the foundation for the provision of quality and effective nursing practice. It is imperative that the home healthcare nurse recognize the limits of their practice and collaborate with other healthcare professionals to assure that the patient's needs are met. Consider the case of Mr. Corneau.

Mr. Corneau

Mr. Corneau is an 84-year-old patient with uncontrolled diabetes. His inability to control his diabetes has resulted in many complications. The latest and most serious complication is a right, below-the-knee amputation. As a result, he receives daily nursing visits for wound care on his right, below-the-knee amputation stump. In addition to nursing, he receives physical therapy twice a week for strengthening and home healthcare aide services three times a week for personal care and assistance with showering.

Despite intensive home health services, the wound has not shown any improvement. In an effort to debride the wound, the physician is now ordering Mr. Corneau to attend an outpatient clinic for whirlpool treatments. At first glance, what seems like a very slight change in Mr. Corneau's plan of care requires you, his home healthcare nurse, to coordinate many changes including:

- Explaining to Mr. Corneau the benefits and risks of this treatment change;

- Coordinating transportation to the outpatient clinic;

- Rearranging the schedule and amending the home healthcare aide's plan of care so that Mr. Corneau is dressed and ready for his appointments;

- Assisting Mr. Corneau in avoiding an insulin reaction by understanding the importance of getting up early enough to eat an adequate breakfast;

- Teaching him to adjust the times that he takes his pain medications and diuretics;

- Reminding Mr. Corneau to contact the agency that provides his homemaking and shopping service to change his scheduled time;

- Encouraging Mr. Corneau to contact the Meals-On-Wheels delivery service to have his meals delivered to a neighbor's apartment on Monday, Wednesday and Friday since he will be attending the outpatient clinic; and

- Contacting the therapist at the outpatient clinic for updates and progress reports on Mr. Corneau's treatment and progress.

Mr. Corneau's case illustrates how one small change in a treatment plan can result in many changes for the patient. Unless the physician or nurse making treatment recommendations has had any exposure to home healthcare, they will not be aware of the repercussions of this small change.

The inclusion of additional disciplines into the plan of care does not diminish the nursing role or contribution. In fact, Mr. Corneau's case illustrated that the multidisciplinary approach to patient care heightens the need for the nurse to coordinate the patient's care and safeguard the patient's right to self-determination and informed decision making.

STANDARD VII: RESEARCH

Unless directly participating in research initiatives, it is doubtful that the generalist nurse will question: "What is the latest research in this area?" However, through participation in continuing education activities, the generalist nurse is usually exposed to the most current information. This information is commonly presented in a way that it can be evaluated and incorporated into day-to-day patient care activities. Standard VII requires the nurse to "utilize best available evidence, preferably research data, to implement the assessment, plan of care, interventions, and evaluation activities" (ANA, 1999, p. 17).

Does Standard VII require that every nurse subscribe to and read journals of nursing research cover to cover? Although exposure to "pure" research is beneficial to every nurse's practice and critical thinking skills, it is not realistic for every home healthcare nurse. What is realistic is making a personal commitment to subscribe and read journals, newsletters or other professional publications that relate directly to the contemporary practice of home healthcare nursing.

Despite the growth in home healthcare, there continues to be comparatively little research that is based in home healthcare. Nurses often have to evaluate research that was conducted in other practice settings to determine its applicability to home healthcare. Although there are many home healthcare resources in hard copy and on the world wide web, the *Home Healthcare Nurse Journal* is the only peer reviewed journal that is directed to both the generalist nurse and the advanced practice home healthcare nurse. This journal is an excellent resource for addressing contemporary issues in home healthcare (Humphrey, 2002).

STANDARD VIII: RESOURCE UTILIZATION

Standard VIII, Resource Utilization, is the final standard outlined in the *Scope and Standards of Home Health Nursing Practice*. It is naïve and unprofessional to think that the role of the professional nurse in home healthcare should not include addressing issues of resource utilization and costs of care. Regardless of the individual nurse's comfort level in discussing these issues, the patient has the right to be informed about "the risks, benefits and cost of planning and delivering patient care" (ANA, 1999, p. 17).

In the United States, healthcare and the availability of health insurance is not an inalienable right. In fact, the National Academy of Sciences', Institute of Medicine estimates there are approximately 58 million uninsured or underinsured Americans (Health Insurance is a Family Matter, 2002). The competent home healthcare nurse has to demonstrate the ability to aid the patient in identifying services that will assist in the management of their healthcare needs within reimbursement restraints.

SUMMARY

The *Scope and Standards of Home Health Nursing Practice* published by the American Nurses' Association provides the home healthcare nurse with expectations for the personal and professional integrity of nurses (ANA, 1999). The document "expresses an agreed-upon level of excellence that has been developed to characterize, to measure, and to provide guidance for achieving excellence in practice (ANA, 1986, p. 1)."

For the purpose of discussion and illustration, this author separated the *Code of Ethics for Nurses* discussed in Chapter 2 from the Standards of Care and the Standards of Professional Performance presented in Chapters 3 and 4. In reality, this has been a simplified approach and the practice of home healthcare requires nurses who can integrate all of these expectations into their day-to-day activities.

Every patient, family, community, nurse, colleague and employer of home healthcare nurses has the right to expect the level of practice outlined in these three chapters. Clearly, the expectations are high.

To some, home healthcare remains a setting where nurses with "less skill" practice or where nurses go when they do not want to work hard. Home healthcare nurses possess the same skills as many of the nurses practicing in the most advanced intensive care units. What the home healthcare nurse does not have is: High tech equipment to monitor the patient, another nurse who can be called from down the hall to "come take a look at this," a physician in the building, control of every minute of the patient's day or visiting hours that allow the nurse to control the patient's interaction with family and friends.

What the home healthcare nurse does have is a set of sharp clinical and assessment skills, the ability to build consensus and to assist the patient in reaching their full potential within the limits of their disease process or disabilities. Are home healthcare nurses better than nurses who practice in other settings? Certainly not. Are home healthcare nurses less skilled than nurses who practice in a hospital or clinic setting? Certainly not.

No matter what the background of the home healthcare nurse or whether they are a generalist or specialist, the standards described above apply equally. When agencies, managers and peers recognize and promote the strengths of all nurses, patient care is optimized.

EXAM QUESTIONS

CHAPTER 4
Questions 34-42

34. Although most home care agencies employ nurses with varied educational backgrounds, the American Nurses' Association *Scope and Standards of Home Health Nursing Practice* recommends the minimum level of nursing preparation for a generalist nurse to be a(n)

    a. practical or vocational nursing license.

    b. Diploma in nursing.

    c. Associate degree and passed the state licensing exam.

    d. Baccalaureate degree in nursing.

35. The nurse generalist

    a. has no role in the agency's performance improvement activities.

    b. often represents the patient's perspective and provides the agency with an understanding of the impact changes in policy and process might have on them.

    c. should only participate in performance improvement activities when requested.

    d. does not have the educational preparation to participate in performance improvement activities.

36. Many agencies organize their performance improvement activities around standards established by accrediting bodies. Agencies typically monitor activities that are

    a. high volume, low volume, high risk or problem prone.

    b. performed by new employees.

    c. identified as problematic on survey.

    d. delegated to home healthcare aides or provided by contract employees.

37. By participating in the agency's performance improvement activities the home healthcare nurse

    a. can reduce the number of visits they are required to make.

    b. should be compensated at the management level.

    c. should take on management responsibilities.

    d. can influence the development of recommendations to improve the effectiveness of nursing practice.

38. A complete and thorough performance appraisal is best described as one that includes input from

    a. peer review.

    b. self-evaluation.

    c. peer review, self-evaluation, and managerial evaluation.

    d. verbal or written information provided by patients, their families, and physicians.

39. The goal of the performance appraisal is to identify areas of practice that may be enhanced by additional education. Standard III

    a. requires the nurse to acquire and maintain current knowledge and competency in nursing practice.

    b. requires that the nurse only participate in mandatory agency programs.

    c. requires the nurse to seek additional education only when mandated by the state licensing board.

    d. only considers attendance at formal college classes as suitable to be considered additional education.

40. Standard IV defines collegiality as

    a. an uncommon phenomena only associated with nurses who practice in home health-care.

    b. a phenomena that is typically associated with nurses who practice in hospitals or other facility-based settings.

    c. any interaction that contributes to the professional development of peers and other healthcare practitioners.

    d. important only to nurses who are in college, or have returned to college to continue their formal education.

41. Standard VI requires the nurse to collaborate with all members of the home healthcare team including the physician and payer. The goal of this collaborative effort should be to

    a. delegate distasteful tasks to other members of the team.

    b. formulate the patient's goals and develop a plan of care.

    c. minimize the amount of time the nurse has to spend documenting and communicating the patient's plan.

    d. force the patient to find alternative mechanisms to get their needs met.

42. The home healthcare nurse

    a. cannot possibly participate in nursing research.

    b. cannot practice without an extensive knowledge of current nursing research.

    c. can utilize the best available evidence to implement the patient assessment and to plan care, interventions, and evaluation activities.

    d. should be expected to conduct at least one clinical trial once they receive a Master of Science degree.

CHAPTER 5

AGENCY STRUCTURE

CHAPTER OBJECTIVE

At the completion of this chapter, the reader will be able to list the eight key components of an agency and recall their interrelationships. In addition, the reader will be able to recognize the Medicare Conditions of Participation.

LEARNING OBJECTIVES

After studying this chapter, the reader will be able to

1. list at least three strategies the agency may use to market its services.

2. list the three major functions of the Intake Department.

3. recall the role of each professional discipline customarily associated with clinical home healthcare.

4. identify four major functions of the fiscal component of an agency.

5. recognize the function of the quality assurance/performance improvement component of the agency.

6. choose the primary function of the medical records component.

7. identify the role of the information systems component as it relates to all other agency components.

8. list the five major functions of the human resources component.

9. recall at least two reasons that Medicare certification is important to a home healthcare agency.

INTRODUCTION

A small hospital may treat 5000 inpatients in a year. A medium sized home healthcare agency may treat just as many. The primary difference between these settings is that the 5000 patients treated by the hospital, received treatment at a **single** facility whereas the thousands of home healthcare patients received services in many unique and individualized settings. Providing patient care in the home requires even the smallest agency to be complex and highly organized.

As discussed in Chapter 1, freestanding not-for-profit visiting nurse associations provided the majority of home healthcare services until the 1980s. These organizations were community-based and until 1965, primarily supported by the generosity of philanthropic citizens and organizations.

Due to economic pressures, hospital-based agencies emerged in the 1950s and 1960s. Hospital administrators recognized home healthcare as both a financial and patient care opportunity. In theory, hospital-based agencies could function as an extension of the hospital's services. Once a patient was discharged from the inpatient setting, home healthcare kept the patient "connected" to the organization.

The Staggers lawsuit of 1987 gave entrée to proprietary organizations into the home healthcare arena. Large national corporations developed strategic plans that included participating in the home healthcare industry. This was accomplished by opening numerous branch offices in hundreds of cities and towns. Examples of these organizations can be found in any community in the United States. Despite the differences in evolution, mission and size, the 3M National Expert Design Project identified the eight components outlined below as common to all home healthcare agencies.

THE 3M EXPERT DESIGN PROJECT

In 2000, Fazzi Associates Inc., a home healthcare consulting and research firm facilitated the Expert Design Project. The goal of the project was to identify the key components common to all home healthcare organizations (3M National Expert Design Project, 2000). This national project was funded by the 3M Company, the National Association for Home Care and Fazzi Associates, Inc. and included the participation of many industry leaders and experts. As a result of this effort, the following eight components were identified as common to all home healthcare organizations regardless of the agency's size and structure.

Marketing

Home healthcare is a highly competitive business. All agencies are dependent on new patient referrals to survive. The 3M National Expert Design Project identified marketing as a key organizational component (3M National Expert Design Project, 2000). The summary report defined marketing as the component "dedicated to increasing referrals by implementing a marketing plan that targets an appropriate case mix for the agency. The

marketing component is also the one (not the only one) that has a responsibility of developing and maintaining positive relationships with referral sources" (3M National Expert Design Project, 2000, p. 11).

The marketing of agency services typically occurs using a wide range of methods. Advertising agency services in print or on the radio or television might be the first thoughts of an agency's marketing strategy. If it is, you might think, "Well my agency could certainly improve in this area." However, the 3M National Expert Design Project describes the agency's marketing strategy as one that must be "dedicated to increasing referrals" (3M National Expert Design Project, 2000, p. 11). With that being said, one must question if using these traditional methods are effective mechanisms to increase the number of patients referred to the agency.

An agency's marketing plan should be much more strategic in nature and target those who provide referrals to the organization, such as hospitals, physician offices, insurance companies, and other health and human service providers in the community. The development of positive, productive working relationships with key individuals in each of these organizations may be the agency's primary and most effective marketing objective.

Marketing strategy can be influenced by a number of issues, such as the agency's mission, scope of services and changes in the local or regional community. Understanding the mission and scope is necessary for those in charge of the agency's marketing endeavors. For example, recall from Chapter 2 the case of My Town VNA and the issues related to the use of epidural and intrathecal pain management. Before the agency decided to train all of its staff to manage these patients clinically, the agency had to decide if the provision of care to these patients was within the agency's scope of services and consistent with the agency's mission.

My Town VNA determined that the provision of epidural pain management services was within the agency's mission and scope and dedicated the resources necessary to train the staff to care for these patients. In this case, the allocation of agency resources to increase the clinical competence of the staff provides an example of how the agency sought to develop and maintain a working relationship with Dr. Landry as a new referral source.

Although agencies may have one person or department responsible for the development of a marketing plan, this can not be done in isolation. In essence, every clinician making home visits is marketing the services of the agency. Excellence in customer service is the agency's most effective strategy. The home healthcare nurse who demonstrates courtesy, competence and caring is fulfilling the most effective marketing strategy.

Some agencies provide health promotion and prevention services as a way to market the agency. Some examples include:

- Annual flu and pneumonia vaccination clinics at a reduced fee or free of charge;

- Blood pressure screenings at elderly housing complexes or local businesses;

- Community education programs about public health issues such as Lyme disease and HIV transmission;

- Presentations at local philanthropic organizations such as Rotary Club or Kiwanis about health related issues: smoking cessation or domestic violence; or

- Conducting hypo/hyperglycemia screenings at health fairs.

Participating in these events allows the agency to develop name recognition by potential or future recipients of the agency's services.

Additional marketing strategies include working with local media to highlight human interest stories or celebrating occasions such as Nurses' Week or Home Health Care Week and Rehabilitation and Hospice/Palliative Care month.

Whatever marketing strategies are used by an agency, the responsibility for the development of positive relationships extends to every employee. Everyone has a role in marketing the agency as the best and easiest to work with from the Chief Executive Officer who meets with insurance companies to negotiate contracts, to the receptionist answering the phone, to the medical records clerk.

The success of the marketing component directly affects every other component of the agency. The most immediate effects will be felt by the Intake Department.

Intake

The 3M National Expert Design Project identified the intake function as a key organizational component. Intake is the "component responsible for taking referrals, verifying their appropriateness, and collecting information needed by the clinical admissions staff" (3M National Expert Design Project, 2000, p. 11).

Depending on the size of the agency, there will be a single individual or an entire department dedicated to this function. Most agencies are organized in a manner that facilitates the acceptance of referrals 24 hours a day, 365 days per year. The Intake Department may be one that is open and staffed ready to accept telephone referrals from morning until night. Some agencies may have the capability to accept on-line referrals, while others only have an intake representative available by pager. Regardless of the method used to actually facilitate the intake process, agencies strive to have a streamlined convenient process that promotes referral source satisfaction.

In addition to the basic patient demographic data (name and age) that are collected, the Intake Department also requires information about where the patient is staying and the phone number at that address. Almost every home healthcare nurse has had a patient who lives at one address but is staying at another. Sometimes the agency is unable to locate the patient until the physician or a family calls in to complain about the lack of home care services. It is at this point that the agency realizes that the Intake Department did not get complete and accurate information at the time of the referral. Figure 5-1 provides an example of the forms that might be used by the Intake Department.

The agency must also obtain physician-related information, i.e., the physician requesting the service and the physician who will be following the patient and signing the plan of care and other orders. The completed intake documents will also include insurance information to identify any payment and eligibility issues.

During intake, clinical information such as the medical diagnoses and any surgical procedures is documented. Depending on the referral source, information related to medications, diet restrictions, equipment needs and psychosocial issues may or may not be available.

The final piece of information required for a complete referral is the physician orders. Orders may be explicit and detailed, or they may be vague requiring the home care nurse to make a visit and then call the physician with a report of the findings. In either case, the skilled home healthcare nurse can take the information and conduct a thorough and efficient home visit.

A successful and efficient Intake Department must work closely with the marketing, clinical and fiscal components of the agency. Intake personnel must be fully aware of the agency's marketing strategy, clinical capacity and competence of the visiting staff. They must be knowledgeable about the agency's admission policy and apply it consistently. The staff working in the Intake Department must be able to triage calls to assure that only appropriate referrals are accepted while striving to maintain referral source satisfaction. Consider My Town VNA's admission policy noted in Figure 5-2.

Although My Town VNA is committed to providing care regardless of the patient's disease or disability, due to recent staffing issues, My Town VNA has lost the services of its psychiatric nurse. The Intake Department receives a referral for a patient whose primary diagnosis is schizophrenia. The referral is from a local psychiatric facility that is clearly looking for the skills of a psychiatric nurse. If you were the Intake nurse on the phone with the referral source, what would your agency expect you to do to guarantee referral source satisfaction? Would they require you to:

- Take the referral and forward it to the clinical department to "figure" out;

- Inform the referral source that due to staffing issues your agency can not accept the referral; or

- Take the referral information and notify the referral source that you will be forwarding it to another agency that can provide the necessary service?

It is important to explore the notion of appropriate referrals. Not every inquiry handled by the Intake Department does or should result in a referral for the Clinical Service Department, particularly when referrals come from health and human service providers or other community organizations. It is not uncommon for the Intake Department to receive inquiries about the type and means to obtain other community-based services. For example, the Intake Department may receive calls to:

- Identify where a family can arrange private duty services;

- Receive information related to Meals-On-Wheels or personal response systems; or

- Receive requests for referrals to "good" doctors.

Some agencies use a liaison nurse to facilitate the referral process. The role of the liaison nurse differs from marketing in that the marketing component is responsible for developing new relationships; whereas the liaison nurse provides assistance to a referral source after the relationship/contact has already been made. For example, a long-term care facility is planning the discharge of a patient to their home. The liaison nurse is called to participate in the discharge planning meeting to assist in identifying an agency and other community based services that might be available to the patient.

In the hospital setting, patients are required to receive a list of all the home healthcare providers in their geographic area. Once the patient chooses a home healthcare agency, the liaison nurse may be called in to visit the patient and facilitate the discharge process and home healthcare services.

Clinical Service

Once the Intake Department completes the referral process, the patient information is forwarded to the Clinical Service Department for admission. The 3M National Expert Design Project (2000) defines the clinical service component as the one responsible for admitting, servicing and discharging the patients.

Depending on the agency's size and scope of services, the clinical component can be highly complex or relatively simple. The structure of the clinical service component includes a Clinical Director, Clinical Manager and direct care staff. In a small agency, it is not uncommon for the Chief Executive Officer (C.E.O.) to serve as the Clinical Director. In large agencies, the C.E.O. role might be distinct, and there may be one or more Clinical Directors who report to a Chief Operating Officer or the C.E.O.

Regardless of an agency's size and structure, Medicare certified agencies are required, by regulation, to have at least a Bachelor's prepared Registered Nurse providing clinical direction. In some hospital-based agencies, the home care department is managed by a director who is a Registered Nurse. The agency may also have additional managerial support from a nurse that is affili-

ated with the hospital, a Medical Director or the hospital's Chief Nurse.

Chapters 2, 3, and 4 outlined the role and function of the home care nurse. The clinical service component of any agency encompasses additional disciplines including, but not limited to, physical, occupational, speech-language, nutrition, and respiratory therapy. In addition, the services of the medical social worker and home healthcare aide are crucial to the success of the entire home healthcare team and plan. These disciplines may be generated from agency staff or contracted from an outside agency.

Although many nurses are exposed to these disciplines in facility-based settings, home care requires the nurse to have a detailed understanding of the functions, capabilities, and scope of practice for each of the disciplines. The following sections contain descriptions of each of the disciplines, the populations they serve, and their basic educational preparation.

Physical Therapy

The majority of physical therapists are Masters prepared clinicians. All physical therapists are required to take a national exam and then be licensed by the state in which they practice.

The physical therapist's role is broad in scope and includes helping patients with orthopedic problems to regain optimal function and minimize pain. In any setting, physical therapists "are experts in the examination and treatment of musculoskeletal and neuromuscular problems that affect peoples' abilities to move the way they want and function as well as they want in their daily lives" (Guccione, 1999, p. 3). In home healthcare, physical therapy services are provided to patients who are recovering from surgery or trauma and chronically ill or deconditioned patients who require strength and endurance training.

Historically, the physical therapist has also had a role in illness and injury prevention and in health

FIGURE 5-1: MY TOWN VNA REFERRAL FORM EXAMPLE

My Town Visiting Nurse Association   Request for Admission

DEMOGRAPHICS   Pg. 1 of 3

Patient Name: _____Gender: ❏ M ❏ F ____Medical Record #: _____

Address:_____Phone #: _____

City: _____ State:_____Zip Code: _____

DOB: _____ SS#: _____

Language: _____ Lives with:_____

Temporary Address: _____ Phone #: _____

CONTACT INFORMATION

Name: _____

Address:_____

City: _____State:_____Zip: _____

Phone: _____

Relationship to patient:_____

SOURCE OF ADMISSION

❏ Transfer from another HHA   ❏ Transfer from a SNF

❏ Readmission to same HHA   ❏ HMO Referral

❏ Clinic referral   ❏ Emergency room

❏ Transfer from another healthcare facility   ❏ Court/Law enforcement

❏ Transfer from a hospital facility   ❏ Information not available

REFERRAL SOURCE

Referred by: _____Phone #: _____

Primary Institution: _____Admit Date: _____D/C Date: _____

Prior Facility: _____Admit Date: _____D/C Date: _____

Referring Physician:_____License Exp. Date: _____

  Address: _____

  Phone #: _____

Attending Physician: _____License Exp. Date: _____

  Address: _____

  Phone #: _____

Consulting Physician: _____License Exp. Date: _____

  Address: _____

  Phone #: _____

INSURANCE INFORMATION

Medicare #: _____Managed by HMO ❏ Yes ❏ No

Medicaid #: _____Managed by HMO ❏ Yes ❏ No

Insurance Company: _____Subscriber's Name: _____

  Address: _____Policy #: _____

  Phone #: _____Group #: _____

Contact/Case Mgr.: _____Type of policy: ❏ Individual ❏ Family

Initial authorization needed? ❏ Yes ❏ No   Effective Date: _____

Person Contacted: _____Termination Date:_____

Service Approved: _____Signature & Date Referral Taken: _____

Authorization #: _____

FIGURE 5-1: MY TOWN VNA REFERRAL FORM EXAMPLE (CONTINUED)

MEDICAL INFORMATION   Pg. 2 of 3

Medical Diagnosis: ICD9 Code: Symptoms/other information reported:

_____   _____   _____

_____   _____   _____

_____   _____   _____

_____   _____   _____

_____   _____

Surgical intervention/procedures: ICD9 Code: Symptoms/other information reported:

_____   _____   _____

_____   _____   _____

_____   _____   _____

                                                                                  _____

Confirmed infection: ❑ MRSA   ❑ VRE   ❑ C-Diff   ❑ Other

SERVICE REQUESTED

❑ RN   To assess: ❑ C/P status   ❑ Weight   ❑ Pain control   ❑ Medication compliance
                            ❑ Other (specify)

                                                                                                          _____

         To perform: ❑ Wound care   Site ___   Frequency ___   Rx. _____
                            ❑ Wound care   Site ___   Frequency ___   Rx. _____
         To teach: ❑ Medications   ❑ Diet   ❑ Other
                            ❑ IV Care*   ❑ Pacemaker* ❑ Tube feeding*   * SEE ATTACHED
❑ PT   Evaluation   Restricted Weight bearing or ROM ?   ❑Right   ❑Left
❑ OT   Evaluation   Restricted ROM ?   ❑Right   ❑Left
❑ ST   Evaluation   Restrictions? (specify) _____
❑ MSW   Evaluation   _____
❑ HHA   Evaluation   _____
❑ Hospice   ❑ Palliative   ❑ Cardiac   ❑ Telemonitor   ❑ Wound   ❑ EMD   ❑ Psych
   Evaluation   Care   Team   Team   Visit   Nurse

DIET, ALLERGIES & MEDICATIONS

Diet: _____ Allergies: _____
Medications: ❑ Refer to hospital discharge information

1. _____   6. _____

2. _____   7. _____

3. _____   8. _____

4. _____   9. _____

5. _____   10. _____

Special Instructions/Information: _____

_____

_____

_____

_____

*THIS PATIENT REQUIRES AUTHORIZATION SEND EVALUATION & NOTES TO INTAKE ASAP

FIGURE 5-1: MY TOWN VNA REFERRAL FORM EXAMPLE (CONTINUED)

| IV, TUBE FEEDING & PACEMAKER ORDERS | Pg. 3 of 3 |

❏ Peripheral line   Flush with every infusion or daily if not in use

❏ Heparin Lock   3 cc of Normal Saline

     3cc of 10u/ml Heparin

     Other per vender (specify): _____

Catheter Length:_____ (inches/cm)   Length Exposed:_____ (inches/cm)

❏ PICC   Flush with every infusion or daily for all ports not in use

❏ Midline   5 cc. Normal Saline

❏ CVP   3cc of 100u/ml Heparin

❏ Hickman   Other per vender (specify): _____

❏ Groshong Catheter   Flush with every infusion or weekly if not in use

     5 cc. Normal Saline

     Other per vender (specify): _____

Port-a-cath   Flush with every infusion or weekly if not in use

❏ Single   5 cc. Normal Saline

❏ Double   5cc of 100u/ml Heparin

Flush Due (date):_____   Other per vender (specify): _____

Site: _____   Date of insertions: _____

Dressing Change: ❏ Weekly   ❏ 3xweek   Other (specify): _____ Due: _____

Cap Change: ❏ Weekly   Other (specify): _____ Due: _____

Method of Infusion: ❏ Dial-a-flow   ❏ Gravity   ❏ Push   ❏ Pump _____

     Cassette Change   ❏ q24hrs   ❏ q48hrs

IV Solution: ❏ Hydration (specify) _____ ❏ TPN (specify) _____

     ❏ Additives/Medications (specify) _____

Vender: _____ Phone #: _____ Delivery Time:_____

TUBE FEEDING

❏ Peg   ❏ J-tube   ❏ G-tube   Size

❏ Clamped ❏ Bolus   ❏ Gravity ❏ Pump   ❏ Flush (specify) _____

Feeding Solution (specify):_____ Volume & Rate (specify): _____

Vender: _____ Phone #: _____ Delivery Time:_____

PACEMAKER/AICD

❏ AICD   ❏ Pacemaker   Type _____ Low rate _____ High rate _____

     Mode set at _____ Rate responsiveness: _____

     Site: _____ Site care (specify):_____

Name: _____ Date: _____

FIGURE 5-2: ACCEPTANCE/NONACCEPTANCE OF PATIENTS POLICY

My Town VNA, will admit patients, and provide care and services making decisions based on the following criteria:

- Patients shall be accepted for treatment without regard to age, race, religion, sex, mental or physical handicap, national origin, sexual preference, communicable disease or payment source. Acceptance of a patient will be based on the reasonable expectation that their nursing, rehabilitative and social service needs, in conjunction with family and/or other community resources, can be met adequately by My Town VNA in the patient's place of residence.

- Consideration for acceptance will be based on the adequacy and suitability of agency personnel within My Town VNA's scope of services. If the patient's needs exceed My Town VNA's serviceability, the patient will be referred to an appropriate source for care.

- There is the reasonable expectation that My Town VNA will receive reimbursement for services rendered. My Town VNA will assist families in exploring financial resources that may be available to eligible patients, including the patient care fund for indigent patients.

- Patients are expected to reside within the communities serviced by My Town VNA.

- When it is reasonably determined that unsafe conditions at a particular time and location place an employee in jeopardy, additional protocols may be implemented.

- Patients shall be accepted for care when the home situation is safe and beneficial to the patient; i.e., the patient has adequate or potential support services to be safely cared for in the community. Support services can be defined as family, friends, substitute caregivers or community organizations. The patient's home has adequate and safe physical facilities and equipment for the nurse, therapist and/or homemaker-home health aide to provide safe care. The patient and/or family has made plans to meet medical emergencies.

- Unless otherwise specified or indicated at the time of referral, an initial contact will be made with the patient/family within 24 hours of My Town VNA's receiving a request for service.

- When the home environment is assessed to be inadequate to safely meet the patient's needs or the care required by the patient is assessed to be beyond the scope of My Town VNA services, the admitting clinician will review their findings with the Clinical Nurse Manager. The patient/family will be notified at that time of My Town VNA's concerns. The patient/family and physician will be notified within 48 hours of My Town VNA's decision not to admit the patient and every attempt will be made by My Town VNA to find a suitable environment for the patient's care.

- Before patients are accepted for home care services from long-term facilities (nursing homes, rehabilitation hospitals, etc.), a registered nurse may make an evaluation visit to the facility to determine whether My Town VNA can safely meet the patient's needs in the community.

- Before patients are accepted, a plan of care is initiated by the patient's physician. This plan of care is signed by the physician and forwarded to My Town VNA for the case to continue. Exception: An initial patient assessment may be made by a clinician without a physician's order to determine an individual's need for service or ongoing medical treatment.

- The patient or caregiver provides written consent for care.

- My Town VNA is committed to providing service to persons meeting admission criteria inclusive of those whose primary language is not English.

- My Town VNA reserves the right not to accept those patients who do not meet the acceptance criteria stated above.

- Hospice patients must be certified as terminally ill. The patient's attending physician must attest that the patient has a medical prognosis of six months or less, and the hospice physician must concur.

promotion in a variety of settings. This role has also been extended to the home setting. Home healthcare nurses and other referral sources request physical therapy services for home safety evaluations, fall prevention plans and evaluations to prevent further loss of functional ability.

Physical therapists employ techniques such as joint mobilization or manipulation to extend a patient's range of motion, as well as massage, ultrasound, and hot or cold pack therapy. Some of the more progressive agencies utilize their physical therapy staff to provide electrical stimulation to heal chronic wounds.

Like the relationship between the registered nurse, the licensed practical (LPN) or licensed vocational nurse (LVN), the physical therapist may work collaboratively with a physical therapy assistant (PTA) in the provision of patient care. A physical therapy assistant is a licensed professional who must complete a two-year educational program and work under the direct supervision of the physical therapist. The PTA is limited by their scope of practice and is not allowed to complete patient assessments or establish a patient's plan of care/treatment. However, the PTA is qualified to carry out a plan of care that has been established by the physical therapist.

Occupational Therapy

"Occupational therapy is a skilled treatment that helps individuals achieve independence in all facets of their lives" (American Occupational Therapy Association, 2002, p. 1). A wide variety of conditions and deficits are treated by these skilled professionals. In home healthcare, occupational therapy services may be requested to address issues such as limitations that result from chronic degenerative conditions like arthritis or neurological disorders; traumatic or sudden onset conditions such as stroke, heart attack, spinal cord injury, broken bones or amputation; or children with birth injuries or developmental delays.

TABLE 5-1: LIST OF ACTIVITIES OF DAILY LIVING (ADLS)
• Grooming
• Ability to dress upper and lower body
• Bathing
• Toileting
• Transferring
• Ambulation/locomotion
• Feeding or eating

TABLE 5-2: INSTRUMENTAL ACTIVITIES OF DAILY LIVING (IADLS)
• Transportation
• Planning and preparing light meals
• Laundry
• Housekeeping
• Ability to use the telephone
• Shopping

The occupational therapist (OT) develops and implements treatment plans that focus on improving the patient's ability to perform both activities of daily living (ADLS) and instrumental activities of daily living (IADLS). (See Tables 5-1 and 5-2.)

In addition to assessment and treatment, the OT has a wealth of knowledge related to the use and availability of adaptive equipment. As part of the occupational therapist's plan of care, they will teach the patient and the patient's caregiver to utilize equipment in a manner that is safe, maximizes independence and promotes the return to optimal function.

Occupational therapists may be prepared at the Baccalaureate, Masters or Doctoral level. Regardless of the program, OTs must complete clinical internships in various supervised healthcare settings. Like physical therapists, occupational therapists must also pass a national certification exam and, in most states, are required to obtain licensure.

Many settings, including home healthcare, employ certified occupational therapy assistants (COTA). Certified occupational therapy assistants typically graduate from an Associate degree program and, like the occupational therapist, is trained in both the classroom and clinical setting. The COTA works under the direct supervision of the occupational therapist by following the treatment plans established by the OT.

Speech-Language Pathologist

In home healthcare, the speech-language pathologist (SLP) is consulted for patients who are having difficulty swallowing (dysphagia), communicating or maintaining adequate nutrition. The speech-language pathologist must be proficient in addressing dysphagia in both adults and children (American Association of Speech-Language-Hearing Association, 2002).

The speech-language pathologist will complete a comprehensive medical history to evaluate the severity of the patient's symptoms and deficits. The assessment will include an evaluation of the strength and movement of the muscles involved in swallowing or communication.

The skills of the SLP may be requested to intervene with patients who have suffered birth defects, stroke, brain, or spinal cord injury or neurological disorders such as multiple sclerosis, muscular dystrophy or cerebral palsy. In addition, the SLP may be asked to treat patients with problems affecting the patient's head or neck such as cancer, injury, surgery or dental problems (American Association of Speech-Language-Hearing Association, 2002).

The certified speech-language pathologist is a graduate of a Masters degree program which includes a classroom and clinical component. The SLP is also required to pass a national certification exam and, in many states, must be licensed

(American Association of Speech-Language-Hearing Association, 2002).

Respiratory Therapy

The registered respiratory therapist's (RRT) expertise is in treating patients with breathing and oxygenation difficulties and deficits. Patients diagnosed with both acute and chronic lung problems such as asthma, bronchitis and emphysema are often referred to the registered respiratory therapist. The RRT's skills are also valuable in the treatment and management of heart attacks, accident victims, premature infants and patients with cystic fibrosis or lung cancer (American Association of Respiratory Care, 2002).

In home healthcare, the registered respiratory therapist (RRT) participates in the patient's plan of care by teaching the patient to maximize their respiratory function and capacity. The skills of the RRT may be required to teach the patient and caregiver to efficiently perform pulmonary toileting, chest physical therapy, or oxygen and equipment management.

Like all professional disciplines, the RRT is a graduate of an accredited respiratory therapy program that included both a classroom and clinical component. The RRT typically holds at least an Associate degree and, in most states, must be licensed to practice.

Registered Dietician

The services of a registered dietician (RD) have become an integral part of the home healthcare team. Through training and education, the RD is knowledgeable about "the effects of nutrients on human life, health, and diseases including dietary deficiency disease" (Dietetics and Nutrition, 2002).

In home healthcare, the RD is responsible for assisting the patient and their family in establishing and implementing prescribed therapeutic diets and goals. For the patient to achieve compliance, it is essential that the RD display a positive and motivating attitude and work well as part of the team. The registered dietician must demonstrate an understanding of people of all ages, backgrounds, temperaments, and tastes (Dietetics and Nutrition, 2002).

The registered dietician usually has a Bachelor of Science degree and is required to complete graduate level education resulting in a Master of Nutrition Science degree. Most states require the RD to obtain a license to practice.

In home healthcare, the registered dietician may be an agency employee or made available to patients by contract. In addition to visiting patients with tube feedings or parenteral nutrition, some agencies screen patients for nutritional risk factors and refer them to the RD for intervention. Over the last few years, home healthcare clinicians have increased their use of the RD and frequently request this service for patients with wounds, respiratory, cardiac, developmental, or gastrointestinal disorders.

MEDICAL SOCIAL WORKER

Social work is a profession that is organized to assist people in improving their lives and circumstances. Medical social workers (MSW) have specialized skills to help patients and their families cope with acute, chronic or terminal illness. Through their counseling skills, the MSW helps patients and their families to identify their concerns, consider effective solutions and mobilize necessary resources to improve the situation or circumstance. The MSW follows through with patients to assure that they make use of the available services.

In home healthcare, the MSW is knowledgeable about the availability of supportive health and human services in each community, as well as state and federal assistance programs. The MSW is essential to support the patient through almost any crisis or to facilitate the placement of a compromised elder in long-term care facilities. As an integral part of the home healthcare team, the MSW helps other team members to identify strategies to manage issues that might limit the patient's return to optimal function and independence.

To practice as a MSW, an individual must be prepared at the graduate level and hold a Masters degree. The MSW must complete at least 900 hours of supervised clinical experience before they are qualified to practice independently (Medical Social Worker, 2002).

HOME HEALTHCARE AIDE

The home healthcare aide (HCA) is usually the only paraprofessional that is part of the home healthcare team. The HCA is assigned to assist patients who cannot meet their personal care needs independently or require assistance to follow a plan of care that has been established by a qualified therapist. The HCA works under the direct supervision of the registered nurse or physical therapist, and in a Medicare certified agency, must be supervised at least every two weeks.

To a certain extent, the individual state regulates the tasks that may be delegated to the home healthcare aide. For example, the aide can assist a patient with a shower or the applications of prosthetic devises, but in some states, the home healthcare aide cannot apply a prescription lotion or cream to a patient who has compromised skin integrity. Most agencies require the HCA to follow the instructions on an individualized patient assignment list. The HCA should not be performing duties that they have not been assigned.

Professional clinicians must always remember that it is not within the scope of the home healthcare aide to assess a patient. Instead, the HCA must be taught what patient-related issues should be observed and reported to the agency. For example, it is within the scope of the HCA to observe a patient with a Foley catheter for signs and symptoms of a urinary tract infection; however, it is not appropriate for the HCA to notify the physician of such findings.

FINANCE COMPONENT

Prior to the federal law resulting in the Balanced Budget Act of 1997, the clinical and financial components of many agencies functioned somewhat separately. The Clinical Service Department performed the patient visits and the Fiscal Department billed the appropriate payer. Fiscal-clinical interaction was usually the result of billing problems that were created by clinical errors or omissions.

Since the Balanced Budget Act required the Center for Medicare and Medicaid Services to control home healthcare expenditures, it created an incentive for all of the agency components/departments to work more closely and efficiently than ever. Today, the financial health of the agency is directly related to the efficient management of agency operations, accurate patient assessment and streamlined efficient plans of care. More now than ever, the agency's staff has had access to information related to patient acuity and the cost of providing care to every single Medicare patient. The Fiscal Department is largely responsible for generating this information in reports that are easily read and used to facilitate decision making and strategic planning.

In addition to the billing function customarily associated with the Fiscal Department of the agency, there are many roles and functions that must be efficiently performed; yet, they are usually invisible to clinical staff. Some of the more common functions are outlined below.

Depending on the scope and size of the agency there may be a single billing clerk or an entire department dedicated to this function. For the purposes of this course, billing is described as the function of producing a bill (either electronically or on paper) that outlines the charges for agency services. In addition to bills for home visits, some agencies may generate bills for additional lines of business such as adult day care, hospice, home infusion services and medical supplies. An agency may generate hundreds or thousands of bills to 10, 20 or even 100 different payers in a month.

The accounts receivable function assures that once the agency has billed for services, payment is actually received (either electronically or in cash) and recorded appropriately. In addition, accounts receivable tracks delinquent, unpaid and partially paid claims. In some instances, accounts receivable must also substantiate and verify recoupments, payment adjustments and process donations or charitable gifts.

The person who functions in the accounts payable role is responsible for paying all of the bills that are incurred by the agency in a timely manner. In addition to paying for necessities like the agency's rent, mortgage or utilities, the accounts payable function releases payment for other business expenses like equipment and office supplies.

In an effort to maintain tight control on spending, many agencies have developed a requisition or purchase order process by which designated signatures are required before the item(s) are ordered and paid. The Accounts Payable Clerk often has the responsibility to verify that the process has been followed and all required approvals have been obtained.

Depending on the size of the agency, there may be a single person in charge of making all agency purchases or an entire department may be necessary to expedite this function. The individual responsible for purchasing typically works very closely with the Accounts Payable Clerk.

There are generally two categories of items purchased by the agency. The first to be discussed are patient-related purchases. Patient-related purchases include items used directly in the provision of patient care, such as gloves, wound supplies, catheters, or intravenous supplies. The second type, agency-related supplies, are generally those supplies that the organization requires to function. Items such as furniture, computers, software, forms, and general office supplies fall into this category.

Payroll is a function that may be found in the finance component or the human resources component of the agency. For the purposes of this course, payroll will be described as a financial component of the organization. The primary responsibility of the Payroll Department is to assure that all employees receive accurate payment for the hours they have worked. If the agency provides fringe benefits to its employees, the Payroll Department assures that benefits are accrued accurately and timely.

Regardless of the size or structure of the agency, there is usually one person who manages the fiscal component of the organization. Whether the manager is a Chief Financial Officer, Vice President or Business Manager, they assure that the agency receives payment for the services it has rendered. This person may report directly to the Chief Executive Officer, the agency's Board of Directors/Trustees or to a Vice President in a hospital system. Regardless of the reporting structure, the manager of the financial component is typically required to prepare monthly financial statements, negotiate rates with various contractors and venders, and prepare or participate in financial audits.

QUALITY ASSURANCE/ PERFORMANCE IMPROVEMENT

The quality assurance/performance improvement (QA/PI) component of the agency is one that "works with other components to develop, monitor, trend and continually update meaningful performance measures and to implement processes that use the data to improve performance" (3M National Expert Design Project, 2000, p. 11).

Since the Balanced Budget Act and the mandatory use of the OASIS assessment, this component of the organization has become highly organized and sophisticated. Although in many agencies the QA/PI functions have primarily impacted clinical and patient-related functions, the implementation of the Medicare prospective payment system has provided new incentives to develop performance measures for all departments. Examples of QA/PI goals for each of the eight agency components are outlined in Table 5-3.

In addition to the functions outlined above, the QA/PI component has a role in the management of the day-to-day operations of the agency. QA/PI functions may be centralized in a single department, disseminated among agency managers or a combination of both. Some of the day-to-day activities of the QA/PI component include:

- Review of admission documents, paperwork and assessment and plans of care;

- Evaluation of recertification of plans of care;

- Review of agency Adverse Event Reports;

- Orientation of new staff to agency documents and expectations for documentation; and

- Responding to Medicare and other payer's requests for additional documentation.

In many organizations, the QA/PI person is extremely knowledgeable of Medicare rules and regulations and is often used as a resource by all clinicians and staff.

TABLE 5-3: EXAMPLES OF QA/PI GOALS FOR EACH OF THE EIGHT AGENCY COMPONENT	
Marketing:	As a result of marketing efforts, the agency will receive three to five new patients from newly identified referral sources per week.
Intake:	All referrals will be processed and forwarded to the clinical department for admission within one hour of receipt in the department.
Clinical:	All patients will be screened for safety risk and referred to the rehabilitation department for evaluation.
Fiscal:	All agency purchases will be accompanied by an authorized purchase order which includes the date and signature of the authorizing agent.
QA/PI:	The agency will maintain a Medicare denial rate of less than 5%.
Medical Records:	Filing will be placed in the medical record within 72 hours of receipt into the department.
Information Systems:	All agency computers will have a screen saver password activated whenever the computer is unattended.
Human Resources:	All new hires will receive a criminal background check before they are allowed to enter patient homes.

MEDICAL RECORDS

The medical records component is responsible to "safeguard complete and accurate information on the patient" (3M National Expert Design Project, 2000, p. 11). All Medicare certified agencies are required to maintain a complete and accurate patient-specific medical record. Therefore, the primary and overriding responsibility of the Medical Records Department is to keep track of every patient record in a manner that protects confidentiality while making sure the information is readily accessible to the clinicians who need it. Although it is estimated that 50% of all agencies have made the transition to a computerized/electronic medical record, that fact does not diminish the responsibility of this component.

Regardless of the type of medical record that the agency uses, the Medical Records Department is also responsible for the storage of completed or discharged records. Each state regulates the length of time that an agency has to keep a record available. Typically, agencies are required to maintain patient records for at least seven years for adult patients and up to 30 years for pediatric patients.

Other functions of the Medical Records Department might include tracking of physician orders to assure that they are returned, signed and dated; management and maintenance of agency forms and paperwork; and providing photocopies of medical records as necessary.

INFORMATION SYSTEMS

The 3M National Expert Design Project (2000) defines information systems as the component of the agency that "responds to needs of other components for Information Systems support and data" (p. 11). Virtually all home healthcare organizations are computerized to some degree. Whether the agency only has its billing component computerized or has a completely computerized electronic medical record, somebody has to provide support to the staff using the hardware and the software.

As agencies become more and more sophisticated, the information systems (IS) component will become larger and larger. For example, the IS component may be supporting (implementing, troubleshooting and maintaining) voice mail systems, answering systems, OASIS and other electronic data submission requirements. If the agency has a web site and/or email, the IS Department supports all of these functions. If the agency uses software to track donations, maintain a telemonitoring program or participates in a patient satisfaction program, information systems will be essential to the success of these initiatives. All it takes is one day when the voice mail or email system does not function properly, and it quickly becomes clear how crucial the IS system is in the daily operations of the agency. The information systems component may also play a role in the education of new staff to agency systems or updating the skills of current staff to software improvements and enhancement.

Regardless of the agency size, structure and level of computerization, information systems management exists somewhere. Although many field clinicians are not aware of who's responsibility it is to assure "things" function properly or what the IS component "does," rest assured that if this component of the agency is weak or non-functioning, it will be felt by all agency components.

One of the final responsibilities of the IS component is to utilize their skill in conducting research. In addition to seeking resources that might be available on the internet, the IS component is usually responsible for generating reports that reflect agency operations.

Although the generation of reports might not be considered research in the purest sense, creating reports that are useful require the IS component to assist the agency in asking the "right" questions and developing a hypothesis. Once the hypothesis is clear, the IS component is skilled at assisting to identify all of the variables that might affect the results such as age, referring physician, number of visits and discharge disposition. Skilled IS personnel can assist agency staff to uncover the detailed agency data that are necessary for both clinical and organizational operations.

HUMAN RESOURCES

The function of the human resources component is "to meet the staffing needs of the organization" (3M National Expert Design Project, 2000, p. 11). The human resources (HR) component may be part of the organization as a freestanding agency, or the organization may tap into the human resources component of a larger organization such as a hospital or facility-based organization. The human resources component of the agency has five major functions: Compliance with laws designed to protect the rights of the employer and employee; retention of current employees; recruitment of new employees; competency evaluation; and maintenance and fringe benefits administration.

Both the federal and state governments have enacted many laws that protect the rights of workers. The human resources component assures that the agency does not violate any of these laws. Violations of a worker's rights can result in heavy fines and penalties to the agency. For example, workers have a right to a lunch and break period after six hours of work; they have the right to be paid for all hours worked and the right to work in a safe environment.

With the shortage of nursing and other healthcare workers, retention of current employees is one of the primary functions of the human resources component. In addition to the lack of qualified employees, the expense associated with recruitment of new employees can be staggering. It is estimated that the cost associated with recruiting one new employee can be $3000 to $5000. Clearly, it is more cost effective to retain the agency's current employees than to recruit new ones. Expenses that contribute to this cost include the cost of advertising, interviewing the candidate, verifying the health of the candidate, evaluating the candidate's competency, and assuring that the new employee receives a thorough orientation to the duties of the job.

In some agencies, the Human Resources Department maintains the competency of the agency's staff. This may be accomplished through on-the-job training, in-servicing, continuing education programs and self-learning modules. Depending on the size of the organization, this function is likely to be shared with the clinical and other components of the organization.

Finally, the Human Resources Department administers the agency's fringe benefits. Depending on the complexity of the agency's benefit package, this function is extremely important and detailed. HR assures that all employees entitled to benefits receive them. Any change in an employee's status may have an effect on their benefits. For example, if a nurse increases/decreases the hours that they work, this may trigger a change in health insurance, life insurance, or vacation accruals. The HR component of the organization must track all these changes and make the necessary adjustments with absolute attention to detail and accuracy.

MEDICARE CERTIFICATION

Medicare is the single largest purchaser of home care in the United States (Medicare Payment Advisory Commission, 2003). The privilege of participating in the Medicare program can mean the difference of existing or not for a home healthcare agency.

Throughout this course, the phrases "Medicare certified" or "Medicare certification" have been used repeatedly. For an agency to receive reimbursement for services provided to Medicare beneficiaries, it must be certified to participate in the Medicare program. Certification requires the agency to meet and continuously adhere to the standards that are outlined in the *Home Health Conditions of Participation*. Once an agency "proves" that it meets the conditions, it is issued a Medicare provider number. The agency's provider number is unique and must be in all billing and other correspondence with the Center for Medicare and Medicaid Services.

Not only is "certification" required to participate in the Medicare program, but other insurance companies that provide a home healthcare benefit require the agencies that they contract with to be meeting the standards outlined in the *Home Health Conditions of Participation*. Failure to achieve and maintain Medicare standards can effectively eliminate the agency from providing any home healthcare services. Although there are numerous agencies that also provide home health services, regulations usually limit them to the provision of non-skilled services such as homemaking and personal care assistance. These services are paid "out of pocket" by the patient or their family, since traditional insurance plans do not cover non-skilled services.

Once an agency is certified, it is required to remain in compliance with the *Home Health Conditions of Participation* at <u>all</u> times. The Center of Medicare and Medicaid Services conducts surveys (usually unannounced) of agencies to assure compliance. If an agency fails to maintain compliance with the standards outlined in the *Home Health Conditions of Participation,* it may face fines, payment denials, or closure.

If an agency knowingly commits fraud or abuses the privilege of participating in the Medicare program, the consequences can be severe. Consequences may range from the owner or administration being subjected to criminal charges, incarceration or revocation of the privilege of ever participating in any CMS/Medicare funded programs in the future. To date, there are over 25 thousand individuals/entities that have been excluded

TABLE 5-4: CONDITIONS OF PARTICIPATION FOR HOME HEALTHCARE AGENCIES

Section and Conditions

484.1	Basis and scope
484.2	Definitions
484.4	Personnel qualifications
484.10	Condition of Participation: Patient rights
484.11	Condition of Participation: Release of patient identifiable OASIS information
484.12	Condition of Participation: Compliance with federal, state and local laws, standards and principles
484.16	Condition of Participation: Group of professional personnel
484.16	Condition of participation: Organization, services, and administration
484.18	Condition of Participation: Acceptance of patients, plan of care and medical supervision
484.20	Condition of participation: Reporting OASIS information
484.30	Condition of Participation: Skilled nursing services
484.32	Condition of Participation: Therapy services
484.34	Condition of Participation: Medical social services
484.36	Condition of Participation: Home health aide services
484.38	Condition of Participation: Qualifying to furnish outpatient physical therapy or speech pathology services
484.48	Condition of Participation: Clinical records
484.52	Condition of Participation: Evaluation of agency's program
484.55	Condition of Participation: Comprehensive assessment of patients

Source: Conditions of Participation. Chapter IV-Health Care Financing Administration, Department of Health and Human Services. (1999) [Available online: http://www.access.gpo.gov/nara/cfr/waisidx_99/42cfr484_99.html]

from participating in any CMS/Medicare (Office of Inspector General, 2003).

Although a lifetime exclusion from participating in Medicare programs might sound severe, it is important to remember that CMS uses public funds (collected through taxation) to purchase healthcare services for Medicare beneficiaries. Since public funds are used, safeguards have been put in place to assure that the funds are spent judiciously. As a certified provider, the agency is acting as a guardian of the Medicare trust fund, which is an asset of the American public. This responsibility is taken seriously by the Center of Medicare and Medicaid Services and the Office of the Inspector General and should be taken seriously by all agencies and providers. For all intent and purposes, committing Medicare fraud and abuse is viewed as stealing money from the American taxpayers and is dealt with swiftly and severely.

CONDITIONS OF PARTICIPATION

The 16 Conditions of Participation (COPS) are found in the Federal Register under Title 42, Chapter IV-healthcare Financing Administration, Department of Health and Human Services, Part 484. They are also easily accessible on the internet. Although the COPS provide a very detailed and extensive explanation of the requirements for Medicare certification, this chapter will only provide a brief overview. In addition, Table 5-4 provides a summary list of the conditions to be discussed.

The COPS begin with an outline of the minimum qualifications of the administrative, managerial and direct care staff. Standard 484.4 requires the Administrator of the agency to be either a licensed physician, registered nurse, or a person who has at least one year of training and experience in administration in home healthcare or a related healthcare field (Health Care Financing Administration...,

1999). In addition to outlining the experience and training requirements of the Administrator, this section of COPS details the minimum requirements for the following disciplines and services:

- Audiologist,
- Home Healthcare Aide,
- Occupational Therapist,
- Occupation Therapy Assistant,
- Physical Therapist,
- Physical Therapy Assistant,
- Medical Doctor,
- Licensed Vocational or Licensed Practical Nurse,
- Registered Nurse,
- Social Work Assistant,
- Social Worker, and
- Speech Language Pathologist.

The second condition of participation provides a very detailed outline of the rights of home healthcare patients. Chapter 3 of this course provided a detailed discussion of patient rights, and although the details will not be repeated here, it is not intended to minimize their importance. Both the state and federal regulating agencies treat violations of patient rights very seriously. Therefore, agencies should be judicious in the administration of these rights and assure that violations are dealt with swiftly. The standards in the COPS include requirements for:

- Notifying the patient of their rights;
- Respect for property and person;
- Informing and allowing the patient to participate in the care planning process;
- Confidentiality;
- Liability for payment;
- Informing the patient of the home health state hotline to register complaints about care treatment or services;

- Formulation of an advance directive; and
- Disclosure of agency ownership (Conditions of Participation, 1999).

As will be discussed in Chapter 6, the implementation of OASIS is highly regulated. Condition 484.11 outlines an agency's responsibility to maintain all patient identifiable OASIS data with the strictest level of confidentiality (Conditions of Participation, 1999). Condition 484.20 also outlines the federal requirements for the agency to encode, lock and transmit the OASIS data in accordance with the time frames outlined in Chapter 6 (Conditions of Participation, 1999).

Agencies are required to operate in compliance with all local, state and federal laws. The staff is required to provide services that are in accordance with the state laws and standards of professional practice. Not every state requires home health agencies to be licensed to operate. However, if the agency is operating in a state that does require licensure, failure to obtain a license is considered a violation of a local/state law as well as a violation of this condition of participation.

The *Home Health Conditions of Participation* outline the basic organizational and oversight structure required for the certified home health agency. Outlined in this section is the requirement that the agency have written policies and procedures that outline the administrative, supervisory and direct care staff functions, including those functions that may be delegated and who is held accountable if issues arise.

The ten standards that comprise Condition 484.14 begin with a description of the minimum services/disciplines that a Medicare certified agency must provide (Health Care Financing Administration..., 1999). Although there is no limit to the number of services that the agency can provide, Medicare certified agencies are required to provide skilled nursing and the services of at least one other discipline. The second discipline may be physical, speech or occupational therapy, social work or home healthcare aide service. Once the agency meets the two discipline requirement, additional services may be purchased from other healthcare providers or staffing agencies.

All Medicare certified agencies are required to have a governing body which assumes the legal authority for the operations of the agency (Health Care Financing Administration..., 1999). In many agencies, the governing body is referred to as the Board of Directors or Trustees. The governing body is also responsible to oversee the management and fiscal affairs of the agency. This is usually accomplished by the appointment of an agency administrator who reports directly to the governing body. As previously stated the Administrator may be a physician, nurse or professional who possesses relevant experience and credentials.

Other responsibilities that the governing body may delegate to the Administrator include the responsibility to assure that the agency employs an adequate number of personnel and that the staff employed is qualified to meet patient care needs (Health Care Financing Administration..., 1999). The Administrator is also responsible for the financial soundness of the agency and is held accountable for assuring that the agency's system of accounting is reliable and accurate. In the absence of the Administrator, written authorization of a qualified person to act in the Administrator's absence must be provided.

Regardless of whether or not the Administrator is a nurse or other healthcare professional, the *Home Health Conditions of Participation* require Medicare certified agencies to provide all services under the direction of a physician or registered nurse. Typically, this position is titled the Clinical Director or Director of Clinical Services. The Director is responsible for patient care services and must be available during all times that patient care is being delivered (Health Care Financing

Administration..., 1999). If the Director is not available to participate in all activities associated with professional services, the agency is required to identify a similarly qualified person who is.

The *Home Health Conditions of Participation* establish standards for human resource management. Medicare certified agencies are required to have written personnel policies and demonstrate practices that support the provision of patient care (Health Care Financing Administration..., 1999). Agencies are required to maintain a personnel record for all employees. At a minimum, the personnel record is required to identify the employee's qualifications and validate that the person is licensed to practice in their respective state.

The *Home Health Conditions of Participation* require the agency to establish a Group of Professional Personnel (GPP). The role of the GPP is to act as a professional advisory committee and provide guidance in the areas of clinical practice and issues. Section 484.16 requires the agency to include at least one physician, one registered nurse (preferably with home healthcare experience) and representation from other disciplines such as physical therapy, social services or nutrition (Health Care Financing Administration..., 1999). Some agencies also invite consumers to participate on their GPP. In a Medicare certified agency, the GPP is required to review agency policy and procedure, and conduct an evaluation of the agency's services at least annually. In addition to the evaluation of clinical programs, the GPP has a responsibility to conduct a review of the administration's ability to promote patient care that is within the accepted standards of professional practice and assure that it is provided in a manner that is efficient and maximizes its patient outcomes.

As part of the agency evaluation, Condition 484.52 requires the agency to conduct a clinical record review at least quarterly (Health Care Financing Administration..., 1999). The record review should include a sample of all disciplines/services provided by the agency and should include both active and discharged patients.

A Medicare certified agency can only accept patients if there is a reasonable expectation that the agency can meet the patient's medical, nursing, rehabilitation, social and personal care needs. Condition 484.18 requires the agency to establish a written admission policy that outlines the agency's admission criteria and the services provided to the patient (Health Care Financing Administration..., 1999). In addition, Condition 484.18 requires the agency to establish an individualized plan of care and provide all services under medical supervision. All changes and amendments to the plan must be obtained through the use of a physician order that is dated, signed, and maintained as part of the patient's medical record.

Conditions 484.30, 484.32, 484.34, 484.36 outline the educational, licensure and performance expectations for skilled nursing, therapy, social work and home health aide services (Conditions of Participation, 1999). Condition 484.30 outlines the expectations of the registered nurse in home healthcare (Health Care Financing Administration, 1999). The standards that comprise this condition are very similar to the Standards of Professional Performance discussed in earlier chapters. This COP requires the nurse to: "Make an initial evaluation visit, regularly reevaluate the patient's nursing needs, initiate the plan of care and necessary revisions, furnish those services requiring substantial and specialized nursing skill, initiates appropriate preventative and rehabilitative nursing procedures, prepares clinical and progress notes, coordinates services, informs the physician and other personnel of changes in the patient's condition and needs, counsels the patient and family in meeting nursing and related needs, participates in in-service programs, and supervises and teaches other nursing personnel" (Health Care Financing Administration..., 1999, p. 442).

Condition 484.32 requires the qualified therapist (either physical, occupational or speech) to: "Assist the physician in evaluating level of function, helps develop the plan of care (revising it as necessary), prepares clinical and progress notes advises and consult with the family and other agency personnel and participates in in-service programs" (Health Care Financing Administration..., 1999, p. 442). In addition, this condition includes a standard that states the expectation of the physical or occupational therapist is to supervise the care, treatment, and services provide by therapy assistants.

If the agency provides social work services, Condition 484.34 outlines the role as inclusive of: "Assisting the physician and other team members in understanding the significant social and emotional factors related to the health problems, participates in the development of the plan of care, prepares clinical and progress notes, works with the family, uses appropriate community resources, participates in discharge planning and in-service programs, and acts as a consultant to other agency personnel" (Health Care Financing Administration..., 1999, p. 442). If the agency utilizes a social work assistant, the agency is required by this standard to provide direct supervision by a qualified social worker.

In most instances, the home healthcare aide (HCA) is considered the "same as" a certified nursing assistant found in other settings. However, the *Home Health Conditions of Participation* recognize that the provision of personal care and support services to a patient in the home environment requires an additional set of skills. Condition 484.36 provides a detailed outline of the training that a HCA must complete before entering clinical practice (Health Care Financing Administration..., 1999).

Every HCA is required to complete 75 hours of classroom training, 16 of which must be in a clinical-like setting. The HCA must demonstrate competence in areas such as communication, recording of vital signs, infection control techniques, an understanding of basic bodily functions, maintenance of a clean and safe patient environment and recognition of developmental and cultural needs, of the patient (Health Care Financing Administration..., 1999). This COP also requires the agency to assure that all HCAs receive 12 hours of in-service and training every year. Like the other services provided by "assistant" staff, the HCA must be supervised by a licensed professional (Health Care Financing Administration..., 1999). In fact, this condition requires the agency to assure that the HCA is supervised in the patient's home at least every two weeks (Health Care Financing Administration..., 1999). Typically, these supervisory visits are completed by the registered nurse and must be documented in the patient's medical record.

The final condition to be discussed is the requirement for the agency to maintain a comprehensive medical record. Condition 484.48 requires the agency to maintain a medical record for every patient in accordance with professional standards and practices (Health Care Financing Administration..., 1999). In addition to requiring agencies to retain patient medical records for a specified number of years, this condition also outlines the expectation for protection of the medical record from unauthorized use and safeguards it against loss.

SUMMARY

Millions of Americans received home healthcare services every year. It is important to remember that each of these patients is cared for in a unique setting, their home. The provision of patient care in the home healthcare setting requires a sophisticated, highly organized agency. The 3M National Expert Design Project identified the eight components that are common to all agencies regardless of size, structure, or location.

Changes in the industry have required agency departments/components to work closely together to assure that operations are efficient and streamlined. Weakness in interdepartmental cooperation and collaboration has the potential to threaten the viability of the entire organization.

Although the *Home Health Conditions of Participation* discussed in this chapter seem to be reasonable and straightforward, there are over 700 home healthcare agencies, owners or administrators who have been excluded from participating in the Medicare program (Office of Inspector General, 2003). All agency employees have the responsibility to understand the *Home Health Conditions of Participation* and work to assure that all violations are avoided.

EXAM QUESTIONS

CHAPTER 5
Questions 43-52

43. An effective marketing strategy is one that

    a. increases the number of patient referrals to the agency.

    b. regularly advertises on the radio and television by highlighting human interest stories.

    c. participates in community-based health fairs and health prevention and promotion activities.

    d. strives to strengthen relationships with the physicians who customarily refer to the agency.

44. The Intake Department must work cooperatively with all agency components and

    a. take all referrals to assure referral source satisfaction.

    b. consider the financial and insurance resources of every patient before accepting the referral.

    c. assure that the agency only takes referrals that will be financially lucrative and decline referrals that might be complex or require large amounts of service.

    d. triage calls to assure that only appropriate referrals are accepted, while striving to maintain referral source satisfaction.

45. The 3M National Expert Design Project identified the clinical service component as the

    a. largest of all agency components.

    b. one that is most often plagued with inefficiency and duplication.

    c. most important of all agency components because it is the one responsible for direct patient care.

    d. one responsible for admitting, servicing and discharging patients.

46. Depending on the agency's size and structure, the fiscal component of the agency is usually comprised of billing, accounts receivable, accounts payable, payroll, and

    a. marketing.

    b. human resources.

    c. information systems.

    d. purchasing.

47. The QA/PI component of the organization

    a. is to focus solely on the financial performance of the company.

    b. is to focus solely on the clinical functions of the agency.

    c. is to assist in the development of performance measures for agency components.

    d. has been eliminated due to financial constraints.

48. The function of the medical records component of the agency

    a. will essentially be eliminated as agencies move to complete electronic medical records.

    b. is to safeguard complete and accurate information on the patient.

    c. is considered nonessential.

    d. will most likely be merged with another agency component to save time and money.

49. The information systems component

    a. is only really important in agencies that have an electronic medical record

    b. is responsible to primarily work with the fiscal department to assure timely billing

    c. will most likely be eliminated due to the expense associated with this component

    d. may be responsible to support voice mail systems, telephone answering systems, and electronic data submission software.

50. Meeting the staffing needs of the organization is the primary function of

    a. quality assurance.

    b. human resources.

    c. intake.

    d. marketing.

51. The *Home Health Conditions of Participation* require the agency to establish a group of professional personnel, complete an annual evaluation of the agency's programs and services and

    a. provide all nursing specialties, including pediatrics, psychiatric, and rehabilitation.

    b. provide free care to patients who are indigent but over the age of 50.

    c. conduct clinical record reviews at least quarterly.

    d. establish a relationship with a local hospital that will provide clinical oversight to the agency.

52. The 3M Expert Design Project identified eight components common to all agencies regardless of size and structure. The project also determined that

    a. the marketing component is the most important of all components.

    b. the clinical component is the most important of all components.

    c. no one component is more important than any other, in fact the success of the organization is dependent on all components functioning in concert with one another.

    d. the fiscal component is the most important component of any business, including the home healthcare agency.

CHAPTER 6

OUTCOME ASSESSMENT INFORMATION SET (OASIS)

CHAPTER OBJECTIVE

At the completion of this chapter the reader will be able to recognize the OASIS assessment and its indications for use.

LEARNING OBJECTIVES

After studying this chapter, the reader will be able to

1. define which patients are excluded from the OASIS requirements.

2. identify the time frames allowed to complete the OASIS.

3. differentiate between the uses of each OASIS document.

4. list the rules that guide the completion of the OASIS documents.

5. recall the relationship between the 485 and the OASIS.

INTRODUCTION

Like any "mature" industry home healthcare has had to evolve and expand to meet the changing needs and expectations of its customers. In any agency, nurses might be heard reminiscing about the "good old days." If a home healthcare nurse is asked when the "good old days" were, they would likely say, "Before OASIS!"

If you have no home healthcare experience, you might think it is odd that an oasis represents something negative or overwhelming. In fact, an oasis is commonly defined as a "situation of place preserved from surrounding unpleasantness; a refuge" (The American Heritage Dictionary..., 2000). In home healthcare, an OASIS is an acronym for an Outcome Assessment Information Set. The home healthcare OASIS is a standardized patient assessment that must be completed for the majority of patients admitted to a Medicare certified home health agency.

The OASIS document was developed by the Center for Health Care Policy and Research (CHCPR). The CHCPR was commissioned by the Federal Department of Health and Human Services to develop a standardized patient data collection/assessment tool. The collection of a standardized information set was intended to provide the federal government a means to measure the quality of an agency's services. From the assessment, patient outcomes (results) of care could be calculated, and agencies could then be compared to identify the most effective service providers.

As a result, the Center for Medicare and Medicaid services would then be able to identify agencies that demonstrated the "best" patient outcomes. Their "best practices" would then be shared with all other agencies, thereby improving the care of all home healthcare patients. This sounds like a noble and worthwhile effort. How can one argue with initiatives aimed at improving the quality of patient care? Is it not our professional obligation to participate in initiatives to improve patient care?

In addition to the quality improvement applications, OASIS information also created the foundation to build the home healthcare prospective payment system (PPS) of reimbursement that will be discussed in Chapter 8. These two factors were the impetus to require all Medicare certified home healthcare agencies to implement OASIS data collection in July 2000. A detailed and specific set of implementation instructions was published in the Federal Register (Prospective Payment System for Home Health Agencies, 2000). The implementation of OASIS required agencies to change many of their policies, procedures and clinical documentation forms. The sections that follow outline a synopsis of the OASIS regulations and processes.

OASIS IMPLEMENTATION

To achieve the measurement of quality goals of the Center for Medicare and Medicaid Services, thousands of home health agencies were required to implement OASIS. To maximize the effectiveness of the quality initiative, all nurses working in home healthcare had to be taught to interpret over 100 questions in a manner that was consistent with the intent of the questions. To facilitate the education and training of agency staff, the *Outcome Assessment Information System User's Manual* was published by the Health Care Finance Administration. The user's manual provided agencies with hundreds of pages of instructions for the implementation of the OASIS system. As part of the implementation, agencies were required to:

- Collect OASIS data on all eligible patients;

- Complete the patient assessment within the required timeframes; and

- Encode, lock, and electronically transmit the data within the required timeframes.

ELIGIBLE PATIENTS

The guidelines require agencies to complete the appropriate document on all patients admitted to home healthcare for the receipt of skilled nursing therapy services. For the most part, the OASIS regulations require that the nursing discipline complete the assessment even if nursing and therapy are both necessary services. However, if therapy services are the only ones requested at the time of admission, the therapist may complete the OASIS document.

Patients who are admitted to the agency for non-skilled services such as homemaking are excluded from the OASIS regulations. In addition, patients admitted with a maternity or post partum diagnosis are excluded. Finally, it is important to note that the OASIS is not designed to be administered to the pediatric population; therefore, patients who are under 18 years of age are also excluded from the OASIS requirements.

Although some home healthcare agencies also provide hospice services, only home health patients are subject to the OASIS regulations. Since the hospice patient's overall condition is expected to decline and the expected outcome is a comfortable and dignified death, it would be inappropriate to use the OASIS functional assessment for these patients.

TIMEFRAMES

The OASIS regulations require agencies to pay attention to at least eight different time frames. The best way to illustrate the time frame requirements is to relate them to a patient example; therefore, consider the case of Mr. Hunt. Mr. Hunt was admitted to My Town VNA on November 1st. Since this is the date of the first skilled visit provided to Mr. Hunt, it is also his home health start of care date (SOC).

The first OASIS timeframe that the agency must consider is the requirement to conduct a start of care visit within 48 hours of receiving a patient referral. If the agency is unable to accommodate the 48-hour requirement, the regulations require the agency to inform the referral source and provide them the option of referring the patient to an agency that can meet the patient's needs in a more timely fashion. If the agency does not or cannot make the visit within 48 hours, the patient's medical record should reflect the reason that the visit was not made and that the referral source, physician and patient were notified.

In some instances, there are appropriate exceptions to this rule. For example, the physician may request that the agency visit the patient in one week to remove postoperative staples or in one month to administer a vitamin B12 injection or flush a venous access device. In any case, this should be clearly documented in the patient's medical record.

The second OASIS timeframe is the 60-day episode. There is no limit to the number of 60-day episodes that a patient can have. However, the agency must be mindful that each 60-day episode is discrete and cannot overlap another episode in any way. In the case of Mr. Hunt, his 60-day episode runs from November 1st to December 30th. If Mr. Hunt receives a visit on December 31st, that visit would have occurred on the first day of his second episode of care.

The completion of the Start of Care OASIS (Appendix B) might be perceived as an overwhelming task by both the home healthcare nurse and by the patient. In deference to this perception, the OASIS regulations allow the agency up to five days to complete the Start of Care OASIS, which seems like a reasonable consideration. However, since OASIS is designed to capture the patient's status at the beginning of the episode, most agencies require their staff to complete the Start of Care

OASIS based on the condition of the patient at the first visit.

The reality of home healthcare is that a patient may present very differently from one visit to next. For example, after a hospitalization a patient may "bounce back" once they are home for a few days. Therefore, most agencies consider the OASIS a snapshot and require that it be completed on the basis of one visit and not a video that can be viewed over a five-day period. Typically, it can be expected that the OASIS will be completed within 24 to 48 hours of the start of care visit.

As mentioned earlier, the intent of OASIS data collection is to provide a measure for patient outcomes and compare one agency's performance to that of all other agencies. In order to accomplish this goal, OASIS regulations require agencies to encode and transmit all Medicare and Medicaid patient data to the federal government for analysis.

Simply stated, agencies are required to enter answers found on each patient OASIS assessment into a computer software program. In essence, the software packages the information in a way that protects confidentiality, yet makes retrieval and analysis of the information possible. The process of computerizing and sending the OASIS data is also called encoding, locking and transmitting.

Like all aspects of OASIS, there is a time requirement associated with the encoding of OASIS data. In this instance, agencies are allowed seven days after the OASIS is completed to encode (computerize) the patient's information. The detail to pay attention to in this statement is "seven days after the OASIS is completed." If one agency requires their staff to complete the OASIS within 24 hours of the start of care visit, the agency has seven additional days to encode and lock the data. This brings the agency to the ninth day of the episode. If the agency's policy allows the staff to take up to five days to complete the OASIS, the agency has until the twelfth day of the episode to encode and lock the data.

In the case of Mr. Hunt, assume that My Town VNA requires its staff to complete the OASIS within 24 hours of the start of care visit (November 1st). Therefore, the agency has until November 9th to encode and lock his data. If the agency utilizes a paper based medical record, that means the nurse has to complete the initial OASIS paperwork, have it checked for errors and omissions, correct the errors or complete the omissions and return the document to data entry for encoding and locking. Although this sounds like a reasonable timeframe, only 77% of agencies are able to meet this requirement (Benchmark of the Week #38, 2002).

Once the agency encodes and locks the assessment, it then has 30 days to transmit the data to its respective State OASIS Coordinator. The State OASIS Coordinator acts as a facilitator for the federal government by electronically packaging the data received from all of the home healthcare agencies in the state and then sending it along to the federal computer system. The State OASIS Coordinator also provides technical support and assistance to agencies in relation to problems with encoding, locking and transmitting the data.

In the case of My Town VNA, Mr. Hunt's data must be encoded and locked by November 9th. Agencies that fail to send the information in a timely fashion will be notified by the State OASIS Coordinator of their delinquence in the form of an electronic validation report.

From the OASIS perspective, a patient may experience three events which require the completion of an additional and specific assessment within a required timeframe. Whenever a patient is transferred to an inpatient facility (i.e., hospital or rehab facility) for more than 24 hours, the agency is required to complete a Transfer to Inpatient Facility OASIS assessment (Appendix C). This document must be completed within 48 hours of being noti-

fied that the patient was admitted. The detail to pay special attention to is the phrase "within 48 hours of being notified."

It is not uncommon for the agency to be unaware that the patient was transferred to an inpatient facility. For some, the first notification that the patient was hospitalized occurs when the agency is notified that the patient will be retuning home and services should resume. When this scenario occurs, the agency must still complete the Transfer OASIS within 48 hours so that it accurately reflects the sequence of events even though the patient has already returned home!

The second event occurs whenever an agency resumes the care of a patient after an inpatient stay. The OASIS regulations require the agency to complete a Resumption of Care OASIS. This document must be completed on the first visit after the patient returns home. The Resumption of Care (ROC) OASIS is the same exact document as the Start of Care OASIS found in Appendix B.

Since one of the uses of OASIS is to measure patient outcomes, the CHCPR has provided agencies with an assessment to capture unanticipated changes in the patient's status. The Significant Change in Condition (SCIC) assessment is the exact same document that is used to complete a Follow-Up Assessment (Appendix D) and is used to document the unanticipated clinical changes.

The SCIC assessment must be completed on the visit that the home healthcare nurse identified the unanticipated change. The most obvious example of a significant change in a patient's condition occurs when a patient develops an open wound or requires the services of a discipline that was not ordered at the patient's start or resumption of care, i.e. physical therapy.

One of the most difficult OASIS time frames to track has been termed the 5-day window. The 5-day window affects only patients who receive home healthcare services for subsequent 60-day episodes. The OASIS regulations require the agency to reassess the patient before the beginning of each subsequent episode of care. To operationalize this requirement, the CHCPR determined that the patient should be assessed any time after the 55th day of the episode but before the end of the 60th day.

To illustrate this point, once again consider the case of Mr. Hunt. Assume he was not discharged from My Town VNA by the end of the 60th day of the start of care episode, and his physician ordered plan of care requires him to continue to receive care into a second episode. OASIS regulations mandate that the agency make a home visit,

reassess his status and document the findings using a Follow-Up OASIS assessment (Appendix D). All of these steps must occur anywhere in the 5-day window of the current episode. When applied to the calendar, Mr. Hunt will have to receive a visit anytime from December 26th (day 56 of the episode) through December 30th (day 60 of the episode).

The final timeframe that the home healthcare nurse must be aware of is the time allotted to complete, encode and lock the Discharge OASIS. Most agencies require their staff to complete the Discharge OASIS within 48 hours of the last visit. OASIS regulations allow the agency seven days to

TABLE 6-1: MR. HUNT'S OASIS TIMEFRAMES AND SCHEDULES		
Event #1: Referral received by agency on 10/31		
	Time allowed to complete:	To be completed by:
SOC Visit	Within 48 hours of referral	11/2
SOC OASIS	5 days	11/7
Encode and lock	7 additional days	11/14
Event #2: Agency notified of inpatient transfer on 12/1		
	Time allowed to complete:	To be completed by:
Transfer OASIS completed	Within 48 hours of notification	12/3
Encode and lock	7 additional days	12/10
Event #3: Patient re-referred on 12/5 to resume services 12/6		
	Time allowed to complete:	To be completed by:
ROC Visit	Within 48 hours of referral	12/8
ROC OASIS completed	Within 48 hours of visit	12/10
Encode and lock	Within 7 days of completion	12/17
Event #4: Patient requires services into a subsequent episode. **5-day window 12/26 through 12/30**		
	Time allowed to complete:	To be completed by:
Follow-Up OASIS completed	Within 48 hours of visit made on 12/26	12/28
Episode end	60 days from start of care	12/30
Encode and lock	Within 7 days of completion	1/4
Event #5: Patient is discharged on 1/6		
	Time allowed to complete:	To be completed by:
Discharge OASIS completed	Within 48 hours of discharge	1/8
Encode and lock	Within 7 days of completion	1/15

encode and lock the assessment. Table 6-1 provides a summary of the OASIS timeframes using Mr. Hunt's schedule for illustration and clarification.

Now that a review of the OASIS time frames has been completed, it is necessary to review the actual OASIS documents that are provided in appendices B through E, and the rules that must be followed when completing them.

RULES FOR COMPLETION OF OASIS DOCUMENTS

It is imperative that, when completing the OASIS documents, the home healthcare nurse is familiar with the rules as they are presented in the OASIS regulations. The five basic rules are outlined below.

- **Rule 1:** OASIS questions are incorporated into the agency's comprehensive patient assessment. OASIS items are identified by the prefix M0 followed by a number. Agencies are not allowed to take liberties with the wording or punctuation of any of the OASIS questions. If it suits the needs of the agency, the questions can be sequenced differently as long as the M0 designations are not changed.

- **Rule 2:** When completing the OASIS items, the nurse must pay careful attention to the directives that are included in each of the questions. Some questions direct the nurse to "Mark all that apply" or follow predetermined skip patterns. For example, if the home healthcare nurse marks that the patient has not experienced an impatient stay, the directives included in the question instruct the nurse to skip all questions that relate to an inpatient stay.

- **Rule 3:** Although many of the questions provide the option of choosing "Unknown" as an answer, this should be avoided as often as possible. Unknown responses eliminate the possibility of the agency measuring the patient's outcome on the question.

- **Rule 4:** The OASIS assessments are not interview questionnaires. The nurse should use all of their assessment and observation skills to identify the answer that most accurately describes the patient's status or function.

- **Rule 5:** The OASIS document is designed to capture the patient's usual status. However, it is not uncommon that a patient's functional abilities may vary from day to day. Therefore, the home healthcare nurse is directed to answer the questions based on the patient's status most of the time on the day the patient assessment is being conducted (Outcome Assessment Information Set User's Manual, 1999).

To clarify this point, consider the patient who receives outpatient chemotherapy. The home care nurse visits the patient the day after the treatment, when the patient is most debilitated. While conducting the assessment, the patient reports that this will be the worst day of the week, and he is too fatigued and nauseous to participate in any activities of daily living such as showering or dressing. The patient expects that as the week progresses he will also be progressively better and able to get into the shower and dress. He reports that his usual routine is to get dressed every day after his morning shower. Following the instructions in the OASIS user's manual, the nurse must answer the questions based on the patient's status as he presents at the time of the assessment. In this case, the OASIS will reflect the patient's worst condition. If the assessment were conducted later in the week, a more positive presentation would be documented.

START OF CARE/ RESUMPTION OF CARE OASIS DOCUMENT

Any professional nurse who reviews the OASIS assessments provided in the appendices will quickly recognize that the OASIS questions are primarily functional in nature. In no way will the completion of the OASIS items provide the home healthcare team with an adequate clinical picture of the patient. Despite the scope of the

OASIS documents, they were never intended to replace the documentation of the patient's clinical and physical status. In fact, they were designed as adjunctive documents to be incorporated into the agency's existing clinical assessments.

Outlined below is a review of each of the OASIS assessments, including points that require special attention form the home healthcare nurse. The Start of Care OASIS basically collects 13 types of information which include:

- Demographic;

- Patient history;

- Current living arrangements;

- Availability of supportive assistance;

- Sensory status;

- Integumentary status;

- Respiratory status;

- Elimination status;

- Neuro/emotional/behavioral status;

- ADLS/IADLS;

- Ability to manage medications;

- Ability to manage medical equipment; and

- The patient's anticipated need for physical, speech, and occupational therapy.

Demographics and Patient History

There are 12 questions that capture patient data in this section of the assessment, eight that describe issues related to an inpatient stay. The remaining five questions primarily address the patient's prognosis and the risk factors that have potential to impact the patient's ability to maximize their potential. While reviewing OASIS questions, you will notice some instructions directing the nurse to either mark all that apply, or skip ahead to other questions. Below, question M0175 exemplifies both of these instructions.

(M0175) From which of the following **Inpatient Facilities** was the patient discharged during the past 14 days? **(Mark all that apply).**

☐   1-   Hospital

☐   2-   Rehabilitation facility

☐   3-   Skilled nursing facility

☐   4-   Other nursing home

☐   5-   Other (specify) _____

☐   NA Patient was not discharged from an inpatient facility
          [If NA, go to M0200]

If the patient was referred to the agency from a physician's office or perhaps a community referral was received, it is likely that the patient did not experience an inpatient facility discharge within the last 14 days. The home healthcare nurse is then instructed to skip all of the questions related to an inpatient facility discharge (M0180, and M0190) and go ahead to the questions that address a change in the patient's medical condition and plan of treatment beginning with question M0200.

If the patient was referred as a result of a hospitalization or other inpatient facility, all of the following questions must be answered.

(M0180) Inpatient Discharge Date (most recent):

_____/_____/_____ UK- Unknown
Month   Day   Year (4 digits)

(M0190) Inpatient Diagnoses and ICD code categories (three digits required; five digits optional) <u>for only those conditions treated during an inpatient stay within the last 14 days</u> (no surgical or V-codes)

<u>Inpatient Facility Diagnoses</u>	<u>ICD</u>
a _____	(_ _ _ . _ _)
b _____	(_ _ _ . _ _)

(M0200) Medical or Treatment Regimen Change Within Past 14 Days: Has this patient experienced a change in medical or treatment regimen (e.g., medication, treatment, or service change due to new or additional diagnosis, etc.) within the last 14 days?

☐ 0- No **[If No, go to M0220]**

☐ 1- Yes

When moving ahead to question M0210, the nurse must determine whether or not the patient experienced a change in their medical or treatment regimen within the past 14 days. Changes in a medical treatment regimen might include something as simple as a new medication or a change that is more complex such as the insertion of a Foley catheter for urinary retention.

(M0210) List the patient's **Medical Diagnoses** and ICD code categories (three digits required; five digits optional) <u>for those conditions requiring changed medical or treatment regimen</u> (no surgical or V-codes):

Changed Medical Regimen Diagnosis	ICD
a _____	(_ _ _ . _ _)
b _____	(_ _ _ . _ _)
c _____	(_ _ _ . _ _)
d _____	(_ _ _ . _ _)

Patients who are referred without a treatment change might include those who have lost the assistance of a caregiver and now have to be taught to take all of their medications independently or a patient who is referred from the physician's office who appears to be noncompliant with the diet and medication regimen that had been established on previous visits.

Regardless of whether or not the patient has experienced a change in their treatment regimes, M0220 must be answered for all patients. If the patient did not experience a change in their medical regimen or an inpatient stay in the past 14 days, the

nurse will mark option NA and move onto question M0230/M0240.

(M0220) Conditions Prior to Medical Treatment Regimen Change or Inpatient Stay Within Past 14 Days: If this patient experienced an inpatient facility discharge or change in medical or treatment regimen within the past 14 days, indicate any conditions which existed prior to the inpatient stay or change in medical or treatment regimen. **(Mark all that apply.)**

☐ 1- Urinary Incontinence

☐ 2- Indwelling/suprapubic catheter

☐ 3- Intractable pain

☐ 4- Impaired decision-making

☐ 5- Disruptive or socially inappropriate behavior

☐ 6- Memory loss to the extent that supervision required

☐ 7- None of the above

☐ NA- No inpatient facility discharge and no change in medial or treatment regimen in past 14 days

☐ UK- Unknown

As mentioned earlier, some of the questions on the OASIS are very simple and straight forward, and others are more complex and require the nurse to pay close attention to the details that differentiate one category from the next. M0230 and M0240 are relatively complex and require the use of standardized definitions to classify patient severity. Outlined below are the definitions provided by the CHCPR to facilitate rating in a consistent manner. The nurse must use these five definitions for all questions that require a severity rating.

(M0230/M0240) Diagnoses and Severity Index: List each medical diagnosis or problem for which the patient is receiving home care and ICD-9 code category (three digits required, five digits optional-no surgical or v codes) and rate them using the following severity index. (Choose one value that represents the most severe rating appropriate for each diagnosis.)

Severity Rating

0- Asymptomatic, no treatment needed at this time

1- Symptoms well controlled with current therapy

2- Symptoms controlled with difficulty, affecting daily functioning; patient needs ongoing monitoring

3- Symptoms poorly controlled, patient needs frequent adjustment in treatment and dose monitoring

4- Symptoms poorly controlled, history of rehospitalizations

Using the definitions above, the home health-care nurse must identify the patient's home care diagnoses and rate the severity in questions M0230 and M0240.

(M0230) Primary Diagnosis	ICD	Severity Rating
a_____	(___.__)	☐1 ☐2 ☐3 ☐4 ☐5

(M0240) Other Diagnosis	ICD	Severity Rating
a_____	(___.__)	☐1 ☐2 ☐3 ☐4 ☐5
b_____	(___.__)	☐1 ☐2 ☐3 ☐4 ☐5
c_____	(___.__)	☐1 ☐2 ☐3 ☐4 ☐5
d_____	(___.__)	☐1 ☐2 ☐3 ☐4 ☐5
e_____	(___.__)	☐1 ☐2 ☐3 ☐4 ☐5
f_____	(___.__)	☐1 ☐2 ☐3 ☐4 ☐5

As part of the patient's medical plan of treatment, M0250 requires the nurse to indicate which nutrition and intravenous therapies a patient receives at home.

(M0250) Therapies the patient receives at home: **(Mark all that apply)**

☐ 1- Intravenous or infusion therapy (excludes TPN)

☐ 2- Parenteral nutrition (TPN or lipids)

☐ 3- Enteral nutrition (nasogastric, gastrostomy, jejunostomy, or any other artificial entry into the alimentary canal)

☐ 4- None of the above

Some of the most "difficult" questions that home care nurses are expected to answer are related to the patient's prognosis and life expectancy. Some nurses report that these questions make them "uncomfortable" and object by stating it is not within their scope of practice to make these determinations.

The OASIS user's manual provides guidance in this area instructing the nurse to "Consider diagnosis and the referring physician's expectations for this patient, based on the information received from these data sources, make informed judgment regarding the patient's overall and rehabilitative prognosis" (Outcome and Assessment Information Set, 1999, p. 8.44).

(M0260) Overall Prognosis: BEST description of patient's overall prognosis for recovery from this episode of illness.

☐ 0- Poor: little or no recovery is expected and/or further decline is imminent

☐ 1- Good/Fair: partial to full recovery is expected

☐ UK- Unknown

(M0270) Rehabilitative Prognosis: BEST description of patient's prognosis for functional status.

☐ 0- Guarded: minimal improvement in functional status is expected; decline is possible

☐ 1- Good: marked improvement in functional status is expected

☐ UK- Unknown

(M0280) Life Expectancy:

(Physician documentation is not required.)

☐ 0- Life expectancy is greater than 6 months

☐ 1- Life expectancy is 6 months or fewer

These three questions, M0260, M0270 and M0280, are subjective in nature and can be influenced by both patient-related and nurse-related factors. For instance, a patient's ability to recover from an episode of illness may be influenced by the physician ordered plan of treatment, the patient's level of motivation, or the level of supportive assistance provided by the patient's family or caregiver.

How the home care nurse responds to these items may be influenced by their experience in caring for patients with a particular diagnosis. For example, if the nurse has not cared for many patients with a primary diagnosis of Multiple Sclerosis or Cystic Fibrosis, determining the patient's rehabilitative prognosis may not be as clear cut as if the primary diagnosis was something more common such as diabetes or asthma. This part of the assessment also requires the home healthcare nurse to identify the risk factors that may impact the patient's health status and ability to recover from their current illness.

(M0290) High Risk Factors characterizing this patient **(Mark all that apply.)**

- ☐ 1- Heavy smoking
- ☐ 2- Obesity
- ☐ 3- Alcohol dependency
- ☐ 4- Drug dependency
- ☐ 5- None of the above
- ☐ UK- Unknown

Once again, the nurse must use their judgement to answer this question. The OASIS user's manual does not provide guidance on whether the patient has to be actively participating in these behaviors or merely have a history of such behavior.

Living Arrangement and Supportive Assistance

This section of the OASIS is comprised of six questions that require the home healthcare nurse to assess the patient's current living arrangements and the supportive assistance available to the patient.

(M0300) Current Residence:

- ☐ 1- Patient's owned or rented residence (house, apartment, or mobile home owned or rented by patient/couple/significant other)
- ☐ 2- Family member's residence
- ☐ 3- Boarding home or rented room
- ☐ 4- Board and care or assisted living facility
- ☐ 5- Other (specify)

(M0340) Patient lives with: (Mark all that apply.)

- ☐ 1- Lives alone
- ☐ 2- With spouse or significant other
- ☐ 3- With other family member
- ☐ 4- With friend
- ☐ 5- With paid help (other than home care agency staff)
- ☐ 6- With other than above

(M0350) Assisting Person(s) other than Home Care Agency Staff: (Mark all that apply.)

- ☐ 1- Relative, friends, or neighbors living outside the home
- ☐ 2- Persons residing in the home (EXCLUDING paid help)
- ☐ 3- Paid help
- ☐ 4- None of the above **[If None of the above, go to M0390]**
- ☐ UK- Unknown **[If Unknown, go to M0390]**

(M0360) Primary Caregiver taking lead responsibility for providing or managing the patient's care, providing the most frequent assistance, etc. (other than home care agency staff):

☐ 0- No one person

[If No one person, go to M0390]

☐ 1- Spouse or significant other

☐ 2- Daughter or son

☐ 3- Other family member

☐ 4- Friend or neighbor or community or church member

☐ 5- Paid help

☐ UK- Unknown **[If unknown, go to M0390]**

(M0370) How Often does the patient receive assistance from the primary caregiver?

☐ 1- Several times during day and night

☐ 2- Several times during day

☐ 3- Once daily

☐ 4- Three or more times per week

☐ 5- One to two times per week

☐ 6- Less often than weekly

☐ UK- Unknown

(M0380) Type of Primary Caregiver Assistance: (Mark all that apply.)

☐ 1- ADL assistance (e.g., bathing, dressing, toileting, bowel/bladder, eating/feeding)

☐ 2- IADL assistance (e.g., meds, meals, housekeeping, laundry, telephone, shopping, finances)

☐ 3- Environmental support (housing, home maintenance)

☐ 4- Psychosocial support (socialization, companionship, recreation)

☐ 5- Advocates or facilitates patient's participation in appropriate medical care

☐ 6- Financial agent, power of attorney, or conservator of finance

☐ 7- Health care agent, conservator of person, or medical power of attorney

☐ UK- Unknown

Once again, the home healthcare nurse must pay close attention to the question and follow the instructions carefully. For example, M0350 instructs the nurse to mark all that apply. If option

number four or the unknown option is selected, the nurse is instructed to skip the remaining questions in this section and move ahead to the sensory status questions beginning with question M0390.

Sensory Status

The patient's ability to see, hear, experience pain, understand spoken language, verbally express themself are captured in questions M0390 to M0430 and are outlined below.

(M0390) Vision with corrective lenses if the patient usually wears them

☐ 0- Normal vision: sees adequately in most situations; can see medication labels, newsprint.

☐ 1- Partially impaired: cannot see medication labels or newsprint, but can see obstacles in path, and the surrounding layout, can count fingers at arm's length

☐ 2- Severely impaired: cannot locate objects without hearing or touching them or patient nonresponsive

(M0400) Hearing and Ability to Understand Spoken Language in patient's own language (with hearing aids if the patient usually uses them):

☐ 0- No observable impairment. Able to hear and understand complex or detailed instructions and extended or abstract conversations.

☐ 1- With minimal difficulty, able to hear and understand most multi-step instructions and ordinary conversation. May need occasional repetition, extra time, or louder voice.

☐ 2- Has moderate difficulty hearing and understanding simple, one step instructions and brief conversation; needs frequent prompting or assistance

☐ 3- Has severe difficulty hearing and understanding simple greetings and short comments. Requires multiple repetitions, restatements, demonstrations, and additional time.

☐ 4- Unable to hear and understand familiar words or common expressions consistently, or patient nonresponsive.

(M0410) Speech and Oral (Verbal) Expression of Language (in patient's own language):

☐ 0- Expresses complex ideas, feelings and needs clearly, completely, and easily in all situations with no observable impairment.

☐ 1- Minimal difficulty in expressing ideas and needs (may take extra time; makes occasional errors in word choice, grammar or speech intelligibility; need minimal prompting or assistance).

☐ 2- Expresses simple ideas or needs with moderate difficulty (needs prompting or assistance, errors in word choice, grammar organization or speech intelligibility). Speaks in phrases or short sentences.

☐ 3- Has severe difficulty expressing basic ideas or needs and requires maximal assistance or guessing by listener. Speech is limited to single words or short phrases.

☐ 4- Unable to express basic needs even with maximal prompting or assistance but is not comatose or unresponsive (e.g. speech is nonsensical or unintelligible).

☐ 5- Patient nonresponsive or unable to speak.

(M0420) Frequency of Pain interfering with patient's activity or movement

☐ 0- Patient has no pain or pain does not interfere with activity or movement

☐ 1- Less often than daily

☐ 2- Daily, but not constantly

☐ 3- All of the time

(M0430) Intractable Pain: Is the patient experiencing pain that is not easily relieved, occurs at least daily, and affects the patient's sleep appetite, physical or emotional energy, concentration, person

relationships, emotions, or ability or desire to perform physical activity?

☐ 0- No
☐ 1- Yes

Although these questions appear very straightforward, M0400 should be considered in depth. Consider a patient who is profoundly deaf. The patient can read lips and communicate their needs by writing notes on a pad of paper that is always kept with them. How would the nurse answer M0400? The patient cannot hear; therefore, options one through three cannot be chosen to describe the patient. Option four does not adequately describe the patient because although they cannot hear, they can understand familiar words or common expressions consistently.

Similarly, M0420 creates some confusion when nurses attempt to answer it. Some nurses report difficulty answering for patients who take medication to manage their pain. If a patient has daily pain but is able to control it with medication so that it does not interfere with activity or movement, how should this question be answered? Option zero states the patient has no pain or pain does not interfere with activity or movement. Once the patient takes medication, is option zero the correct option for the patient? If the patient does not take their medications, option one, two, or three might be more appropriate. When answering this question, home healthcare nurses might seek assistance of a manger or the agency's OASIS coordinator to assure that this question is interpreted in accordance with agency and OASIS policy.

Integumentary Status

With few exceptions, the majority of the questions to this point have been relatively simply stated and easy to answer. When reviewing the 13 questions that comprise the Integumentary Status portion of the OASIS assessment, questions that are detailed and more complex are noted.

These questions require the home healthcare nurse to accurately differentiate between a pressure and a stasis ulcer.

A review of questions M0440 to M0488 illustrated that, to complete an OASIS accurately, the home healthcare nurse must be knowledgeable about the accepted definitions and description of wounds and wound related issues. The home healthcare nurse has to learn to describe the status of wounds very rigidly.

The first wound question encountered is M0440. If the nurse answers "No" to this question, all of the subsequent wound questions will be skipped, and the next question answered is to evaluate the patient's respiratory status. For the purposes of this OASIS, a "lesion is a broad term used to describe an area of pathologically altered tissue. Sores, skin tears, ulcers, rashes, surgical incisions, crusts etc. are all considered lesions" (Outcome Assessment Information Set User's Manual, 1999, p. 8.62).

(M0440) Does this patient have a **Skin Lesion** or an **Open Wound**? This excludes "OSTOMIES"

☐ 0- No **[If No, go to M0468]**
☐ 1- Yes

The OASIS user's manual defines a pressure ulcer as "skin inflammation, sore, or ulcer resulting from tissue hypoxia due to prolonged pressure. Pressure ulcers most often occur over bony prominences" (Outcome Assessment Information Set User's Manual, 1999, p. 8.63). Patients at most risk for developing pressure ulcers include those with limited mobility or patients who experience bowel and/or bladder incontinence. Patients with inadequate nutrition or sensory-perceptual deficits might also be at risk for developing pressure ulcers.

(M0445) Does this patient have a **Pressure Ulcer**?

☐ 0- No **[If No, go to M0468]**
☐ 1- Yes

Although most clinicians can readily identify the presence of a pressure ulcer, some difficulty might arise when answering M0450, which requires the nurse to differentiate between the stages of the pressure ulcer. When responding to M0450, it is important to read the detailed description of each stage and answer the questions as accurately as possible. OASIS requires that wounds with eschar be classified as non-observable and has provided an option to capture this scenario.

In addition to staging the pressure ulcer, the clinician must also identify which pressure ulcer is most problematic. For instance, a patient may have more than one pressure ulcer at two different stages of healing. More specifically, the patient may have a Stage 4 ulcer that demonstrates active and progressive healing in addition to a Stage 3 ulcer that is infected and filled with slough. Therefore, it is important to pay close attention when answering M0460 and M0470.

(M0460) Stage of Most Problematic (Observable) Pressure Ulcer:

☐ 1- Stage 1
☐ 2- Stage 2
☐ 3- Stage 3
☐ 4- Stage 4
☐ NA No observable pressure ulcer

(M0464) Status of Most Problematic (Observable) Pressure Ulcer:

☐ 1- Fully granulating
☐ 2- Early/partial granulation
☐ 3- Not healing
☐ NA No observable pressure ulcer

A stasis ulcer is defined as an "ulcer caused by inadequate venous circulation in the area affected (usually lower legs). This lesion is often associated with stasis dermatitis" (Outcome and Assessment Information Set, 1999, p. 8.67).

(M0468) Does this patient have a **Stasis Ulcer?**

☐ 0- No [If No, go to M0482]
☐ 1- Yes

(M0450) Current Number of Pressure Ulcers at Each Stage: (Choose one response for each stage.)

Pressure Ulcer Stages   Number of Pressure Ulcers

a)   Stage 1: Nonblanchable erythema of intact skin;
the heralding of skin ulceration. In darker-pigmented
skin, warmth, edema, hardness, or discolored skin
may be indicators.   ☐ 0   ☐ 1   ☐ 2   ☐ 3   ☐ 4 or more

b)   Stage 2: Partial thickness skin loss involving epidermis
and/or dermis. The ulcer is superficial and presents
clinically as an abrasion, blister or shallow crater. ☐ 0   ☐ 1   ☐ 2   ☐ 3   ☐ 4 or more

c)   Stage 3: Full thickness skin loss involving damage or
necrosis of subcutaneous tissue, which may extend
down to, but not through underlying fascia. The ulcer
presents clinically as a deep crater with or without
undermining of adjacent tissue.   ☐ 0   ☐ 1   ☐ 2   ☐ 3   ☐ 4 or more

d)   Stage 4: Full thickness skin loss with extensive
destruction, tissue necrosis, or damage to muscle, bone
or supporting structures (e.g., tendon, joint capsule, etc.) ☐ 0   ☐ 1   ☐ 2   ☐ 3   ☐ 4 or more

e)   In addition to the above, is there at least one pressure ulcer
that cannot be observed due to the presence of eschar or
nonremovable dressing including casts?

☐ 0- No

☐ 1- Yes

(M0470) Current Number of Observable Stasis Ulcer(s):

☐ 0-   Zero
☐ 1-   One
☐ 2-   Two
☐ 3-   Three
☐ 4-   Four or more

(M0474) Does this patient have at least one **Stasis Ulcer that Cannot be Observed** due to the presence of a nonremovable dressing?

☐ 0-   No
☐ 1-   Yes

(M0476) Status of Most Problematic (Observable) Stasis Ulcer:

☐ 1-   Fully granulating
☐ 2-   Early/partial granulation
☐ 3-   Not healing
☐ NA No observable stasis ulcer

In addition to documenting the presence of pressure and stasis ulcers, the home healthcare nurse must also identify the status of any surgical wound(s). Although the first of these three questions is pretty straight forward, answering the fourth question, M0488, has created some difficulty.

(M0482) Does this patient have a **Surgical Wound**?

☐ 0-   No **[If No, go to M0490]**
☐ 1-   Yes

(M0484) Current Number of (Observable) Surgical Wounds: (If a wound is partially closed but has more than one opening, consider each opening as a separate wound.)

☐ 0-   Zero
☐ 1-   One
☐ 2-   Two
☐ 3-   Three
☐ 4-   Four or more

(M0486) Does this patient have at least one Surgical Wound that Cannot be Observed due to the presence of a nonremovable dressing?

☐ 0- No
☐ 1- Yes

(M0488) Status of Most Problematic (Observable) Surgical Wound:

☐ 1- Fully granulating
☐ 2- Early/partial granulation
☐ 3- Not healing
☐ NA No observable surgical ulcer

M0488 describes the stages of an actively healing surgical wound. Healed surgical wounds are scars, not wounds. For the purposes of OASIS documentation, a scar is characterized as a skin lesion or wound, by answering "Yes" to M0440 and answering "No" to M0482. To clarify this in the medical record, many agencies require the nurse who completes the assessment to make a notation about the presence of a healed surgical scar on the visit note associated with the visit or in the physical assessment portion of the document.

Respiratory Status

The next two questions on the Start of Care OASIS directs the nurse to assess the patient's respiratory status.

(M0490) When is the patient dyspneic or **noticeably Short of Breath**?

☐ 0- Never, patient is not short of breath
☐ 1- When walking more than 20 feet, climbing stairs
☐ 2- With moderate exertion (e.g. while dressing, using commode or bedpan, walking distances less than 20 feet)
☐ 3- With minimal exertion (e.g. while eating, talking or performing other ADLSs) or with agitation
☐ 4- At rest (during day or night)

Although the first question, M0490, does not direct the nurse how to answer if the patient utilizes oxygen, the OASIS user's manual does. The nurse must determine whether or not the patient uses oxygen, and if they do, the nurse must then identify whether or not the patient uses it intermittently or continuously.

If the patient uses oxygen intermittently, the nurse should answer M0490 after assessing the patient without the oxygen on. If the patient uses oxygen on a continuous basis, the nurse should assess the patient while using the oxygen (Outcome Assessment Information Set User's Manual, 1999).

(M0500) Respiratory Treatments utilized at home: **(Mark all that apply.)**

☐ 1- Oxygen (intermittent or continuous)
☐ 2- Ventilator (continually or at night)
☐ 3- Continuous positive airway pressure
☐ 4- None of the above

Elimination Status

There are five questions that are intended to assess the patient's bowel and bladder function. These questions, M0510 through M0550, are relatively straight forward and require simple answers.

(M0510) Has this patient been treated for a **Urinary Tract Infection** in the past 14 days?

☐ 0- No
☐ 1- Yes
☐ NA Patient on prophylactic treatment
☐ UK Unknown

(M0520) Urinary Incontinence or Urinary Catheter Presence:

☐ 0- No incontinence or catheter (includes anuria or ostomy for urinary drainage) **[If No, go to M0540]**
☐ 1- Patient is incontinent

☐ 2- Patient requires a urinary catheter (i.e., external, indwelling, intermittent, suprapubic) **[Go to M0540]**

(M0530) When does **Urinary Incontinence** occur?

☐ 0- Timed-voiding defers incontinence
☐ 1- During the night only
☐ 2- During the day and night

(M0540) Bowel Incontinence frequency:

☐ 0- Very rarely or never has bowel incontinence
☐ 1- Less than once weekly
☐ 2- One to three times weekly
☐ 3- Four to six times weekly
☐ 4- On a daily basis
☐ 5- More often than once daily
☐ NA Patient has ostomy for bowel elimination
☐ UK Unknown

(M0550) Ostomy for Bowel Elimination: Does this patient have an ostomy for bowel elimination that (within the last 14 days): a) was related to an inpatient facility stay, or b) necessitated a change in medical or treatment regimen?

☐ 0- Patient does not have an ostomy for bowel elimination.
☐ 1- Patient's ostomy was not related to an inpatient stay and did not necessitate change in medical or treatment regimen.
☐ 2- The ostomy was related to an inpatient stay or did necessitate change in medical or treatment regimen.

Neuro/Emotional/Behavioral Status

This section of the assessment is detailed and intended to uncover difficulties that might inhibit the patient from achieving an optimal level of function. This is the only section of the assessment that directs the nurse to answer questions based on what is "Reported or Observed" during the assessment process. The OASIS user's manual does not provide the nurse with any guidance about how to answer these questions if a conflict arises between the perceptions of the nurse and the behaviors reported by the patient or caregiver.

When reviewing the following questions, it can be noted that many of the responses are detailed and characterized by subtle variations. Ideally, when answering these questions, the nurse should read each of the options and pay careful attention to the subtle differences of each. Answering requires the nurse to use their professional judgment to choose the option that best describes what they have observed. If there is inconsistency between the nurse, patient or caregiver, the nurse should be sure to make a notation that describes the inconsistent views or conflicts in the patient's medical record.

(M0560) Cognitive Functioning: (Patient's current level of alertness, orientation, comprehension, concentration, and immediate memory for simple commands.)

☐ 0- Alert/oriented, able to focus and shift attention, comprehends and recalls task directions independently.
☐ 1- Requires prompting (cueing, repetition, reminders) only under stressful or unfamiliar conditions.
☐ 2- Requires assistance and some direction in specific situations (e.g., on all tasks involving shifting of attention), or consistently requires low stimulus environment due to distractibility.
☐ 3- Requires considerable assistance in routine situations. Is not alert and oriented or is unable to shift attention and recall directions more than half of the time.
☐ 4- Totally dependent due to disturbances such as constant disorientation, coma, persistent vegetative state, or delirium.

(M0570) When Confused (Reported or Observed):

- ☐ 0- Never
- ☐ 1- In new or complex situations only
- ☐ 2- On awakening or at night only
- ☐ 3- During the day and evening, but not constantly
- ☐ 4- Constantly
- ☐ NA Patient nonresponsive

(M0580) When Anxious (Reported or Observed):

- ☐ 0- None of the time
- ☐ 1- Less often than daily
- ☐ 2- Daily, but not constantly
- ☐ 3- All of the time
- ☐ NA Patient nonresponsive

(M0590) Depressive Feelings Reported or Observed in Patient: (Mark all that apply.)

- ☐ 1- Depressed mood (e.g., feeling sad, tearful)
- ☐ 2- Sense of failure
- ☐ 3- Hopelessness
- ☐ 4- Recurrent thoughts of death
- ☐ 5- Thoughts of suicide
- ☐ 6- None of the above feelings observed or reported

(M0610) Demonstrated at Least Once a Week (Reported or Observed): (Mark all that apply.)

- ☐ 1- Memory deficit: failure to recognize familiar persons/places, inability to recall events of past 24 hours, significant memory loss so that supervision is required
- ☐ 2- Impaired decision-making failure to perform usual ADLs or IADLs , inability to appropriately stop activities, jeopardizes safety through actions
- ☐ 3- Verbal disruption: yelling, threatening, excessive profanity, sexual references, etc.
- ☐ 4- Physical aggression: aggressive or combative to self and others (e.g. hits self, throws objects, punches, dangerous

maneuvers with wheelchair or other objects)

- ☐ 5- Disruptive, infantile, or socially inappropriate behaviors (excludes verbal actions)
- ☐ 6- Delusional, hallucinatory, or paranoid behavior
- ☐ 7- None of the above behaviors demonstrated

(M0620) Frequency of behavior Problems (Reported or Observed) (e.g., wandering episodes, self abuse, verbal disruption, physical aggression, etc.):

- ☐ 0- Never
- ☐ 1- Less than once a month
- ☐ 2- Once a month
- ☐ 3- Several times each month
- ☐ 4- Several times a week
- ☐ 5- At least daily

(M0630) Is this patient receiving **Psychiatric Nursing Services** at home provided by a qualified psychiatric nurse?

- ☐ 0- No
- ☐ 1- Yes

Activities of Daily Living (ADLS) and Instrumental Activities of Daily Living (IADLS)

The Start of Care OASIS assessment includes 14 questions that require the nurse to evaluate the patient's mental and physical ability to perform ADLS and IADLS. The guidelines provided in the OASIS user's manual instruct the home healthcare nurse to differentiate between the patient's ability **not** willingness to perform ALDS and IADLS. To highlight the difference between ability and willingness, consider the following patient scenarios.

Mrs. Leger is a 68-year-old woman who tells the home healthcare nurse that she has never taken a shower. She tells the nurse that she grew up only taking sponge baths and prefers not to get into the tub or shower. Does this mean she is unable?

Mr. Shoesmith is an elderly gentleman who has been recently widowed after being married all of his adult life. He reports to the nurse that he could not possibly perform grocery shopping, because his wife had always performed this chore. Does that mean he is unable?

In addition to answering the ADL and IADL questions based on the patient's current status, the home healthcare nurse will also have to document the patient's prior ability. The OASIS regulations recognize that a patient may experience variation in their ability on a day-to-day basis and instructs the nurse to "choose the response describing the ability more than 50 percent of the time" (Outcome Assessment Information Set User's Manual, 1999, p. 8.91).

When completing the questions that require the nurse to document the patient's "prior" ability to perform ADLS and IADLS, the nurse is to consider the patient's ability **exactly** 14 days prior to the current day. Even in cases where the patient may have been in the hospital or operating room, the OASIS instructions require the nurse to adhere "rigidly" to the 14-day rule, and the nurse should estimate the patient's functional ability at that time. If the patient were in the operating room, their ability to perform any ADLS or IADLS would be minimal and should be documented accordingly on the OASIS.

(M0640) Grooming: Ability to tend to personal hygiene needs (i.e., washing face and hands, hair care, shaving or make up, teeth or denture care, fingernail care).

Prior Current

☐ ☐ 0- Able to groom self unaided, with or without the use of assistive devices or adapted methods.

☐ ☐ 1- Grooming utensils must be place within reach before able to complete grooming activities.

☐ ☐ 2- Someone must assist the patient to groom self.

☐ ☐ 3- Patient depends entirely upon someone else for grooming needs.

☐ UK Unknown

(M0650)Ability to Dress Upper Body (with or without dressing aids) including undergarments, pullovers, front opening shirts and blouses, managing zippers, buttons and snaps

Prior Current

☐ ☐ 0- Able to obtain clothes out of closets and drawers, put them on, and remove them from the upper body without assistance

☐ ☐ 1- Able to dress upper body without assistance if clothing is laid out or handed to the patient

☐ ☐ 2- Someone must help the patient put on upper body clothing

☐ ☐ 3- Patient depends entirely upon another person to dress the upper body

☐ UK Unknown

(M0660) Ability to Dress Lower Body (with or without dressing aids) including undergarments, slacks, socks or nylons and shoes

Prior Current

☐ ☐ 0- Able to obtain, put on, and remove clothing and shoes without assistance

☐ ☐ 1- Able to dress lower body without assistance if clothing and shoes are laid out or handed to the patient

☐ ☐ 2- Someone must help the patient put on undergarments, slacks, socks or nylons and shoes

☐ ☐ 3- Patient depends entirely upon another person to dress the lower body

☐ UK- Unknown

(M0670) Bathing: Ability to wash entire body. Excludes grooming (washing face and hands only).

Prior Current

☐ ☐ 0- Able to bathe self in <u>shower or tub</u> independently.

☐ ☐ 1- With the use of devices, is able to bathe self in shower or tub independently

☐ ☐ Able to bathe in shower or tub with the assistance of another person

    (a) For intermittent supervision or encouragement or reminders, <u>OR</u>

    (b) To get in and out of the shower or tub, <u>OR</u>

    (c) For washing difficult to reach areas.

☐ ☐ 3- Participates in bathing self in shower or tub, but requires presence of another person throughout the bath for assistance or supervision

☐ ☐ 4- <u>Unable</u> to use the shower or tub and is bathed in <u>bed or bedside chair.</u>

☐ ☐ 5- Unable to effectively participate in bathing and is totally bathed by another person

☐ UK- Unknown

(M0680) Toileting: Ability to get to and from the toilet or bedside commode.

Prior Current

☐ ☐ 0- Able to get to and from the toilet independently with or without a device.

☐ ☐ 1- When reminded, assisted, or supervised by another person, able to get to and from the toilet.

☐ ☐ 2- <u>Unable</u> to get to and from the toilet but is able to use a bedside commode (with or without assistance).

☐ ☐ 3- <u>Unable</u> to get to and from the toilet or bedside commode but is able to use a bedpan/urinal independently.

☐ ☐ 4- Is totally dependent in toileting
☐ UK Unknown

(M0690) Transferring: Ability to move from bed to chair, on and off toilet or commode, into and out of tub or shower, and ability to turn and position self in bed if patient is bedfast.

Prior Current

☐ ☐ 0- Able to independently transfer.
☐ ☐ 1- Transfers with minimal human assistance or with use of an assistive device.

☐ ☐ 2- Unable to transfer self but is able to bear weight and pivot during the transfer process.

☐ ☐ 3- Unable to transfer self and is unable to bear weight or pivot when transferred by another person.

☐ ☐ 4- Is totally dependent in toileting
☐ ☐ 5- Bedfast, unable to transfer but is able to turn and position self in bed.

☐ UK Unknown

(M0700) Ambulation/Locomotion: Ability to walk, once in a standing position, or use a wheelchair, once in a seated position, on a variety of surfaces.

Prior Current

☐ ☐ 0- Able to independently walk on even and uneven surfaces and climb stairs with or without railings (e.g., needs no human assistance or assistive device).

☐ ☐ 1- Requires use of a device (e.g.. cane, walker) to walk alone or requires human supervision or assistance to negotiate stairs or steps on uneven surfaces.

☐ ☐ 2- Able to walk only with super-vision or assistance of another person at all times.

☐ ☐ 3- Chairfast, unable to ambulate but is able to wheel self inde-pendently.

☐ ☐ 4- Chairfast, unable to ambulate and is unable to wheel self.

☐ ☐ 5- Bedfast, unable to ambulate or be up in a chair.

☐   UK Unknown

(M0710) Feeding or Eating: Ability to feed self meals and snacks. **Note: This refers only to the process of <u>eating</u>, <u>chewing</u>, and <u>swallowing</u>, <u>not</u> <u>preparing</u> the food to be eaten.**

Prior Current

☐ ☐ 0- Able to independently feed self.

☐ ☐ 1- Able to feed self independently but requires:
(a) meal set-up; <u>OR</u>
(b) intermittent assistance or supervision from another person; <u>OR</u>
(c) a liquid, pureed or ground meat diet.

☐ ☐ 2- <u>Unable</u> to feed self and must be assisted or supervised throughout the meal/snack.

☐ ☐ 3- Able to take in nutrients orally and receives supplemental nutrients through a nasogastric tube or gastrostomy.

☐ ☐ 4- <u>Unable</u> to take in nutrients orally and is fed nutrients through a nasogastric tube or gastrostomy.

☐ ☐ 5- Unable to take in nutrients orally or by tube feeding.

☐   UK Unknown

(M0720) Planning and Preparing Light Meals (e.g., cereal, sandwich) or reheat delivered meals:

Prior Current

☐ ☐ 0- (a) Able to independently plan and prepare all light meals for self or reheat delivered meals: <u>OR</u>
(b) Is physically, cognitively, and mentally able to pre-pare light meals on a regu-lar basis but has not rou-tinely performed light meal preparation in the past

(i.e., prior to this home care admission)

☐ ☐ 1- <u>Unable</u> to prepare light meals on a regular basis due to physical, cognitive, or mental limitations.

☐ ☐ 2- Unable to prepare any light meals or reheat any delivered meals.

☐ UK Unknown

(M0730) Transportation: Physical and mental ability to safely use a car, taxi, or public transportation (bus, train, subway).

<u>Prior</u> <u>Current</u>

☐ ☐ 0- Able to independently drive a regular or adapted car; <u>OR</u> uses a regular or handicap-accessible public bus.

☐ ☐ 1- Able to ride in a car only when driven by another person; <u>OR</u> able to use a bus or a handicap van only when assisted or accompanied by another person.

☐ ☐ 2- Unable to ride in a car, taxi, bus or van, and requires transportation by ambulance.

☐ UK Unknown

(M0740) Laundry: Ability to do own laundry - to carry laundry to and from washing machine, to use washer and dryer, to wash small items by hand.

<u>Prior</u> <u>Current</u>

☐ ☐ 0- (a) Able to independently take care of all laundry tasks; <u>OR</u>

(b) Physically, cognitively, and mentally able to do laundry and access facilities, <u>but</u> has not routinely performed laundry tasks in the past i.e., prior to this home care admission.

☐ ☐ 1- Able to do only light laundry, such as minor hand wash or light washer loads. Due to physical cognitive, or mental limitations, needs assistance with heavy laundry such as carrying large loads of laundry.

☐ ☐ 2- <u>Unable</u> to do any do any laundry due to physical limitation or needs continual supervision and assistance due to cognitive or mental limitations.

☐ UK Unknown

(M0750) Housekeeping: Ability to safely and effectively perform light housekeeping and heavier cleaning tasks.

<u>Prior</u> <u>Current</u>

☐ ☐ 0- (a) Able to independently perform all housekeeping tasks; <u>OR</u>

(b) Physically, cognitively, and mentally able to perform <u>all</u> housekeeping tasks, <u>but</u> has not routinely participated in housekeeping tasks in the past (i.e., prior to this home care admission.

☐ ☐ 1- Able to perform only <u>light</u> housekeeping (i.e., dusting, wiping kitchen counters) task independently.

☐ ☐ 2- Able to perform housekeeping tasks with intermittent assistance or supervision from another person.

☐ ☐ 3- <u>Unable</u> to consistently perform any housekeeping tasks unless assisted by another person throughout the process.

☐ ☐ 4- Unable to effectively participate in any housekeeping tasks.

☐ UK Unknown

(M0760) Shopping: Ability to plan for, select, and purchase items in a store and carry them home or arrange delivery

Prior Current

☐ ☐ 0- (a) Able to plan for shopping needs and independently perform shopping tasks including carrying packages; OR

(b) Physically, cognitively, and mentally able to take care of shopping, but has not done shopping in the past (i.e., prior to this home care admission.

☐ ☐ 1- Able to go shopping, but needs some assistance:

(a) By self is able to do only light shopping and carry small packages, but needs someone to do occasional major shopping; OR

(b) Unable to go shopping alone, but can go with someone to assist.

☐ ☐ 2- Unable to go shopping, but is able to identify items needed, place orders, and arrange home delivery.

☐ ☐ 3- Needs someone to do all shopping and errands.

☐   UK Unknown

(M0770) Ability to Use Telephone: Ability to answer the phone, dial numbers, and effectively use the telephone to communicate.

Prior Current

☐ ☐ 0- Able to dial numbers and answer calls appropriately and as desired.

☐ ☐ 1- Able to use a specially adapted telephone (i.e., large numbers on the dial, teletype phone for the deaf) and call essential numbers.

☐ ☐ 2- Able to answer the telephone and carry on a normal conversation but has difficulty placing calls.

☐ ☐ 3- Able to answer the telephone only some of the time or is able to carry on only a limited conversation.

☐ ☐ 4- Unable to answer the telephone at all but can listen if assisted with equipment.

☐ ☐ 5- Totally unable to use the telephone.

☐ ☐ NA Patient does not have a telephone.

☐   UK Unknown

Medication Management

The next three OASIS questions are intended to determine the patient's ability to prepare and take all prescribed medications. Like the ADL and IADL questions the nurse is required to document the patient's current and prior ability.

(M0780) Management of Oral Medications: Patient's ability to prepare and take all prescribed oral medications reliably and safely, including administration of the correct dosage at the appropriate times/intervals. **Excludes injectable and IV medications. (NOTE: this refers to ability, not compliance or willingness.)**

Prior Current

☐ ☐ 0- Able to independently take the correct oral medication(s) and proper dosage(s) at the correct times.

☐ ☐ 1- Able to take medication(s) at the correct times if:

   (a) individual dosages are pre-
      pared in advance by anoth-
      er person; OR

   (b) given daily reminders; OR

   (c) someone develops a drug
      diary or chart.

☐ ☐ 2- <u>Unable</u> to take medications
         unless administered by some-
         one else.

☐ ☐ NA No oral medications prescribed

☐   UK Unknown

(M0790) Management of Inhalant/Mist Medications: <u>Patient's ability</u> to prepare and take <u>all</u> prescribed inhalant/mist medications (nebulizers, metered dose devices) reliably and safely, including administration of the correct dosage at the appropriate times/intervals. **<u>Excludes</u> all other forms of medication (oral tablets, injectable and IV medications).**

<u>Prior</u> <u>Current</u>

☐ ☐ 0- Able to independently take the
         correct medication and proper
         dosages at the correct times.

☐ ☐ 1- Able to take medications at the
         correct times if:

   (a) individual dosages are pre-
      pared in advance by anoth-
      er person; OR

   (b) given daily reminders; OR

☐ ☐ 2- <u>Unable</u> to take medications
         unless administered by some-
         one else.

☐ ☐ NA No inhalant/mist medications
         prescribed.

☐   UK Unknown

(M0800) Management of Injectable Medications: <u>Patient's ability</u> to prepare and take <u>all</u> prescribed injectable medications reliably and safely, including administration of the correct dosage at the appropriate times/intervals. **<u>Excludes</u> IV medications).**

<u>Prior</u> <u>Current</u>

☐ ☐ 0- Able to independently take the
         correct mediation and proper
         dosages at the correct times.

☐ ☐ 1- Able to take medications at the
         correct times if:

   (a) individual syringes are pre-
      pared in advance by anoth-
      er person.

   (b) given daily reminders; OR

☐ ☐ 2- Unable to take injectable med-
         ications unless administered by
         someone else.

☐ ☐ NA No injectable medications pre-
         scribed.

☐   UK Unknown

Answering these questions also require the nurse to document the patient's ability, not willingness or compliance. When answering these questions the nurse should use their best judgment of the patient's cognitive and physical ability. The nurse should disregard whether or not the patient has demonstrated compliance when completing the OASIS but should document any compliance issues in the patient's medical record.

Equipment Management

The ability of the patient or caregiver to manage oxygen or intravenous therapy equipment could be the deciding factor in determining whether a patient can remain home or be transferred to an inpatient facility. Like the previous questions, ability is differentiated from willingness or compliance. When answering these questions, the nurse should pay close attention to the varying degrees of ability in each of the responses.

(M0810) Patient Management of Equipment (includes ONLY oxygen, IV/Infusion therapy, enteral/parenteral nutrition equipment or supplies): <u>Patient's ability</u> to set up, monitor and change equipment reliably and safely, add appropriate fluids or medication, clean/store/dispose of equipment or supplies using proper technique. **(NOTE: This refers to ability, not compliance or willingness).**

Prior Current

☐ ☐   0-   Patient manages all tasks related to equipment completely independently.

☐ ☐   1-   If someone else sets up equipment (i.e., fills portable oxygen tank, provides patient with prepared solutions), patient is able to manage all other aspects of equipment.

☐ ☐   2-   Patient requires considerable assistance form another person to mange equipment, but independently completes portions of the task.

☐ ☐   3-   Patient is only able to monitor equipment (i.e., liter flow, fluid in bag) and must call someone else to manage the equipment.

☐ ☐   4-   Patient is completely dependent on someone else to manage all equipment.

☐ ☐   NA   No equipment of this type is used in care **[If NA, go to M0825]**

☐   UK   Unknown

(M0810) Caregiver Management of Equipment (includes ONLY oxygen, IV/Infusion equipment, enteral/parenteral nutrition, ventilator therapy equipment or supplies): Caregivers's ability to set up, monitor, and change equipment reliably and safely, add appropriate fluids or medication, clean/store/dispose of equipment or supplies using proper technique. **(NOTE: This refers to ability, not compliance or willingness).**

Prior Current

☐ ☐   0-   Caregiver manages all tasks related to equipment completely independently.

☐ ☐   1-   If someone else sets up equipment, caregiver is able to manage all other aspects.

☐ ☐   2-   Caregiver requires considerable assistance from another person to manage equipment, but independently completes significant portions of the task.

☐ ☐   3-   Caregiver is only able to complete small portions of task (i.e., administer nebulizer treatment, clean/store/dispose of equipment or supplies.

☐ ☐   4-   Caregiver is completely dependent on someone else to manage all equipment.

☐ ☐   NA   No caregiver

☐   UK   Unknown

Therapy Need

The final section of the Start of Care/ Resumption of Care OASIS has only one question. The clinician completing the OASIS is required to estimate whether or not the patient will require ten or more therapy visits. A "Yes" answer can be chosen if the patient will receive ten visits from a therapy discipline or will receive any combination of physical, occupational and speech therapy.

This question is only important for Medicare payment purposes. If the home healthcare patient has a payer that is anything other than Medicare, the correct answer is "NA-not applicable".

(M0825) Therapy Need: Does the care plan of the Medicare payment period for which this assessment will define a case mix group, indicate a need for therapy (physical, occupational, or speech therapy) that meets the threshold for a Medicare high-therapy case mix group?

☐ ☐   0-   No
☐ ☐   1-   Yes
☐ ☐   NA- Not applicable

Because this question has significant financial implications, agencies have implemented systems and processes to assure that this question is answered accurately. Some of the systems require a physical therapist to visit the patient before this question is answered or may require the nurse to conduct a case conference with a member of the Rehabilitation Department to assure accuracy.

To this point, a review of the Start of Care OASIS data set has been completed. The Start of Care/Resumption of Care Assessment is the most extensive of the OASIS assessments. The Follow-Up/Significant Change in Condition OASIS assessment is comprised of a selected sample of the questions found on the SOC assessment (Appendix B). A discussion of the financial implication of these assessments will be discussed in Chapter 8.

TRANSFER OASIS DOCUMENT

As discussed earlier, all home healthcare occurs in 60-day episodes of care. A patient may be admitted to a home healthcare agency and be discharged with their goals met or when the patient experiences a transfer to an inpatient facility for acute or rehabilitative care. The OASIS regulations require the agency to "track" what has happened to the patient by completing the appropriate OASIS document.

(M0830)Emergent Care: Since the last OASIS data were collected, has the patient utilized any of the following services for emergent care (other than home care agency services)? (**Mark all that apply.**)

☐ 0- No emergent care services [**If no emergent care, go to M0855**]

☐ 1- Hospital emergency room (includes 23-hour holding)

☐ 2- Doctor's office emergency visit/house call

☐ 3- Outpatient department/clinic emergency (includes urgicenter sites)

☐ NA Unknown [If UK, go to M0855]

(M0840) Emergency Care Reason: For what reason(s) did the patient/family seek emergent care? (**Mark all that apply.**)

☐ 1- Improper medication administration, medication side effects, toxicity, anaphylaxis

☐ 2- Nausea, dehydration, malnutrition, constipation, impaction

☐ 3- Injury caused by fall or accident at home

☐ 4- Respiratory problems (e.g., shortness of breath, respiratory infection, tracheobronchial obstruction)

☐ 5- Wound infection, deteriorating wound status, new lesion/ulcer

☐ 6- Cardiac problems (e.g., fluid overload, exacerbation of CHF, chest pain)

☐ 7- Hypo/hyperglycemia, diabetes out of control

☐ 8- GI bleeding, obstruction

☐ 9- Other than above reasons

☐ UK Reason Unknown

For the purposes of OASIS, an inpatient admission is different than a patient who has a trip to the emergency room and remains in a holding unit/bed and is then discharged home. Making this distinction is sometimes difficult for the home care clinician to determine. Often, the patient is not aware of the difference and cannot provide any assistance to the nurse attempting to answer these questions. It is not uncommon for the representative of the home health agency to call the hospital to try to determine whether or not the patient meets the definition of an inpatient facility admission.

(M0855) To which **Inpatient Facility** has the patient been admitted?

☐   1-   Hospital **[Go to M0890]**
☐   2-   Rehabilitation facility **[Go to M0903]**
☐   3-   Nursing home **[Go to M0900]**
☐   4-   Hospice **[go to M0903]**
☐   NA   No inpatient facility admission

(M0890) If the patient was admitted to an acute care **Hospital,** for what **Reason** was he/she admitted?

☐   1-   Hospitalized for <u>emergent </u>(unscheduled) care
☐   2-   Hospitalized for <u>urgent</u> (scheduled within 24 of admission) care
☐   3-   Hospitalized for <u>elective</u> (scheduled more than 24 hours before admission) care
☐   UK   Unknown

(M0895) Reason for Hospitalization (Mark all that apply.)

☐   1-   Improper medication administration, medication side effects, toxicity, anaphylaxis
☐   2-   Injury caused by fall or accident at home
☐   3-   Respiratory problems (e.g., SOB, infection, obstruction)
☐   4-   Wound or tube site infection, deteriorating wound status, new lesion/ ulcer
☐   5-   Hypo/hyperglycemia, diabetes out of control
☐   6-   GI bleeding, obstruction
☐   7-   Exacerbation of CHF, fluid overload, heart failure
☐   8-   Myocardial infarction, stroke
☐   9-   Chemotherapy
☐   10-   Scheduled surgical procedure
☐   11-   Urinary tract infection
☐   12-   IV catheter-related infection
☐   13-   Deep vein thrombosis, pulmonary embolus

☐   14-   Uncontrolled pain
☐   15-   Psychotic episode
☐   16-   Other than above reasons
Go to M0903

(M0900) For what Reason(s) was the patient **Admitted** to a **Nursing Home? (Mark all that apply.)**

☐   1-   Therapy services
☐   2-   Respite care
☐   3-   Hospice care
☐   4-   Permanent placement
☐   5-   Unsafe for care at home
☐   6-   Other
☐   UK   Unknown

In addition to the questions noted above, the Transfer OASIS document includes some very specific questions related to date of transfer and date of last visit. The questions can be reviewed in Appendix C.

DISCHARGE OASIS DOCUMENT

The Discharge OASIS document is intended to measure the change in the patient's health status at the completion of the home health plan of treatment. In order to identify the change in health status, a comparison of the information on the Start of Care OASIS and the Discharge OASIS must be completed. For that reason, many of the questions found on the previous OASIS documents discussed are repeated on the Discharge OASIS. For the purpose of this course, only the questions that are unique to the Discharge OASIS will be reviewed; however, the complete Discharge OASIS is available in Appendix E.

(M0870) Discharge Disposition: Where is the patient after discharge from your agency? **(Choose only one answer.)**

☐ 1- Patient remained in the community (not in hospital, nursing home or rehab facility)

☐ 2- Patient transferred to a noninstitutional hospice **[Go to M0903]**

☐ 3- Unknown because patient moved to a geographic location not served by this agency **[Go to M0903]**

☐ 4- Other unknown **[Go to M0903]**

(M0880) After discharge, does the patient receive health, personal, or support **Services or Assistance? (Mark all that apply.)**

☐ 1- No assistance or services received

☐ 2- Yes, assistance or services provided by family or friends

☐ 3- Yes, assistance or services provided by other community resources (e.g., meals-on-wheels, home health services, homemaker assistance, transportation assistance, assisted living, board and care)
Go to M0903

(M0890) If the patient was admitted to an acute care **Hospital**, for what **Reason** was he/she admitted?

☐ 1- Hospitalized for emergent(unscheduled) care

☐ 2- Hospitalized for urgent (scheduled within 24 for admission) care

☐ 3- Hospitalized for elective(scheduled more than 24 hours before admission) care

☐ UK Unknown

(M0895) Reason for Hospitalization (Mark all that apply.)

☐ 1- Improper medication administration, medication side effects, toxicity, anaphylaxis

☐ 2- Injury caused by fall or accident at home

☐ 3- Respiratory problems (e.g., SOB, infection, obstruction)

☐ 4- Wound or tube site infection, deteriorating wound status, new lesion/ ulcer

☐ 5- Hypo/hyperglycemia, diabetes out of control

☐ 6- GI bleeding, obstruction

☐ 7- Exacerbation of CHF, fluid overload, heart failure

☐ 8- Myocardial infarction, stroke

☐ 9- Chemotherapy

☐ 10- Scheduled surgical procedure

☐ 11- Urinary tract infection

☐ 12- IV catheter-related infection

☐ 13- Deep vein thrombosis, pulmonary embolus

☐ 14- Uncontrolled pain

☐ 15- Psychotic episode

☐ 16- Other than above reasons
Go to M0903

(M0900) For what Reason(s) was the patient **Admitted** to a **Nursing Home? (Mark all that apply.)**

☐ 1- Therapy services

☐ 2- Respite care

☐ 3- Hospice care

☐ 4- Permanent placement

☐ 5- Unsafe for care at home

☐ 6- Other

☐ UK Unknown

(M0903) Date of Last (Most Recent) Home Visit:

_____/_____/_____
Month   Day   Year (4 digits)

(M0906) Discharge/Transfer/Death Date: Enter the date of the discharge, transfer, or death (at home) of the patient.

_____/_____/_____
Month   Day   Year (4 digits)

NOTICE OF PRIVACY

A complete OASIS assessment obviously provides a very detailed description of the patient's status and functional abilities in many areas. For these reasons, the Center for Medicare and Medicaid services has very strict expectations for the security and confidentiality of the patient's OASIS data.

To demonstrate their commitment, they have required agencies to inform patients of their rights – specifically in relation to this information. Appendix F provides a copy of the federally mandated Privacy Act Statement Health care Records for review. Although this privacy statement is comprehensive, it is not a consent form. Most agencies require a patient to sign a separate consent form that states that the patient has been given the privacy statement, understands the information and agrees to the release of their medical information.

OASIS AND THE 485

Although a significant amount of time has been spent reviewing details of the OASIS questions, it is important to understand that the OASIS is only **part** of the patient's medical record. It is not a document that is intended to "stand alone." It has to be incorporated into the agency's comprehensive patient assessment and the patient's overall plan of

treatment as it is documented on the Medicare 485 (Appendix A).

A review of these documents demonstrated duplication in areas such as patient demographics, functional limitations and activities permitted, Table 6-2 provides an OASIS/485 comparison.

Although this duplication seems benign, it can create difficulties if the nurse does not pay close attention to what they are documenting. If the nurse is not careful, this duplication can lead to inconsistent and contradictory documentation in the medical record. From the agency's perspective, these errors can lead to payment denials, poor patient outcomes, and medical records that would not stand up well if scrutinized in a court of law. For these reasons, it is always a good idea to closely review and compare the answers on the OASIS to those on the 485 and follow the agency's policy to make any corrections or additions if necessary.

SUMMARY

Since the inception of the OASIS, most agencies have worked diligently to follow the instructions and interpret the individual assessment questions consistently. The implementation regulations clearly state that the OASIS was not to be completed as "extra" pieces of paper and required agencies to incorporate the OASIS questions into existing

TABLE 6-2: OASIS/485 COMPARISON		
Indicator:	Medicare 485	OASIS
Principal Diagnosis	Box 11	M0230
Other Pertinent Diagnoses	Box 13	M0240
DME and Supplies	Box 14	M0640-M0800
Safety Measures	Box 15	M0640-M0800
Functional Limitations	Box 18A	M0640-M0800
Activities Permitted	Box 18B	M0640-M0800
Mental Status	Box 19	M0560-M0630
Prognosis	Box 20	M0260-M0280

documents. After reviewing the examples of the OASIS items provided in this chapter, one can appreciate the potential for misinterpretations and inaccuracies in the patient descriptors.

As stated in the beginning of this chapter, the intent of the OASIS was to provide agencies with a mechanism to measure the quality of their services. Although the system is not perfect, it has provided the first set of objective measures that can be applied to almost all patients admitted to home healthcare. As the OASIS assessments evolve, the questions are "fine tuned," and agencies will be able to increase the ability of their staff to answer the questions consistently. The goal of identifying "best practices" will come to fruition, and all home healthcare patients will benefit.

EXAM QUESTIONS

CHAPTER 6
Questions 53-78

53. Collecting, encoding, locking and transmitting OASIS data is

   a. required to comply with the requirements outlined in the OASIS user's manual.

   b. required only of agencies with more than 60 patients.

   c. voluntary until the revised Conditions of Participation are finalized.

   d. necessary to obtain a certificate of compliance.

54. The cohort of a patient that is subject to the OASIS stat collection requirements is best described as all patients

   a. who receive skilled care.

   b. over 18 years of age.

   c. who receive skilled care, except pediatric, maternity, and psychiatric patients.

   d. who receive skilled care except pediatric, Hospice, and maternity patients.

55. OASIS regulations mandate that agencies adhere to many different time frames and schedules. Which of the following is true?

   a. Agencies must complete the start of care visit within 72 hours of receiving the referral.

   b. All episodes are limited to 60 days.

   c. Agencies must complete the Start of Care OASIS within seven days of the visit.

   d. All OASIS documents must be encoded and locked within five days.

56. If a patient experiences a transfer to an inpatient facility, a significant change in condition or returns from an inpatient stay, OASIS regulations mandate that the agency

   a. complete an additional and specific assessment within the required time frame.

   b. notify the physician.

   c. discharge the patient from agency services.

   d. amend the physician ordered plan of care.

57. The electronic packaging and transmission of the entire state's OASIS database to the federal government is the responsibility of the

   a. state OASIS Coordinator.

   b. the nurse or therapist who collected the data.

   c. state's Department of Information Systems and Data Quality.

   d. Department of Public Health.

58. Clinicians should minimize choosing the "Unknown" option found in the OASIS questions because

   a. it does not meet the definition of a comprehensive assessment if too many areas are not thoroughly assessed.

   b. marking this option is associated with poor clinical practice.

   c. the agency might be penalized for failing to take the OASIS mandate seriously.

   d. it eliminates the possibility of measuring the patient's outcome.

59. A referral from a physician to evaluate the patient's technique when self-administering insulin, insert a Foley catheter to treat urinary retention or evaluate a patient's tolerance to a new antidepressant medication

    a. exemplifies changes in the patient's plan of treatment.

    b. represent tasks that do not require the skills of an RN and therefore do not represent a change in the patient's plan of treatment.

    c. are tasks that should be delegated to a home care aide.

    d. are tasks that should be delegated to a licensed practical/vocational nurse.

60. M0260 requires the home healthcare nurse to provide the "best" description of the patient's overall prognosis for recovering from this episode of illness. The nurse

    a. must only consult the physician to determine the correct answer.

    b. should consider information received from all sources.

    c. should not answer this question since it is not within the home healthcare nurse's scope of practice to diagnose a patient's condition or status.

    d. should only answer this question if they are confident in their professional judgment to make this prediction.

61. Determining a patient's ability to recover from an illness may be influenced by the physician ordered plan of care, the level of the patient's motivation and the

    a. supportive assistance available to the patient.

    b. agency's ability to make a financial profit on the care provided.

    c. number of visits approved by the patient's insurance company.

    d. patient's length of stay.

To view the OASIS items referred to in some of the following questions, please see Appendix B.

Mrs. Jones has been deaf since childhood. While conducting her assessment, she gives you a written note that asks you to look directly at her and speak slowly to facilitate her ability to read your lips. She is able to respond to your questions using a combination of signals and written responses.

62. The OASIS assessment requires you to answer M0400 which relates to the patient's ability to hear **and** understand spoken language. The M0400

    a. provides an accurate description of all possible patient scenarios.

    b. should only be answered for a patient who does not have an obvious hearing deficit.

    c. should only be answered if the patient has an obvious hearing deficit.

    d. does not adequately describe the patient who cannot hear **but** is able to understand familiar words or common expressions.

Questions 63 through 67 refer to the case of Mrs. McMillan

After a prolonged hospitalization, Mrs. McMillan is admitted to your home healthcare agency for services. She complains of bilateral heel pain whenever she is in a standing position. Inspection of her heels reveals bilateral blackened areas that are approximately the size of a quarter.

63. The best description of Mrs. McMillan's heels are

    a. pressure ulcers, since they are blackened areas over a bony prominence.

    b. stasis ulcers, since they have occurred on her lower extremities.

    c. not pressure ulcers, since they must be open to be classified as such.

    d. not pressure ulcers, since they must be open, draining and painful to be classified as such.

64. When answering M0450, Mrs. McMillan's heels would be classified as a

    a. Stage 1: Nonblanchable erythema of intact skin; the heralding of skin ulceration. In darker-pigmented skin, warmth, edema, hardness, or discolored skin may be indicators.

    b. Stage 3: Full thickness skin loss involving damage or necrosis of subcutaneous tissue, which may extend down to, but not through underlying fascia. The ulcer presents clinically as a deep crater with or without undermining of adjacent tissue.

    c. Stage 4: Full thickness skin loss with extensive destruction, tissue necrosis, or damage to muscle, bone or supporting structures (e.g., tendon, joint capsule, etc.).

    d. Pressure ulcers that cannot be observed for staging due to the presence of eschar.

65. M0460 asks the clinician to stage the most problematic (observable) pressure ulcer. When answering this question for Mrs. McMillan, the correct response would be

    a. Stage 1: Nonblanchable erythema of intact skin; the heralding of skin ulceration. In darker-pigmented skin, warmth, edema, hardness, or discolored skin may be indicators.

    b. Stage 3: Full thickness skin loss involving damage or necrosis of subcutaneous tissue, which may extend down to, but not through underlying fascia. The ulcer presents clinically as a deep crater with or without undermining of adjacent tissue.

    c. Stage 4: Full thickness skin loss with extensive destruction, tissue necrosis, or damage to muscle, bone or supporting structures (e.g., tendon, joint capsule, etc.).

    d. no observable pressure ulcer since the wounds are covered with blackened eschar.

66. After identifying and staging Mrs. McMillan's heels, item M0464 requires the nurse to describe the status of the most problematic wound. Due to the presence of eschar that fills the wound bed with blackened dead tissue, the correct response would be

    a. wounds are healing and filled with granulation tissue.

    b. wounds are partially healed, and granulation tissue must be present even though it is not easily observed.

    c. wounds are nonhealing due to the presence of eschar.

    d. this determination can only be made by a Certified Wound Ostomy Continence Nurse (CWOCN).

67. When answering M0468, the clinician must also identify whether or not the patient has a stasis ulcer. Stasis ulcers are typically

    a. described as an ulceration caused by inadequate venous circulation in the affected area, and is often associated with stasis dermatitis.

    b. described as an ulceration caused by inadequate arterial circulation in the affected area and typically occur in the trunk.

    c. the result of skin inflammations, sores or ulcers resulting from tissue hypoxia due to prolonged pressure most often occurring over bony prominences.

    d. only diagnosed by nurses who are certified wound-ostomy-continence nurses (CWOCN).

68. M0440 requires the nurse to answer "Yes" if the patient has any alterations in their skin even if the alteration is a well-healed surgical scar. The only way to identify that the wound is actually a scar is to mark

    a. option zero on M0484 .

    b. option one on M0488 – wound is fully granulating.

    c. NA – no observable wound on M0488.

    d. "Yes" on M0440 and make a notation in the patient's medical record that the lesion is a healed wound or a scar.

69. If a patient uses oxygen, the OASIS guidelines instruct the nurse to

    a. answer M0490 after discussing with the patient how many hours they use the oxygen each day and make a decision about whether or not the patient would be assessed with or without the oxygen in place.

    b. assess the patient without their oxygen in place.

    c. assess the patient with their oxygen in place.

    d. skip this question, since the patient has an obvious deficit, and only answer M0500.

70. During your assessment of a female patient, she reports that she experiences urinary incontinence whenever she coughs, sneezes or "waits too long" to go to the bathroom. M0520 requires you to choose the option that best describes her urinary status. The best description is that she is

    a. continent.

    b. anuric.

    c. in need of a urinary catheter.

    d. incontinent.

71. The question in the Neuro/Emotional/Behavioral Status section of the OASIS (questions M0560 through M0630) instruct the nurse to answer the questions based on behaviors reported or observed. If a conflict arises between the nurse's observations and what the patient and caregiver report, the nurse should

    a. answer the questions to the best of their ability.

    b. use their professional judgment to choose the option that best describes the patient and make a notation that clarifies the inconsistency between the observed and reported behaviors.

    c. discuss the correct response with the patient's physician.

    d. request the services of a psychiatric clinical nurse specialist to complete this portion of the assessment.

Case of Mrs. Leger

Mrs. Leger is a 68-year-old woman who tells the home healthcare nurse that she has never taken a shower. She tells the nurse that she grew up only taking sponge baths and prefers not to get into the tub or shower. The nurse observes that her gait is steady, and she is able to easily rise out of a soft cushioned chair or couch.

72. M0670 requires the nurse to describe the patient's ability to wash their entire body. The choice that best describes Mrs. Leger's ability is that she is

    a. able to bathe herself in the shower or tub independently.

    b. able to bathe herself in the shower or tub with the use of an assistive device.

    c. able to bathe herself in the shower or tub with the assistance of another person.

    d. unable to bathe in the shower or tub.

The Case of Mr. Shoesmith

Mr. Shoesmith is an elderly gentleman who has been recently widowed after being married all of his adult life. He is being admitted to your agency after suffering a mild stroke. He has no residual deficits. The physician has ordered skilled nursing assessments of his cardiovascular and neurological status and teaching of his new medications. From the nurse's assessment, it is clear that he has no cognitive limitations. He reports to the nurse that he unwilling to perform any tasks associated with shopping because his wife has always performed that chore. (In answering OASIS questions related to ADLS and IADLS, the nurse must answer considering only the patient's cognitive and physical ability and not their willingness.)

73. Even though Mr. Shoesmith has not had to complete the tasks associated with shopping, from the nurse's assessment, it appears that he

    a. is physically and cognitively able to perform the tasks associated with shopping despite his unwillingness.

    b. able to go shopping but needs some assistance.

    c. unable to go shopping alone.

    d. in need of someone to do all of the shopping and errands.

The Case of Ms. Maury

You are the home healthcare nurse conducting the Start of Care OASIS Assessment of Ms. Maury. She is a 79-year-old woman who has a history of cardiac disease and insulin dependent diabetes. As you evaluate her ability to manage her medication regimen, you note that she is taking all medications correctly except her insulin. As she demonstrates her technique, you note that there is a significant air bubble in the syringe. Ms. Maury does not seem to notice this detail. When you ask her about the presence of the air bubble, she states, "Oh dear, I have been taking insulin so long that I don't worry about such things anymore." You ask her to demonstrate the filling of a second syringe, and she does it without difficulty.

74. Although Ms. Maury is not always careful when prefilling her syringes, which of the following describes her ability to manage her medications? Ms. Maury is

    a. able to independently take the correct medication and proper dosages at the correct times.

    b. able to take medications at the correct times, if individual syringes are prepared in advance by another person

    c. able to take medications at the correct times, if given daily reminders

    d. unable to take injectable medications, unless administered by someone else.

75. Informing the patient of their right to the confidentiality of OASIS data

    a. is optional.

    b. is unnecessary, because everybody knows that healthcare data is kept confidential.

    c. should only be done if the patient requests the information.

    d. is mandated by federal regulations.

76. The OASIS and the 485 should

    a. be separate "stand alone" documents.

    b. never be completed at the same time by the same clinician.

    c. remain separate, since one is for assessment and the other for payment purposes.

    d. be reviewed for inconsistency and contradiction.

77. The agency must assure that a Transfer OASIS is completed when the patient is

    a. transferred to the emergency room.

    b. held in a holding unit.

    c. transferred to Hospice services.

    d. transferred to an inpatient facility for more than 24 hours.

78. The correct answer on M0825 for an HMO patient is always

    a. Yes.

    b. No.

    c. NA.

    d. Unknown.

CHAPTER 7

OUTCOME-BASED QUALITY IMPROVEMENT AND OUTCOME-BASED QUALITY MONITORING

CHAPTER OBJECTIVE:

At the completion of this chapter, the reader will be able to recall how the agency can use OASIS data in its performance improvement activities.

LEARNING OBJECTIVES:

After studying this chapter, the reader will be able to

1. list the three possible patient outcomes.

2. differentiate between process outcomes and patient outcomes.

3. identify the value of determining statistical significance.

4. recall the importance of risk adjusting.

INTRODUCTION

Medicare certified home health agencies have always had performance improvement programs. Until the implementation of OASIS, most initiatives were aimed at improving the process of care (the way care is delivered). Depending on the size of the organization, agencies may have had a person or entire department dedicated to evaluating compliance with policies and procedures. One example of a process that was (and still is) frequently measured is the level of compliance with

conducting home health aide supervision visits every 14 days.

Agencies that were interested in measuring patient outcomes usually did not have an objective measure that could be used. Attainment of the care plan goals was often the only measure of patient outcomes available to staff. For instance, a patient's goal might be to verbalize three signs or symptoms of exacerbation to be reported to the physician. Although this information might be helpful for discharge planning, it did not capture a change in the patient's clinical or functional status.

The implementation of OASIS enables agencies to measure the clinical outcomes of the care provided to the individual patient and/or to an entire group of patients. Before the types of outcomes that can be measured are discussed, it is important to define exactly what is meant by "patient outcome." For the purpose of this course, an outcome is defined as a change in the patient's clinical or functional status between two points in time.

TYPES OF OUTCOMES

To measure an outcome, the agency must be able to compare a patient at two different points in time. OASIS regulations require agencies to collect patient data:

- At the start of care;
- Whenever the patient is transferred to an inpatient facility;

- At the resumption of care;

- With every recertification; and

- At discharge.

The collection of data at these time points provides opportunities to compare the patient's response to the same question at different times.

There are three general types of outcomes that can be measured using OASIS data. The first and most obvious outcome is an improvement. An improvement in status or functional ability occurs whenever a patient moves from a less functional to a more functional status.

Using M0420 as an example, consider a patient who reports that they have pain daily (but not constantly) when first admitted to home healthcare. By the time the patient is discharged, they report that their pain occurs less often than daily. The change from daily to less than daily pain is a positive change, which represents an improved outcome.

(M0420) Frequency of Pain interfering with patient's activity or movement

- ☐   0- Patient has no pain or pain does not interfere with activity or movement

- ☐   1- Less often than daily

- ☐   2- Daily, but not constantly

- ☐   3- All of the time

Conversely, a patient who denies pain at the time of admission and reports **any** level of pain at the time of discharge would have experienced a decline, which represents the second type of general outcome – a negative patient outcome.

The final outcome that can be measured is one where the patient has stabilized; the outcome is said to be null. Stabilization means that the patient's condition did not improve nor did it decline; it was unchanged.

One question that agencies must answer in relation to stabilization outcomes is: "Are stabilized outcomes a reasonable expectation for some patients, or does it illustrate that an agency's services where inadequate?" Would it not be reasonable to expect that after receiving the services of a skilled nurse or therapist that the patient's status would be improved? Consider the case of Mrs. Huff.

Mrs. Huff

Mrs. Huff is a 46-year-old woman who is a quadriplegic. Her caregiver uses a Hoyer lift to transfer her from bed to a specially equipped wheelchair. When in bed or the chair, she is unable to change her position or move any part of her body without the assistance of a caregiver. Is it reasonable to expect that, even with intense home healthcare services, she will demonstrate an improvement in the areas such as M0690 which measures her ability to transfer?

(M0690) Transferring: Ability to move from bed to chair, on and off toilet or commode, into and out of tub or shower, and ability to turn and position self in bed if patient is bedfast.

Prior	Current		
☐	☐	0-	Able to independently transfer.
☐	☐	1-	Transfers with minimal human assistance or with use of an assistive device.
☐	☐	2-	Unable to transfer self but is able to bear weight and pivot during the transfer process.
☐	☐	3-	Unable to transfer self and is unable to bear weight or pivot when transferred by another person.
☐	☐	4-	Bedfast, unable to transfer but is able to turn and position self in bed.
☐	☐	5-	Bedfast, unable to transfer and is unable to turn and position self.
☐		UK	Unknown

Although most patients have the opportunity to achieve any of the three outcomes mentioned above, some do not have the ability to get better, and others could possibly get worse.

To clarify, consider the patient who denies any pain at the start of care. This patient is already at the most functional state and could not possibly get better. On M0420 there are only two possible outcomes for this patient, to stabilize (remain pain free) or destabilize (develop a pain issue) and experience a negative outcome.

The same thinking can also be applied to patients who are in the most dependent functional state. Reconsider the case of Mrs. Huff in light of M0690. She is a quadriplegic and is the most dependent functional state. The only two potential outcomes that she can experience are to stabilize (remain unchanged) or improve by moving to a less dependent state. In reality, it is unlikely that she will demonstrate much improvement in her ability to transfer, so the most likely outcome for her will be to remain stable.

AGGREGATE REPORTS

Not only has the OASIS provided agencies with a mechanism to measure individual patient outcomes, the system also enables an agency to compare its performance to all other agencies who care for Medicare and Medicaid patients. These aggregate reports provide outcome measures for all of the patients cared for in a specified time period.

The ability to compare your agency's performance (benchmark) with the performance of other agencies makes it possible to set realistic patient outcome goals. Although one would hope that patients who receive home healthcare services would experience an improvement in their clinical and functional status, one must question whether that expectation is realistic. Would you think that it is reasonable to expect that 100% of the patients who report pain at the start of care will experience

an improvement by discharge? If a 100% rate of improvement is expected and not achieved, does that mean that an agency's care is inadequate, or does it mean that it is not a realistic goal?

If benchmarking against other agencies reveals that approximately 70% of all home care patients experience an improvement in this outcome, would you consider the 100% expectation as realistic? When looking at your agency's performance, is it important to compare it to a large sample of other agencies? You might question:

- If an agency's performance is better than others, how much better is it? Is it significantly better?

- Can the agency's performance in this area be attributed to a commitment to improve patients' pain?

- Has the agency conducted educational programs for the staff to improve their ability to manage pain?

- If an agency consistently performs better than all other agencies in the area of improvement in pain, have they identified a "best practice" that should be shared with other agencies?

To help answer some of these questions, the Center for Medicare and Medicaid services has facilitated the development of the Outcome-Based Quality Improvement and Outcome-Based Quality Monitoring Reports. These reports are created from analyzing all of the OASIS data that is encoded and transmitted to the state and federal OASIS computers.

Once the statistical analysis is complete, the information is presented in three agency-specific reports. The Adverse Event Outcome Report (Figure 7-1), the Patient Outcome Report (Figure 7-2) and the Case Mix Report (Figure 7-3) all provide the agency with patient outcome results as compared to all other agencies who contributed their OASIS data. Through the use of a secure web site, agencies are able to download their individual reports at will.

OUTCOME-BASED QUALITY MONITORING

Despite an agency's best effort, it is not uncommon for a patient to experience a decline in condition or an adverse event. The Outcome-Based Quality Monitoring Report (OBQM) provides the agency with a means to compare their incidence of adverse event outcomes during a specified time period to all other agencies that contributed data during the same period.

Figure 7-1 provides a sample of one agency's Adverse Event Outcome Report. A preliminary review of the report reveals a list of patients who received emergent care for an injury caused by a fall or accident at home. An agency's incidence is calculated by dividing the number of patients who

experienced the adverse event (9) by the total number of patients in the same time period (572). For this agency their incidence is 1.6%.

Like one blood pressure reading, one adverse event report does not tell the agency much about its overall performance until it is benchmarked (compared). The agency may choose to benchmark its performance from month to month or may choose to benchmark against the performance of all other agencies commonly referred to as the reference group. Whichever option the agency chooses, paying close attention to the adverse events that agency patients experience might provide the agency with some insight into areas of weakness in their clinical services.

When looking at this report, it would not be uncommon for agency staff to become defensive and list a number of reasons why they feel these adverse outcomes occurred. It is important to listen to the staff's theory about why these events

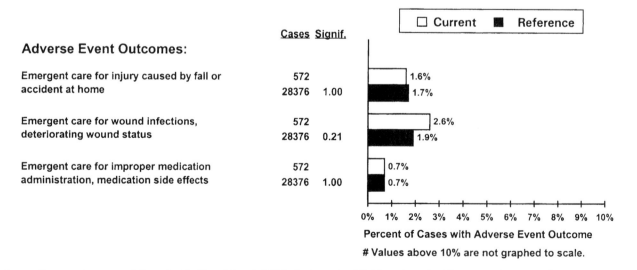

FIGURE 7-1: ADVERSE EVENT OUTCOME REPORT

Agency Name: Faircare Home Health Services
Agency ID: HHA01
Location: Anytown, USA
Medicare Number: 007001
Medicaid Number: 999888001

Requested Current Period: 09/1999-08/2000
Actual Current Period: 09/1999-08/2000
Number of Cases in Current Period: 601
Number of Cases in Reference Sample: 29983
Date Report Printed: 11/30/2000

Adverse Event Outcome Report

Adverse Event Outcomes:	Cases	Signif.	Current	Reference
Emergent care for injury caused by fall or accident at home	572		1.6%	
	28376	1.00		1.7%
Emergent care for wound infections, deteriorating wound status	572		2.6%	
	28376	0.21		1.9%
Emergent care for improper medication administration, medication side effects	572		0.7%	
	28376	1.00		0.7%

0% 1% 2% 3% 4% 5% 6% 7% 8% 9% 10%

Percent of Cases with Adverse Event Outcome

 # Values above 10% are not graphed to scale.

Source: Outcome Assessment Information Set Users Manual. (1999). *Implementing OASIS at a home health agency to improve patient outcomes.* Washington, DC: U.S. Government Printing Office.

occurred, but it is even more important to attempt to identify the actual reason for occurrence. If a lot of time is spent trying to undermine the credibility of the report, the opportunity to avoid future adverse events could be lost. For this reason, many agencies review the medical records of the patients who experienced an adverse event. The review of these records might reveal trends in diagnoses, clinicians or services. If a trend is identified, the agency can then work to identify strategies that might be beneficial in decreasing the occurrence of the adverse event.

When reviewing any of these outcome reports, a column titled "Signif." will be found. The level of significance is a statistical value which identifies the probability that the difference between your agency and the reference group is due to chance. Levels of significance are usually presented as numbers that are less than 1.0. The smaller the number, the more likely (or the higher the probabil-

ity) that the difference in performance is the result of something that the agency is (or is not) doing.

The significance value is an important part of the report because it assists the agency to determine if the difference in their performance when compared to the reference group is a random variation or representative of a true difference in performance. In Figure 7-1, the level of significance was calculated at 1.0, which means the difference between the performance of the agency and the reference group is likely to be the result of random variation and not the result of the agency's performance.

OUTCOME-BASED QUALITY IMPROVEMENT

The second report available to agencies is the Risk Adjusted Outcome Report. This report provides a graphical depiction of their end-result and utilization outcomes.

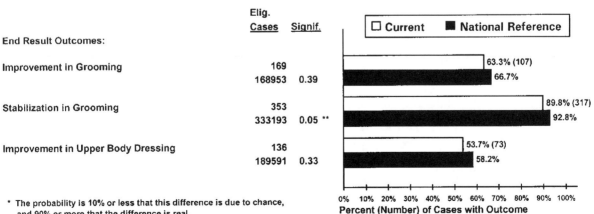

FIGURE 7-2: PATIENT OUTCOME REPORT

Agency Name: FAIRCARE HOME HEALTH SERVICES
Agency ID: HHA01
Location: ANYTOWN, USA
Medicare Number: 007001
Medicaid Number: 999888001

Requested Current Period: 01/2001 - 12/2001
Actual Current Period: 01/2001 - 12/2001
Number of Cases in Current Period: 374
Number of Cases in Natl Ref Sample: 357978
Date Report Printed: 02/28/2002

All Patients' Risk Adjusted Outcome Report

	Elig. Cases	Signif.	
End Result Outcomes:			☐ Current ■ National Reference
Improvement in Grooming	169 / 168953	0.39	63.3% (107) / 66.7%
Stabilization in Grooming	353 / 333193	0.05 **	89.8% (317) / 92.8%
Improvement in Upper Body Dressing	136 / 189591	0.33	53.7% (73) / 58.2%

0% 10% 20% 30% 40% 50% 60% 70% 80% 90% 100%
Percent (Number) of Cases with Outcome

* The probability is 10% or less that this difference is due to chance, and 90% or more that the difference is real.

** The probability is 5% or less that this difference is due to chance, and 95% or more that the difference is real.

Source: Outcome Assessment Information Set Users Manual. (1999). *Implementing OASIS at a home health agency to improve patient outcomes.* Washington, DC: U.S. Government Printing Office.

TABLE 7-1: END-RESULT PATIENT OUTCOMES

<ins>Risk Adjusted</ins>	<ins>Non Risk Adjusted/Descriptive</ins>
• Improvement in Grooming	• Stabilization in Management of Oral Medications
• Stabilization in Grooming	• Improvement in Speech and Language
• Improvement in Upper Body Dressing	• Stabilization in Speech and Language
• Improvement in Lower Body Dressing	• Improvement in Pain Interfering with Activity
• Improvement in Bathing	• Improvement in the Number of Surgical Wounds
• Stabilization in Bathing	• Improvement in Urinary Tract Infection
• Improvement in Toileting	• Improvement in Status of Surgical Wounds
• Improvement in Transferring	• Improvement in Cognitive Functioning
• Stabilization in Transferring	• Stabilization in Cognitive Functioning
• Improvement in Ambulation/Locomotion	• Improvement in Anxiety Level
• Improvement in Eating	• Stabilization in Anxiety Level
• Improvement in Light Meal Preparation	
• Improvement in Behavior Problem Frequency	
• Stabilization in Light Meal Preparation	
• Improvement in Laundry	
• Stabilization in Laundry	
• Improvement in Housekeeping	
• Stabilization in Housekeeping	
• Improvement in Shopping	
• Stabilization in Shopping	
• Improvement in Phone Use	
• Stabilization in Phone Use	
• Improvement in Management of Oral Medications	
• Improvement in Dyspnea	
• Improvement in Urinary Tract Infection	
• Improvement in Urinary Incontinence	
• Improvement in Bowel Incontinence	
• Improvement in Confusion Frequency	

Source: Outcome Assessment Information Set Users Manual. (1999). *Implementing OASIS at a home health agency to improve patient outcomes.* Washington, DC: U.S. Government Printing Office.

As discussed previously, an end-result outcome is defined as the patient's change in health status between two points in time. Although patient outcomes are primarily measured as improvements, it is also possible for a patient to stabilize (experience no change) or to experience a decline in functional or clinical status.

To date, there are 41 patient outcomes included in this report, 26 of which are risk adjusted. (See Table 7-1.) Since the acuity of patients can vary from one agency to the next, the Center for Healthcare Policy and Research applies statistical techniques to the data to minimize the influence of factors that might impact the agency's outcomes. The application of these techniques is commonly known as risk adjusting.

For example, assume that My Town VNA receives a large number of its referrals from a post-

TABLE 7-2: UTILIZATION OUTCOMES	
Risk Adjusted	**Non Risk Adjusted/Descriptive**
• Discharged to the community	• Any Emergent Care Provided
• Acute Care Hospitalizations	

Source: Outcome Assessment Information Set Users Manual. (1999). *Implementing OASIS at a home health agency to improve patient outcomes.* Washington, DC: U.S. Government Printing Office.

acute rehabilitation stroke unit, and the majority of these patients demonstrate a high level of functional dependence. When completing the OASIS, My Town VNA will have low scores in the ADL and IADL section of the assessment. The outcome report for My Town VNA will demonstrate a large number of stabilized outcomes and fewer improved outcomes.

Across town, Global Home Health Care accepts the majority of its referrals from an acute care hospital that is renowned for its care of cardiac patients. Global's patients are usually referred to home care after experiencing a three to four day hospitalization. The typical patient admitted by this agency receives six or seven home healthcare visits and are then discharged to outpatient cardiac rehabilitation. When completing the OASIS, the majority of Global's patients demonstrate a high level of functional independence, and the majority of their patients return to complete independence by the time they are discharged. The Risk Adjusted Outcome Report for Global Home Health Care

reveals a large number of improved outcomes and few that only stabilized.

From the examples above, it is clear that the type of patients an agency admits to its caseload can have an impact on its Patient Outcome Report. The process of risk adjusting is a statistical comparison of the factors that result from the characteristics of the patients. Risk adjusting is necessary to assure that the outcomes reported are the result of patient care and not underlying characteristics of the patient. In essence, risk adjusting allows agencies to compare apples to apples and not apples to oranges.

The utilization outcomes provided in Table 7-2 provide the agency with the type of services their patients used while they were active or the services that their patients required at the time of discharge. As stated above, the utilization outcomes can be greatly influenced by the characteristics of the agency's patient population.

FIGURE 7-3: CASE MIX REPORT

Agency Name: Faircare Home Health Services
Agency ID: HHA01
Location: Anytown, USA
Medicare Number: 007001
Medicaid Number: 999888001

Requested Current Period: 09/1999-08/2000
Actual Current Period: 09/1999-08/2000
Number of Cases in Current Period: 601
Number of Cases in Reference Sample: 29983
Date Report Printed: 11/30/2000

All Patients' Case Mix Profile at Start/Resumption of Care

	Current Mean	Reference Mean	Sig.
Demographics			
Age (average in years)	70.75	72.78	**
Gender: Female (%)	69.4%	62.9%	**
Race: Black (%)	1.7%	10.7%	**
Race: White (%)	97.5%	85.5%	**
Race: Other (%)	0.8%	3.8%	**

Source: Outcome Assessment Information Set Users Manual. (1999). *Implementing OASIS at a home health agency to improve patient outcomes.* Washington, DC: U.S. Government Printing Office.

CASE MIX REPORT

The third and final report is the Case Mix Report. (See Figure 7-3.) Like the two previous reports, this report provides the agency with notations when their results are statistically significant. The Case Mix Report provides the agency with a description of all of the patients who have been included in the two reports previously outlined. The description includes patient demographics such as age, living situation and presence of a primary caregiver. In addition, the Case Mix Report provides a summary of some of the OASIS data collected. The agency is able to identify trends in diagnosis, medical condition and the clinical and functional status of patients in the sample. Finally, the Case Mix Report will provide the agency with information related to discharge disposition and length of stay.

A review of this report assists the agency to identify in detail the characteristics of the patients they serve and may influence the agency's decisions related to resource utilization and allocation. Difference like those between My Town VNA and Global Home Healthcare will become obvious.

OBQM OR OBQI?

Now that the three reports available to agencies have been reviewed, it is important to differentiate between Outcome-Based Quality Monitoring (OBQM) and Outcome-Based Quality Improvement (OBQI). Although these acronyms are often used interchangeably, they do represent different approaches to quality management.

In short, the monitoring of data does not impact the delivery of patient care. For instance, the Adverse Event Outcome Report lists the patients who experienced a negative outcome. The disadvantage to using only this report is that it can only identify variations in the agency's performance after they have occurred, and although the agency can then review the patient's medical record to identify what happened, it is too late to change the negative effect it had on the patient.

The OBQI Report provides the agency with an opportunity to analyze current performance and make the changes in the care delivery process necessary to assure that the patient does not experience a negative or adverse outcome. The use of this report provides an opportunity to identify areas of weakness, to implement measures to improve identified weaknesses and the ability to evaluate the effectiveness of the changes made.

Although the agency's performance on any outcome is only available to the agency, the state department responsible for monitoring the quality of home healthcare services and the Center for Medicare and Medicaid Services are soon to change this. As part of the government's initiative to assure quality, agencies can expect to see their performance published in the local newspapers.

Through the use of home health report cards, consumers, physicians, and other community providers will be able to compare the performance of all of the agencies in their geographic location. This comparison is intended to assist the consumer with choosing the agency that meets their needs and provides the "best" clinical and functional outcomes.

SUMMARY

Through the use of Adverse Event Outcome Reports, Outcome-Based Quality Improvement Reports, and the Case Mix Report, agencies have data that describes their performance as it is compared to reference groups. The identification of statistically significant variations allows the agency to focus their performance improvement efforts on areas that will not only effect care of the individual patient but also put the agency in a position to flourish in a highly competitive and regulated environment.

EXAM QUESTIONS

CHAPTER 7

Questions 79-85

79. Prior to the implementation of OASIS, an agency's performance improvement initiatives were

    a. nonexistent.

    b. subjective in nature.

    c. most often aimed at improving the process of care delivery.

    d. complex and ineffective.

80. An outcome can be determined

    a. at the completion of the OASIS Start of Care Assessment.

    b. whenever the patient achieves the goals on the physician certified plan of care.

    c. when the agency is able to compare the same patient at two points in time.

    d. when the patient returns their post discharge satisfaction survey.

81. Noted below is a comparison of a patient's status at the start of care and at discharge. When reviewing these results, one can determine that the patient experienced which type of outcome?

Start of Care OASIS Assessment

(M0490) When is the patient dyspneic or noticeably Short of Breath?

☐ 0- Never, patient is not short of breath

■ 1- When walking more than 20 feet, climbing stairs

☐ 2- With moderate exertion (e.g. while dressing, using commode or bedpan, walking distances less than 20 feet)

☐ 3- With minimal exertion (e.g. while eating, talking or performing other ADLSs) or with agitation

☐ 4- At rest (during day or night)

Discharge OASIS Assessment

(M0490) When is the patient dyspneic or noticeably Short of Breath?

☐ 0- Never, patient is not short of breath

■ 1- When walking more than 20 feet, climbing stairs

☐ 2- With moderate exertion (e.g. while dressing, using commode or bedpan, walking distances less than 20 feet)

☐ 3- With minimal exertion (e.g. while eating, talking or performing other ADLS) or with agitation

☐ 4- At rest (during day or night)

    a. stabilized

    b. improved

    c. decline

    d. unable to be determined

82. Outcome-based quality monitoring

    a. does not provide the agency with useful data.

    b. should only be used as a quality measure when the agency has identified the existence of a problem.

    c. provides the agency with a means to compare their incidence of adverse event outcomes to those of other agencies.

    d. provides a graphical depiction of end-result and utilization outcomes.

83. Identifying the level of significance

    a. is only important in validating that the agency's performance is better than all others in the reference group.

    b. is only important in validating that the agency's performance is worse than all others in the reference group.

    c. assists the agency to determine if the difference in their performance compared to the reference group is a random variation or representative of a true difference in performance.

    d. is too complex for most agencies to effectively evaluate.

84. A report that provides the agency with a summary of OASIS data for all patients who appear on the agency's End Result Outcome Report is

    a. Start of Care Assessment.

    b. Risk Adjusted Outcome Report .

    c. Outcome-Based Quality Monitoring Report.

    d. Case Mix Report.

85. The process of risk adjustment

    a. is only important in validating that the agency's performance is better than all others in the reference group.

    b. is only important in validating that the agency's performance is worse than all others in the reference group.

    c. assures that the outcomes are the result of the patient care and not the characteristics of the patient.

    d. is too complex for most agencies to effectively evaluate.

CHAPTER 8

REIMBURSEMENT OF HOME HEALTH SERVICES

CHAPTER OBJECTIVE

At the completion of this chapter, the reader will be able to recall the five major principles of the Medicare prospective payment system for home healthcare reimbursement.

LEARNING OBJECTIVES

After studying this chapter, the reader will be able to

1. indicate how case mix management can significantly improve the financial performance of the home healthcare agency.

2. differentiate between episodic and fee-for-service reimbursement methodologies for home healthcare services.

3. differentiate between a full episode, low utilization and a partial episode payment.

4. specify which services are "bundled" into the Medicare episodic payment.

5. identify when a patient experiences a significant change in condition.

INTRODUCTION

Most of us did not choose nursing as a profession because it is glamorous. We are not usually excited to work every other weekend and holiday. Most of us do not enjoy rotating shifts and

being subjected to mandatory overtime. There is no thrill in working short staffed and being required to complete volumes of paperwork to validate our contribution to patient care. We are nurses because of a desire to care for people.

The *Code of Ethics for Nurses* dictates that all patients should receive care regardless of their race, religion, sexual orientation, age or ability to pay (ANA, 2001). However, the reality is that very few nurses volunteer their time, knowledge, and skills to their employers. Nurses expect to be fairly compensated for the skills and services they provide. In fact, by exercising the right to participate in collective bargaining, some nurses have picketed to improve working conditions and wages. At the same time, it is naïve not to acknowledge nursing's role in the financial health of the organizations where they are employed.

More than ever, home health nurses are being held accountable for providing patients with the clinically appropriate level of service. It is imperative that home healthcare nurses differentiate between the "wants" and "needs" of patients. Surely there are hundreds (maybe even thousands) of patients who "want" a daily visit from a home healthcare nurse. The question that must be answered is: Does the patient "need" that level of intensive service? Since the implementation of the Medicare prospective payment system, unnecessary visits can quickly jeopardize the financial health of an entire organization.

In theory, home health reimbursement is simple. There are generally two payment mechanisms for home healthcare, fee-for-service and prospective payment. Since Medicare is the largest purchaser of home healthcare services, the prospective payment system (PPS) will be presented first, followed by a description of fee-for-service payment systems.

THE MEDICARE PROSPECTIVE PAYMENT SYSTEM

Simply stated, Medicare provides one lump sum to the agency to provide all the beneficiary's care required for a 60-day period. This lump sum is adjusted up or down based on the patient's acuity as it is documented on 23 of the OASIS assessment questions.

As with all things, the "devil is in the detail," and Medicare PPS is no exception. Outlined below are the principles that more fully describe the details of PPS.

Principle One: Case Mix

PPS reimbursement to the agency is based on averages. With some patients, the agency may achieve a profitable episode, and with others, the agency may experience a financial loss. Fiscal viability requires agencies to balance profitable and losing episodes closely. If the agency experiences the reverse, it will quickly find its financial soundness in jeopardy. The mechanism by which this balance of profit and loss is achieved is called case mix adjusting or case mix management.

Case mix management requires the agency to understand exactly what types of patients are referred, and the amount of service/visits these patients typically receive. In a small agency, one patient who requires twice-daily home health aide and nursing can lead to financial instability or ruin.

FIGURE 8-1: MR. BAILEY'S OASIS CLINICAL SCORING DETAIL

MO	Question	Response	Point Value
230	Primary Diagnosis	Orthopedic	11
250	Therapies the patient receives at home	4-None of the above	0
390	Vision with corrective lenses if the patient usually wears them	0-Normal vision	0
420	Frequency of Pain interfering with patient's activity or movement	2-Daily, but not constant	5
440	Does this patient have a Skin Lesion or an Open Wound? Excluding "OSTOMIES"	1-Yes	0
450	Multiple Pressure Ulcers	0- None	0
460	Stage of Most Problematic (Observable) Pressure Ulcer:	NA-No observable ulcer	0
476	Status of Most Problematic (Observable) Stasis Ulcer:	NA-Daily, but not constantly	0
488	Status of Most Problematic (Observable) Surgical Ulcer:	3-Not Healing	15
490	When is the patient dyspneic or noticeable Short of Breath?	2-With moderate exertion	5
530	When does Urinary Incontinence occur?	No-incontinence or catheter	0
540	Bowel Incontinence frequency:	0-Very rarely or never	0
550	Bowel Ostomy	0- None	0
610	Behaviors Demonstrated at Least Once a Week (Reported or Observed):	7-None of the above behaviors demonstrated	0
		Total Clinical Points	**36**

Source: Outcome Assessment Information Set Users Manual. (1999). *Implementing OASIS at a home health agency to improve patient outcomes.* Washington, DC: U.S. Government Printing Office.

How can one patient have such an impact? Consider the detailed case of Mr. Bailey outlined below.

Mr. Bailey

Mr. Bailey is an 84-year-old patient who is known to My Town VNA. Mr. Bailey's physician prescribed nursing visits once a month for the injection of vitamin B12 to treat his pernicious anemia. As a result of a fractured hip, the Intake Department received a referral from the local hospital requesting an increase in agency services. Mr. Bailey experienced a postoperative complication resulting in an opening of his surgical wound. The opening is currently infected and requires twice-daily dressing changes. In addition, the hospital is requesting home health aide services and physical therapy.

Although Mr. Bailey is able to ambulate short distances with a walker, the discharge planner has already requested home delivered meals and home-making services. Mr. Bailey is a Medicare beneficiary, and the patient assessment reveals the 23 scored questions OASIS profile outlined in Figures 8-1, 8-2, and 8-3.

From Mr. Bailey's OASIS assessment, it is evident that he has many deficits. Based on the combination of the OASIS answers, the agency will receive approximately $5627 to provide all of Mr. Bailey's care, including dressing supplies and home visits for the next 60-day period.

At Mr. Bailey's start of care, the physician orders in box 21 on the 485/plan of treatment are found in Figure 8-4. At the start of care, the plan of treatment established for Mr. Bailey appears to be clinically appropriate. Now consider the cost of providing this same level of service to him for the next 60-day period. Assume that My Town VNA's average costs per visit are approximately:

- Registered nurse visits =$100/visit,

- Physical Therapy visit =$100/visit,

- Home healthcare aide visit = $25/visit.

By simply performing the math, the cost of Mr. Bailey's plan of treatment is estimated to be a little over $16,000. (See Figure 8.5.) The agency can expect to be reimbursed from Medicare approximately $5600. If this plan of treatment does not

MO	Question	Answer	Point Value
\multicolumn{4}{l}{**FIGURE 8-2: MR. BAILEY'S OASIS FUNCTIONAL SCORING DETAIL**}			
650	Ability to Dress Upper Body (with or without dressing aids)	0- Able upper body without assistance	0
660	Ability to Dress Lower Body (with or without dressing aids)	2- Someone must help the patient dress lower body	4
670	Bathing: Ability to wash entire body. Excludes grooming (washing face and hands only).	2- Able to bathe with the assistance of another person	8
680	Toileting: Ability to get to and from the toilet or bedside commode.	0- Able to get to and from the toilet or commode independently	0
690	Transferring: Ability to move from bed to chair, on and off toilet or commode, into and out of tub or shower	1- Transfers with minimal human assistance or with use of an assistive device	3
700	Ambulation/Locomotion: Ability to SAFELY walk, once in a standing position, on a variety of surfaces.	1- Requires use of a device	6
		Total Functional Points	**21**

Source: Outcome Assessment Information Set Users Manual. (1999). *Implementing OASIS at a home health agency to improve patient outcomes.* Washington, DC: U.S. Government Printing Office.

FIGURE 8-3: MR. BAILEY'S OASIS SERVICE UTILIZATION SCORING DETAIL

MO	Question	Answer	Point Value
175	From which of the following inpatient facilities was the patient discharged during the past 14 days?	1-Hospital	0
825	Therapy Need: Does the care plan indicate the need for 10 or more therapy visits?	1- Yes	4
		Total Service Utilization Points	**4**

Source: Outcome Assessment Information Set Users Manual. (1999). *Implementing OASIS at a home health agency to improve patient outcomes.* Washington, DC: U.S. Government Printing Office.

change, that is if services are not reduced as Mr. Bailey's condition improves, the agency will lose over $10,000 on this one case.

As stated earlier, the Medicare prospective payment system is based on averages. The case of Mr. Bailey illustrates why it is imperative to have a detailed understanding of the patients an agency serves, the expectations of the referring community and the skill of the agency's clinicians. For every patient that represents a significant loss to the

FIGURE 8-4: MR. BAILEY'S PHYSICIAN ORDERED PLAN OF CARE/TREATMENT

Orders for Discipline and Treatments (Specify Amount/Frequency/Duration)

• Skilled Nursing 2 x day x 60 days to perform dressing change to right hip wound. Wound care- Normal Saline wet to dry, lightly pack wound with two Kerlix® sponges, cover with ABD. Skilled Nursing p.r.n. x 4 for excessive drainage, dislodged dressing or complaints of pain. Skilled nursing to perform the administration of Vitamin B12.

• Skilled Nursing to assess 1 x month, vital signs, wound healing, pain, hydration, nutrition, mobility, safety and bowel function.

• Physical Therapy 3 x week up to 9 weeks to perform home safety evaluation, strengthening and gait training. Patient to progress from walker to cane.

• Home Health Care Aide 1 x day x 60 days under the direct supervision of skilled nurse or therapist to assist the patient with ADLs, including transfer to shower.

agency, there must be patients who the agency is able to generate a substantial profit. Mr. Dean represents such a case.

Mr. Dean

Mr. Dean is a 65-year-old patient who was referred to My Town VNA post myocardial infarction (MI) and pacemaker insertion. His hospital course was also complicated by an occurrence of pulmonary edema. Until this MI, Mr. Dean has had a benign medical history.

Mr. Dean lives with his wife who is supportive and is a recently retired certified nurse's aide. He was referred to My Town VNA for medication and diet teaching. Mr. Dean's physician has prescribed a titrating Coumadin® regimen, Atenolol, and sublingual Nitroglycerine tablets. He has also ordered

FIGURE 8-5: COSTS ASSOCIATED WITH MR. BAILEY'S PLAN OF CARE

Skilled Nursing

  2 visits/day x $100/visit = $200/day x 60 days
                                  = $12,000

Physical Therapy

  3 visits/week x $100/visit = $300/week x 8.5
                            weeks = $2550

Home Health Care Aide

  7visits/week x $25/visit = $175/week x 8.5
                            weeks = $1487

                  Cost of Care = $16,037

Anticipated Medicare PPS Payment = $5600

         Agency Profit/Loss = $ (10,437)

a skilled nursing assessment of the pacemaker insertion site. Once the home healthcare nurse completes Mr. Dean's OASIS document, his Medicare PPS score is calculated. (See Figure 8-6, 8-7, and 8-8.)

Like Mr. Bailey's plan of treatment illustrated in Figure 8-9, the cost of providing this level of care to Mr. Dean can be easily calculated. The physician has ordered seven nursing visits for the entire 60-day period. We already know that the cost of a nursing visit at My Town VNA is approximately $100; therefore, the anticipated cost for Mr. Dean's care will be $700. From the OASIS scoring, the agency anticipates a Medicare PPS payment of $1600 which leaves the agency with a profit of $900. (See Figure 8-10.)

From a financial perspective, agencies would clearly prefer to care for patients who are similar to Mr. Dean as opposed to Mr. Bailey. In reality, the most common home healthcare patient falls some-

where between the extreme loss associated with Mr. Bailey and the profit associated with Mr. Dean. It is important to remember that for every patient like Mr. Bailey, the agency needs approximately 11 patients as profitable as Mr. Dean to cover the cost of caring for patients like Mr. Bailey.

These two examples are realistic examples of patients found in home care, and they represent both extremes of care and the associated profit and loss. The General Accounting Office estimates that the average home healthcare profit per Medicare episode is approximately $700 (Medicare Home Health Care..., May, 2002).

From the above examples, it is clear that the agency and its clinicians have to manage patients efficiently to minimize financial losses and maximize agency profits. Case mix management requires agencies to know which patients and diagnoses are most profitable to the agency and market to referral sources for this type of patients. Most

FIGURE 8-6: MR. DEAN'S OASIS CLINICAL SCORING DETAIL

MO	Question	Response	Point Value
230	Primary Diagnosis	Cardiac	0
250	Therapies the patient receives <u>at home</u>:	4-None of the above	0
390	Vision with corrective lenses if the patient usually wears them	0-Normal vision	0
420	Frequency of Pain interfering with patient's activity or movement	2-Daily, but not constant	5
440	Does this patient have a Skin Lesion or an Open Wound? Excluding "OSTOMIES"	1-Yes	0
450	Multiple Pressure Ulcers	0- None	0
460	Stage of Most Problematic (Observable) Pressure Ulcer:	NA-No observable ulcer	0
476	Status of Most Problematic (Observable) Stasis Ulcer:	NA-Daily, but not constantly	0
480	Status of Most Problematic (Observable) Surgical Ulcer:	2-Early/partial granulation	7
490	When is the patient dyspneic or noticeable Short of Breath?	2-With moderate exertion	5
530	When does Urinary Incontinence occur?	No-incontinence or catheter	0
540	Bowel Incontinence frequency:	0-Very rarely or never	0
550	Bowel Ostomy	0- None	0
610	Behaviors Demonstrated at Least Once a Week (Reported or Observed):	7-None of the above behaviors demonstrated	0
		Total Clinical Points	**17**

Source: Outcome Assessment Information Set Users Manual. (1999). *Implementing OASIS at a home health agency to improve patient outcomes.* Washington, DC: U.S. Government Printing Office.

FIGURE 8-7: MR. DEAN'S OASIS FUNCTIONAL SCORING DETAIL

MO	Question	Answer	Point Value
650	Ability to Dress Upper Body (with or without dressing aids)	2-Someone must help the patient put on upper body clothing	4
660	Ability to Dress Lower Body (with or without dressing aids)	0-Able lower body without assistance	0
670	Bathing: Ability to wash entire body. Excludes grooming (washing face and hands only).	0-Able to bathe self in <u>shower or tub</u> independently.	0
680	Toileting: Ability to get to and from the toilet or bedside commode.	0- Able to get to and from the toilet or commode independently	0
690	Transferring: Ability to move from bed to chair, on and off toilet or commode, into and out of tub or shower	0- Able to independently transfer.	0
700	Ambulation/Locomotion: Ability to <u>SAFELY</u> walk, once in a standing position, on a variety of surfaces.	0-Able to independently walk on even and uneven surfaces and climb stairs	0
		Total Functional Points	**4**

Source: Outcome Assessment Information Set Users Manual. (1999). *Implementing OASIS at a home health agency to improve patient outcomes.* Washington, DC: U.S. Government Printing Office.

FIGURE 8-8: MR. DEAN'S SERVICE UTILIZATION SCORING DETAIL

MO	Question	Answer	Point Value
175	From which of the following inpatient facilities was the patient discharged during the past 14 days? (Mark all that apply).	1-Hospital	0
825	Therapy Need: Does the care plan indicate the need for 10 or more therapy visits?	0- No	0
		Total Service Utilization Points	**0**

Source: Outcome Assessment Information Set Users Manual. (1999). *Implementing OASIS at a home health agency to improve patient outcomes.* Washington, DC: U.S. Government Printing Office.

FIGURE 8-9: MR. DEAN'S PHYSICIAN ORDERED PLAN OF CARE/TREATMENT

Orders for Discipline and Treatments (Specify Amount/Frequency/Duration)

• <u>Skilled Nursing</u> 2x week x 1week, then 1 x week x 2 weeks, every other week x 3 week and p.r.n. x 2 for symptom management and complications related to medications or cardiac status. <u>Skilled nurse</u> to teach patient medication regimen, Coumadin titration and diet restrictions. Skilled nursing to assess vital signs, medication and diet compliance, cardiac status, hydration, nutrition and emergency plan.

agencies would not turn a case like Mr. Bailey away, but they certainly would not compete with other agencies to gets lots of referrals like his.

To further illustrate this point, consider the example of Happy Home Health Care (HHHC).

HHHC is the largest provider of home healthcare services in their geographic location. Diabetes is one of the top three diagnoses that this agency admits to service. HHHC has a highly developed diabetes team, which includes:

• A certified diabetes educator (CDE);

FIGURE 8-10: COST ASSOCIATED WITH MR. DEAN'S PLAN OF CARE

Skilled Nursing

7 visits/60 days x $100/visit = $700

Anticipated Medicare PPS Payment = $1600

Agency Profit/Loss = $ 900

- A certified ostomy, wound continence nurse (CWOCN);

- A team of staff nurses who have participated in intensive training demonstrating competence in diabetes management;

- Diabetes care protocols; and

- Collaborative relationships with the local diabetic clinics and endocrinology physician practices.

For every Medicare PPS diabetes episode, HHHC averages a profit of $325; however, the agency is also aware that although psychiatric diagnoses are also one of the top ten diagnoses that it receives, it does not have a highly specialized psychiatric care management team. In fact, they no longer have a psychiatric clinic nurse specialist, and their patient outcomes are not as positive as the agency would like.

HHHC also finds that its clinicians are providing a large number of nursing and home healthcare aide visits to the psychiatric patient population. As a group, the OASIS scoring profile for the psychiatric patients tends to be very low translating into a low clinical and function acuity. For every Medicare beneficiary with a psychiatric diagnosis that HHHC admits to service, the agency loses approximately $250 per 60-day episode.

The Medicare PPS reimbursement system forces the management team at HHHC to face a very important decision. Should the agency continue to admit a category of patients that represent financial losses and inadequate patient outcomes? Figure 8-11 numerically outlines the simple problem that the agency must consider.

The profit generated by the expert and efficient management of the diabetes patients was lost to the agency through the inefficient management of the psychiatric patients. Based on this simplified example, what do you think the management of HHHC should do?

- Manage the agency's case mix by no longer accepting psychiatric cases;

- Increase the agency's marketing efforts to increase the number of diabetic patients to off set the losses incurred from psychiatric patients;

- Reallocate agency resources to increase the skills of the agency's staff and develop a specialty team for psychiatric patients; or

- Develop a partnership or collaborative relationship with other community-based providers of psychiatric services to improve the agency's patient and financial outcomes?

Although there is no "right" answer that is applicable to every agency, the decision to discontinue admitting psychiatric patients is a serious one and will not be taken lightly by the agency's Administrator and/Board of Directors.

The same principles of case mix management can also be applied to physicians or agency staff. Consider the comparison of Dr. Kolb and Dr. Stritter. Both of these physicians have internal medicine practices that provide a large number of referral to your agency. Historically, Dr. Kolb aggressively manages her patients and makes frequent adjustments to her patient's medication regimen based on the patient's response as it is reported by the home healthcare nurse. Dr. Kolb usually implements the heart failure guidelines recommended by the Center for Health Care Policy and Research (CHCPR), and all of her patients are placed on ACE inhibitors.

Dr. Stritter also refers a significant number of heart failure patients to your agency; however, he

FIGURE 8-11: PROFITABILITY OF PATIENTS WITH DIABETES VS. PSYCHIATRIC DIAGNOSES

# Patients	Primary Diagnosis	Average P/(L) per episode*	Aggregate P/(L)*	Patient Outcomes
17	Diabetes	$325	$5565	Excellent
23	Psychiatric	($250)	($5750)	Marginal
			($185)	

* P-profit * (L)-loss

manages his patients very differently than Dr. Kolb. He typically places his patients on Digoxin and Lasix® and tends to avoid the medications recommended by CHCPR stating, "Those drugs are too expensive and have too many side effects." Although this statement has some level of truth, your agency has also noticed that Dr. Stritter's patients have a significantly longer length of stay and require many more skilled nursing visits than do Dr. Kolb's patients. Despite phone calls from the home healthcare nurse, Dr. Stritter rarely changes a home health plan of care without first seeing the patient or recommending that the patient return to the local emergency department instead of attempting to manage the patient's condition in their own home. Figure 8-12 depicts a side-by-side comparison of Dr. Kolb and Dr. Stritter in a three-month period.

Case mix management requires the agency's management team to evaluate whether or not it can afford to continue to take referrals from Dr. Stritter. The agency has clearly identified some differences between the practices of these two physicians and must decide if it is willing to continue to take risk for both financial and patient outcomes.

The same comparative analysis can be applied to agency clinicians. If a nurse or therapist tends to provide "extra" or unnecessary visits to a Medicare beneficiary, it will likely impact the agency's financial situations. As discussed in Chapter 6, the OASIS scoring provides a mechanism to clinically compare patients, and it is reasonable to expect that patients with similar acuity levels will require a similar number of home visits. If large variations in practice occur, it is likely that the agency will

investigate the variations and assist clinicians with understanding the financial impact of their decisions and assist them to develop more reasonable plans of care.

Principle Two: Episodic Payment

The implementation of the Medicare PPS on October 1, 2000 changed reimbursement to home healthcare agencies from a per visit system to one that was episodic. In general, episodic payment is designed to make one payment for all of the home healthcare services that are provided to a beneficiary for a 60-day period.

Medicare PPS reimbursement begins and ends with the completion of a patient assessment. As discussed in Chapter 6, assessment data is collected and documented on the OASIS. As discussed earlier, the OASIS consists of over 100 federally man-

FIGURE 8-12: EFFECTS OF PHYSICIAN PRACTICE ON AGENCY'S PROFITABILITY

	Dr. Kolb	Dr. Stritter
Number of heart failure patients referred	25	27
Average age	83	83
Average acuity	.8703	.8700
Changes in drug regimen	85%	15%
Patients rehospitalized in 60-day period	20%	48%
Average number of RN visits per 60-day period	9	15
Discharge due to goals met	93%	79%
Average profit/loss per 60-day episode	$776	$176

dated questions. Of these, 23 are the core drivers of the agency's episode payment.

The 23 questions are categorized into clinical severity (C), functional status (F), and service utilization (S). Within each of these categories, the patient's acuity is rated on a scale from one to four. There are a total of 81 categories of acuity ranging from low for a patient who has no clinical severity, functional status or service utilization points (C0F0S0) to a patient who is in a completely dependent state and receives a maximum score of C3F4S3.

The CFS score determines the home health resource group (HHRG). The HHRG converts the OASIS score into a number that is similar to an acuity number. This determines the Medicare payment that the agency will receive to provide 60 days of home healthcare services to a patient with that level of acuity.

Although the patient assessment questions that determine the episode payment do not vary, the episode payment is adjusted slightly depending on the geographic region secondary to labor and wage index adjustments. Rural agencies have also been given consideration, and some slight increases have been made to the episode payment. Other than these two adjustments, Medicare payment formula for home health services does not vary. Table 8-1 provides a conversion from the CFS OASIS score to an HHRG and the associated payment. For example, an episode payment for a patient with a C0F0S0 score is approximately $1137. Barring any unexpected changes in this patient's condition, this is all the reimbursement the agency will receive to care for this patient for the next 60 days. The agency will receive approximately $6071 for a patient who scores C3F4S3.

Although episodic payment does not dictate service levels, it does limit the amount that

Medicare will pay for home health services. At first glance, an episodic payment system may seem entirely appropriate and easy to manage; however, consider what happens if:

- The patient is discharged before the end of the 60-day period;

- The patient is discharged and readmitted to the agency in the same 60-day period;

- The patient is hospitalized or dies before the end of the 60-day period; or

- The patient gets unexpectedly worse or better during a 60 day episode.

The answers to these seemingly simple scenarios increase the complexity of PPS.

In theory, a Medicare beneficiary is admitted to the agency, and based on the patient assessment, receives a clinically appropriate number of visits (as defined by the agency and certified by the physician). The patient is then discharged by the agency in an improved state of physical health and functional ability. The agency is in turn reimbursed a lump sum for the care that was provided.

The case of Mr. Dean discussed earlier illustrates what some might call an ideal home health care patient. He was admitted to the agency and required a minimal amount of visits to achieve his goals. He was discharged independent in medication and compliant with his dietary restrictions. He was able to state the emergency procedures to be implemented in case he needed them, and his surgical wound healed without incident. Therefore, the agency will receive a complete episode payment for the service it provided. In fact, the agency will receive a complete episode payment whenever a patient has received at least five visits prior to being discharged whether the reason for discharge is goals met, death, hospitalization or transfer to a Hospice program.

TABLE 8-1: OASIS HHRG CONVERSIONS

HHRG	C=0		C=1		C=2		C=3	
	Weight	Rate	Weight	Rate	Weight	Rate	Weight	Rate
F=0, S=0	0.5265	$1,137	0.6221	$1,343	0.7965	$1,720	1.1973	$2,585
F=0, S=1	0.6074	$1,312	0.7030	$1,518	0.8774	$1,895	1.2782	$2,760
F=0, S=2	1.4847	$3,206	1.5803	$3,412	1.7548	$3,789	2.1556	$4,655
F=0, S=3	1.7364	$3,750	1.8320	$3,956	2.0065	$4,333	2.4073	$5,198
F=1, S=0	0.6213	$1,342	0.7169	$1,548	0.8914	$1,925	1.2922	$2,790
F=1, S=1	0.7022	$1,516	0.7978	$1,723	0.9723	$2,100	1.3731	$2,965
F=1, S=2	1.5769	$3,411	1.6752	$3,617	1.8946	$4,091	2.2504	$4,859
F=1, S=3	1.8313	$3,954	1.9269	$4,161	2.1013	$4,538	2.5021	$5,403
F=2, S=0	0.7249	$1,565	0.8205	$1,772	0.9949	$2,148	1.3957	$3,014
F=2, S=1	0.8058	$1,740	0.9014	$1,946	1.0758	$2,323	1.4766	$3,189
F=2, S=2	1.6831	$3,634	1.7787	$3,841	1.9532	$4,218	2.3540	$5,083
F=2, S=3	1.9348	$4,178	2.0304	$4,384	2.2048	$4,761	2.6056	$5,627
F=3, S=0	0.7629	$1,647	0.8585	$2,216	1.0329	$2,230	1.4337	$3,096
F=3, S=1	0.8438	$1,822	0.9394	$2,390	1.1139	$2,405	1.5147	$3,271
F=3, S=2	1.7212	$3,717	1.8168	$4,285	1.9912	$4,300	2.3920	$5,165
F=3, S=3	1.9728	$4,260	2.0684	$4,828	2.2429	$4,843	2.6437	$5,709
F=4, S=0	0.9305	$2,009	1.0261	$2,216	1.2005	$2,592	1.6013	$3,458
F=4, S=1	1.0114	$2,184	1.1070	$2,390	1.2814	$2,767	1.6822	$3,633
F=4, S=2	1.8887	$4,078	1.0843	$4,285	2.1588	$4,662	2.5596	$5,527
F=4, S=3	2.1404	$4,622	22360	$4,828	2.4105	$5,205	2.8133	$6,071

Source: Home health agencies PPS. (2003). Update (125), 43616-43629. *Federal Register, 67.*

The reality of providing home healthcare to Medicare beneficiaries is that between 20% and 25% of them experience a hospitalization while they are under the care of the home health agency (Benchmark of Week #75, 2003). Some patients get worse and are placed in a nursing home or are referred to Hospice care, while some require equipment only available at outpatient therapy departments or even change agencies in the middle of a 60-day episode. "So what," you might say, "agencies should be flexible and adaptable enough to meet the changing needs of their patients." Fortunately, agencies are; however, the complexities of PPS regulations require agencies to experience payment adjustments and reductions with almost every change in a patient's status.

Principle Three: Low Utilization Payments

The Center for Medicare and Medicaid services anticipated scenarios where a patient may only receive a few home visits and determined that the agency should not receive a full episode payment for these patients. As part of the PPS regulations, the concept of a low utilization payment adjustment (LUPA) was introduced.

A LUPA payment is made to the agency for all sixty-day episodes that require fewer than five visits. Like all PPS rates, the standardized LUPA payment is slightly adjusted based on the geographic location of the agency. The standardized (unadjusted for geographic labor costs) LUPA payment is approximately $100 per visit. Once again, the LUPA payment will depend on the agency's cost per visit and mix of visits provided during the

LUPA episode. For example, the first home health-care visit can be up to two hours long. The nurse admitting the patient sometimes requires an addition 30-40 minutes to complete paperwork in the office, phone the physician to verify the plan of care and make referrals to other disciplines. It is reasonable to assume that the cost of the first home healthcare visit is the most expensive of all visits provided to the patient. In a complete episode, some of this cost is minimized when the agency receives a full payment. Further, if the agency's cost per visit is higher than the per visit LUPA payment, the agency could conceivably lose money on every visit it provided to the patient.

A LUPA episode can be comprised of any mix of home healthcare services or disciplines. A LUPA episode may be four nursing visits; one nursing and three home healthcare aide visits; two physical therapy, a medical social worker and one home healthcare aide visit; or any combination of visits as long as it is fewer than five.

If a LUPA episode can have a negative financial impact on the agency why would agencies have them? It is reasonable to ask why the agency does not "make sure" that no LUPA episodes occur?

Why would a clinician provide three or four visits and then discharges a patient? The occurrence of LUPA episodes is not always in the agency's control or inappropriate. This scenario can happen for a few reasons. The first is the patient may have met their goals and no longer needs home healthcare services. Second, the patient may have returned to the hospital very early in the 60-day episode, and the agency did not get a referral to revisit the patient after they returned home. Third, the patient's plan of care may be that they only require a monthly visit for an injection of vitamin B12 or a Foley catheter change every six to eight weeks.

Although in some instances LUPA episodes are unavoidable, there are also instances where a LUPA episode was the result of inefficient management of the patient's plan of treatment. Take for example the case of Mrs. Spooner.

Mrs. Spooner

Mrs. Spooner is a 73-year-old patient who was admitted to My Town VNA after a right mastectomy. She was discharged home with two Jackson-Pratt (JP) drains in the lateral aspect of her incision. The home healthcare nurse taught Mrs. Spooner how to manage the drains and the signs and symptoms of infection that should be reported. Approximately one week after the surgery, the JP drains were removed and occupational therapy began to strengthen her affected arm. The therapist continued to see Mrs. Spooner twice weekly. During the fifth week, Mrs. Spooner reported a "lump" in her right axilla, dark red foul smelling drainage from the incision and a temperature of 100.8 degrees Farenheit.

Mrs. Spooner returned to her surgeon who opened the incision, evacuated a hematoma, placed her on an antibiotic and ordered daily dressing changes for two weeks. At this point, the wound measured three centimeters long, one centimeter wide and approximately two centimeters deep. The physician ordered plan of treatment required the nurse to pack the wound with Nu-gauze to prevent it from closing prematurely and to continue to assess for worsening of the infection. Mrs. Spooner's plan of treatment continued until she returned to the surgeon during week seven.

At week seven, the surgeon changed his orders and requested that the nurse reduce visits to every other day. The wound care was changed to alginate packing and a dry sterile dressing to facilitate moist wound healing and closure of the wound.

Midway through week eight (day 53) the home healthcare nurse discussed with Mr. and Mrs. Spooner the feasibility of teaching Mr. Spooner the wound care. Once he agreed, the nurse obtained a physician order to begin teaching Mr. Spooner to perform the wound care.

On day 55, the nurse began demonstrating and teaching the wound care to Mr. Spooner. When the nurse visited on day 57, Mr. Spooner attempted to provide a return demonstration of the wound care; however, he was not able to complete the dressing without verbal cueing and assistance from the nurse.

On the 59th day of the episode, Mr. Spooner was able to complete the dressing care independently. He required no verbal cueing or physical assistance from the nurse. He admitted to still being a little nervous about performing the dressing change and stated that after one more "perfect" change he felt he would be able to perform the dressing changes without the nurse. Since the nurse would be returning for one additional visit to validate Mr. Spooner's ability to change the dressing, the OASIS regulations required that the nurse complete a recertification OASIS to plan for the additional visit.

On day 61 (or day one of the second episode), the nurse returned to the patient's home to find out the patient had gone to the surgeon on the previous day, and the wound care was discontinued. Mr. Spooner was instructed to cover the wound with a dressing only to protect it from being irritated by Mrs. Spooner's bra or other clothing. The wound had well approximated edges and no drainage. Both he and Mrs. Spooner were able to list the signs and symptoms that should be reported to the physician and were discharged from agency services.

Since the dressing was being changed every other day and the teaching of Mr. Spooner began late in the first episode, one additional visit into the second episode became necessary. The nurse felt that although Mr. Spooner was able to demonstrate appropriate technique once, a second return demonstration was necessary to be sure. This "extra" visit resulted in an avoidable LUPA episode and payment for the agency.

Principle Four: Significant Change in Condition

The architects of the home health PPS recognized that Medicare beneficiaries could be fragile and subject to unanticipated changes in their medical condition. A significant change can result in a patient who had a low HHRG/acuity score to suddenly require an increased level of service. Without an adjustment in the episodic payment, the agency will be destined to lose money on the episode through no fault of its own.

Reconsider the case of Mrs. Spooner. The development of an infection in her surgical wound could not have been anticipated; therefore, the agency would have to evaluate whether or not she meets the criteria necessary to claim a significant change in condition adjustment (SCIC).

Before this discussion continues, it is important to differentiate between assessment and payment regulations. Whenever a patient experiences a change in their condition, regulations that govern patient care require the agency to conduct a reassessment of the patient. Whether or not an agency uses the OASIS to document the reassessment is left up to each individual agency to decide. The decision to request a SCIC adjustment is an agency decision and the patient does not have to give consent, agree or even be notified of the agency's decision.

If the agency intends to have the patient's episode payment adjusted, the agency must be sure the 23 scoring OASIS items are part of the patient's reassessment. When the clinician gets to M0100, the reason for assessment question option 3 will be selected to indicate that the agency is completing a Resumption of Care Assessment and is requesting a SCIC adjustment.

(M0100) This Assessment is Currently Being Completed for the Following Reason:

Start/Resumption of Care

- [ ] 1   Start of care-further visits planned
- [ ] 3   Resumption of care (after inpatient stay)

In addition to a change in the patient's physical status, the patient's plan of treatment must also be adjusted (Prospective Payment System for Home Health Agencies: Final Rule, 2000). The PPS regulations require the agency to obtain a physician order that reflects the need for a new plan of treatment.

Deciding whether or not to claim a SCIC adjustment to the episode payment is not as simple as identifying the change in the patient and then requesting additional monies. The SCIC adjustment was designed to provide the agency with additional resources for the proportion of the episode that the patient required an increased level of resources/services. The case of Mrs. Leger serves to exemplify this point.

Mrs. Leger

Mrs. Leger is an 82-year-old Medicare beneficiary referred to My Town VNA for assessment of her cardiopulmonary status and medication compliance. Her primary diagnosis is hypertension. The home healthcare nurse conducts a thorough assessment. The OASIS scoring detail can be found in Figures 8-13, 8-14, and 8-15. The agency anticipates an episode payment of $1,137 to provide Mrs. Leger's care for the entire 60 days.

On day 18, Mrs. Leger was hospitalized for a stroke and returns to the agency approximately 13 days later. The OASIS regulations require the agency to complete a Resumption of Care OASIS; however, the agency must investigate if there will be any financial benefit to claiming a SCIC payment adjustment. Figures 8-16, 8-17, and 8-18 depict Mrs. Leger's post-hospitalization OASIS scoring detail and the significant changes in her condition. The agency has obtained a signed physician order to increase the frequency of nursing visits to teach Mrs. Leger her newly prescribed medications and will also add a home health aide for

assistance with personal care and a physical therapist for a safety evaluation.

Since a SCIC adjustment applies only to the proportion of the episode after the change in the patient's status occurred, the agency must identify the:

- Proportion of the original episode payment the agency will receive;

- Number of "non-revenue" days; and

- Proportion of the new episode payment the agency is entitled to receive.

To complete this calculation, the agency must first determine the number of days in each period. Applied to the case of Mrs. Leger, day 1 to day 17 represents the proportion of the original episode. Day 1 is the start of home healthcare services and day 17 is the day of the last billable home visit before she was hospitalized.

Day 18 to day 30 is the first day of her hospitalization to the day before the home healthcare nurse completed the Resumption of Care OASIS. This period represents the "non-revenue" days of the episode.

Day 31 to day 60 represents the proportion of the episode where a new increased HHRG is determined based on the completion of the Resumption of Care OASIS. If the agency decides to request a SCIC episode payment adjustment, it will be proportional to this part of the episode.

Based on the admission OASIS scoring detail, Mrs. Leger's HHRG is C0F0S0, and the corresponding episode payment is approximately $1,137. Based on her post hospitalization OASIS scoring detail, her SCIC adjusted payment could be up to $2,148.

At first glance, the agency appears to be entitled to an additional $1,000 if a SCIC adjustment is requested. Remember, the agency can only request the proportion of higher episode payment that corresponds to the number of days that the patient required the higher level of service. Therefore, the

FIGURE 8-13: MRS. LEGER'S ADMISSION OASIS CLINICAL SCORING DETAIL

MO	Question	Response	Point Value
230	Primary Diagnosis	Hypertension	0
250	Therapies the patient receives at home	4-None of the above	0
390	Vision with corrective lenses if the patient usually wears them	0-Normal vision	0
420	Frequency of Pain interfering with patient's activity or movement	1-Less often than daily	0
440	Does this patient have a Skin Lesion or an Open Wound? Excluding "OSTOMIES"	1-Yes	0
450	Multiple Pressure Ulcers	0- None	0
460	Stage of Most Problematic (Observable) Pressure Ulcer:	NA-No observable ulcer	0
476	Status of Most Problematic (Observable) Stasis Ulcer:	NA-No observable stasis ulcer	0
480	Status of Most Problematic (Observable) Surgical Wound:	NA-No observable surgical wound	0
490	When is the patient dyspneic or noticeable Short of Breath?	5-At rest (during day or night)	5
530	When does Urinary Incontinence occur?	No-incontinence or catheter	0
540	Bowel Incontinence frequency:	0-Very rarely or never	0
550	Bowel Ostomy	0- No	0
610	Behaviors Demonstrated at Least Once a Week (Reported or Observed):	7-None of the above behaviors demonstrated	0
		Total Clinical Points	**5**

Source: Outcome Assessment Information Set Users Manual. (1999). *Implementing OASIS at a home health agency to improve patient outcomes.* Washington, DC: U.S. Government Printing Office.

FIGURE 8-14: MRS. LEGER'S ADMISSION OASIS FUNCTIONAL SCORING DETAIL

MO	Question	Answer	Point Value
650	Ability to Dress Upper Body (with or without dressing aids)	0- Able upper body without assistance	0
660	Ability to Dress Lower Body (with or without dressing aids)	0- Able lower body without assistance	0
670	Bathing: Ability to wash entire body. <u>Excludes</u> grooming (washing face and hands only).	0-Able to bathe self in <u>shower or tub</u> independently	0
680	Toileting: Ability to get to and from the toilet or bedside commode.	0- Able to get to and from the toilet or commode independently	0
690	Transferring: Ability to move from bed to chair, on and off toilet or commode, into and out of tub or shower	0-Able to get to and from the toilet independently with or without a device	0
700	Ambulation/Locomotion: Ability to <u>SAFELY</u> walk, once in a standing position, on a variety of surfaces.	0- Able to independently transfer	0
		Total Functional Points	**0**

Source: Outcome Assessment Information Set Users Manual. (1999). *Implementing OASIS at a home health agency to improve patient outcomes.* Washington, DC: U.S. Government Printing Office.

FIGURE 8-15: MRS. LEGER'S ADMISSION OASIS SERVICE UTILIZATION SCORING DETAIL

MO	Question	Answer	Point Value
175	From which of the following inpatient facilities was the patient discharged during the past 14 days?	Patient was not discharged from an inpatient facility	0
825	Therapy Need: Does the care plan indicate the need for 10 or more therapy visits?	Yes	0
		Total Service Utilization Points	**0**

Source: Outcome Assessment Information Set Users Manual. (1999). *Implementing OASIS at a home health agency to improve patient outcomes.* Washington, DC: U.S. Government Printing Office.

next step in determining if a SCIC payment adjustment should be requested is to calculate the proportions. Figure 8-19 provides an example of the calculations used to make the determination.

It is absolutely essential to calculate each SCIC adjustment with this level of detail. Although, at first glance, one would anticipate that the agency would benefit from claiming the adjustment, a large portion of the gains are undermined by the number of the non-revenue days. A few additional days in the hospital or a skilled nursing facility may completely undermine any possibility of a financial gain the agency might make by requesting a SCIC adjustment.

Home healthcare patients may experience more than one hospitalization during the course of a single episode. Although the patient's condition may worsen each time, the repeated trips to the hospital increase the number of non-revenue days in an episode, which ultimately dilutes the agency's potential of requesting a SCIC payment adjustment.

FIGURE 8-16: MRS. LEGER'S POST-HOSPITALIZATION OASIS CLINICAL SCORING DETAIL

MO	Question	Response	Point Value
230	Primary Diagnosis	CVA	20
250	Therapies the patient receives <u>at home</u>:	4-None of the above	0
390	Vision with corrective lenses if the patient usually wears them	0-Normal vision	0
420	Frequency of Pain interfering with patient's activity or movement	1-Less often than daily	0
440	Does this patient have a Skin Lesion or an Open Wound? Excluding "OSTOMIES"	1-No	0
450	Multiple Pressure Ulcers	0- No	0
460	Stage of Most Problematic (Observable) Pressure Ulcer:	NA-No observable ulcer	0
476	Status of Most Problematic (Observable) Stasis Ulcer:	NA-No observable stasis ulcer	0
480	Status of Most Problematic (Observable) Surgical Wound:	NA-No observable surgical wound	0
490	When is the patient dyspneic or noticeable Short of Breath?	5-At rest (during day or night)	5
530	When does Urinary Incontinence occur?	No-incontinence or catheter	0
540	Bowel Incontinence frequency:	0-Very rarely or never	0
550	Bowel Ostomy	0- No	0
610	Behaviors Demonstrated at Least Once a Week (Reported or Observed):	7-None of the above behaviors demonstrated	0
		Total Clinical Points	**25**

Source: Outcome Assessment Information Set Users Manual. (1999). *Implementing OASIS at a home health agency to improve patient outcomes.* Washington, DC: U.S. Government Printing Office.

The rationale for counting non-revenue days is that although the patient's condition worsened, the agency was not incurring additional expenses providing care to the patient while they were hospitalized or in a skilled nursing facility. The regulations state the intent of creating a SCIC adjustment is to "ensure that the agency would have adequate resources to meet the changing patient needs" (Prospective Payment System for Home Health Agencies: Final Rule, p. 41144). The reality of counting the non-revenue portion of the episode minimizes the positive financial effect of requesting a SCIC payment adjustment.

Principle Five: Bundling of Supplies and Outpatient Therapy

As part of the episodic payment, Medicare requires agencies to provide the beneficiaries with all of the disposable medical supplies that they require. The agency is required to provide items such as dressings, catheters, ostomy, and other supplies – whether or not the agency is actually using the supplies as part of the physician ordered plan of treatment. For example, a patient with a well-estab-

FIGURE 8-17: MRS. LEGER'S POST-HOSPITALIZATION OASIS FUNCTIONAL SCORING DETAIL

MO	Question	Answer	Point Value
650	Ability to Dress Upper Body (with or without dressing aids)	0-Able upper body without assistance	0
660	Ability to Dress Lower Body (with or without dressing aids)	0-Able lower body without assistance	0
670	Bathing: Ability to wash entire body. <u>Excludes</u> grooming (washing face and hands only).	2-Able to bathe in shower or tub with the assistance of another	8
680	Toileting: Ability to get to and from the toilet or bedside commode.	0-Able to get to and from the toilet or commode independently	0
690	Transferring: Ability to move from bed to chair, on and off toilet or commode, into and out of tub or shower	1-Transfers with minimal human assistance or with use of an assistive device	3
700	Ambulation/Locomotion: Ability to <u>SAFELY</u> walk, once in a standing position, on a variety of surfaces.	Requires use of a device	6
		Total Functional Points	**17**

Source: Outcome Assessment Information Set Users Manual. (1999). *Implementing OASIS at a home health agency to improve patient outcomes.* Washington, DC: U.S. Government Printing Office.

FIGURE 8-18: MRS. LEGER'S POST-HOSPITALIZATION OASIS SERVICE UTILIZATION SCORING DETAIL

MO	Question	Answer	Point Value
175	From which of the following inpatient facilities was the patient discharged during the past 14 days? (Mark all that apply).	1-Hospital	0
825	Therapy Need: Does the care plan indicate the need for 10 or more therapy visits?	0- No	0
		Total Service Utilization Points	**0**

Source: Outcome Assessment Information Set Users Manual. (1999). *Implementing OASIS at a home health agency to improve patient outcomes.* Washington, DC: U.S. Government Printing Office.

lished colostomy is admitted to the agency for cardiac or respiratory care. During the assessment process, the nurse discusses the patient's ability to manage the colostomy. The patient has and will continue to manage the colostomy independently. The nurse established a plan of treatment that does not include any interventions related to colostomy, yet the agency is required to provide all of these supplies and pay for them from the episode payment. There is no episode adjustment add-on that the agency can request. When crafting the PPS Medicare determined that the average cost of supplies per Medicare beneficiary was approximately $43 and built that into the episodic payment (Prospective Payment System for Home Health Agencies: Final Rule, 2000).

In an attempt to manage supply costs, some agencies have implemented strict supply management systems, protocols and formularies which restrict the types of supplies available to staff. If careful attention is not paid, the cost of supplies can insidiously or, depending on the volume of supplies ordered, abruptly diminish the profitability of the agency.

Along with the bundling of patient related supplies into the episode payment, the PPS regulations also bundled outpatient therapy services. The bundling of these services requires home health agencies to be financially responsible for all of the services a patient may receive in an outpatient rehabilitation facility. There are few limitations on the provision of physical, occupational and speech therapy in a patient's home, and the majority of home healthcare patients are able to meet their rehabilitation goals without returning to an outpatient therapy department. However, in some instances, a patient may require a piece of equipment that cannot be brought into their home. For example, a patient may return to the outpatient therapy department for the development or adjustment of a prosthetic devise, debridement of a wound in a whirlpool tank, or a testing to evaluate

FIGURE 8-19: CALCULATING A POTENTIAL SCIC PAYMENT ADJUSTMENT

Step 1:
Divide the total episode payment by 60 to obtain a daily rate.

$1,137/60 days = $18.95 per day

Step 2:
Multiply the daily rate by the number of days in that portion of the episode, the start of care to the last billable visit prior to the hospitalization to determine the first partial episode payment.

$18.95 per day x 17 days = $322.15

Step 3:
Determine the number of "non-revenue" days. The day after the last billable visit to the day before the completion of the Resumption of Care.

13 "non-revenue" days

Step 4:
Divide the new episode payment by 60 to obtain the new daily rate.

$2,148/60 days = $35.80 per day

Step 5:
Multiply the daily rate by the number of days in that portion of the episode, the resumption of care to the last billable visit to determine the second partial episode payment.

$35.80 per day x 30 days = $1,074

Step 6:
Add the first partial episode payment to second partial episode payment to determine the total episode payment if a SCIC adjustment is requested.

$322.15 + $1,074 = $1,396.95

Step 7:
To make a decision about whether or not to claim a SCIC adjustment, subtract the original episode payment from the SCIC adjusted payment.

$1,396.95 - %1,137 = $259.15

swallowing. Since the PPS makes the agency financially responsible for patient-related supplies and outpatient therapy services, many agencies have negotiated contracts with suppliers of these services. Not only is a contractual relationship required for most agencies, it also provides that agency with some control over these expenses.

As part of most agencies' admission process, Medicare beneficiaries are notified both verbally and in writing of an agency's responsibility to provide these bundled services at no cost. Patients are often asked to sign, acknowledging that they have received this information. As part of this notification process, patients are informed of their financial responsibility if they choose to use a vender for services that the agency does not have a contract with.

For patients who have relationships with venders that are not contracted with the agency, the bundling of supplies may create a problem. For example, the patient who has a colostomy, feeding tube, or catheter may refuse to have the agency assume the management of their supplies if that means the disruption of a pre-existing relationship. In this case, the patient may be asked to sign a form that outlines their refusal of this service, or the agency may decide to negotiate with the patient's supply vender. In any event, the bundling of supplies has made it easier for the agency to obtain the supplies necessary to appropriately manage patient care. Agencies no longer face barriers because a patient cannot or will not pay for supplies. On the other hand, the bundling of supplies and outpatient therapy services has added to the complexity of the home health PPS.

Principle Six: Therapy Add-On

The provision of physical, occupational and speech therapy is crucial to many home health patients. The architects of the Medicare PPS system recognized the importance of these services to home care patients. In addition, they recognized that the utilization of these services significantly adds cost to the management of the patient. In an attempt to fairly reimburse the agency for the provision of these services, a therapy add-on provision was built into the PPS.

Like all Medicare home health reimbursement, the determination for a therapy add-on payment adjustment is based on the OASIS assessment and the physician ordered plan of treatment. OASIS M0825 specifically asks the clinician (nurse or therapist) to determine whether or not the patient will receive ten or more therapy visits in the episode. For patients who receive at least ten therapy visits, the agency is entitled to approximately an additional $2,000 per episode.

(M0825) Therapy Need: Does the care plan of the Medicare payment period for which this assessment will define a case mix group, indicate a need for therapy (physical, occupational, or speech therapy) that meets the threshold for a Medicare high-therapy case mix group?

Point Value

Zero	0-	No
4	1-	Yes
Zero	NA	Not applicable if patient is not a Medicare beneficiary

---

It is important to remember that episodes are discrete; they are only 60 days in length. Therefore, the counting of therapy visits to establish a therapy add-on payment adjustment must also be done on a 60-day episode as well. Many agencies closely monitor the provision of therapy services and strive to have therapy services begin as early in the episode as possible to avoid instances where the patient would have met the threshold if the timing of service were better. For example, if a patient begins therapy service late in the episode and receives seven visits in the first episode and three or four in the second, neither episode will qualify for the therapy add-on payment adjustment. If the delay in beginning therapy services was the result of poor planning or scheduling difficulties, the agency's management will undoubtedly strive to

FIGURE 8-20: FINANCIAL IMPLICATIONS ASSOCIATED WITH PROVIDING 10 THERAPY VISITS ACROSS TWO SEPARATE EPISODES

Episode One

Cost of 10 nursing visits =	$1,000
Cost of 7 therapy visits =	$700
Cost of 9 home healthcare aide visits =	$225
Total cost of episode one =	$1,925
Episode payment =	$2,100
Agency profit/loss for episode one =	$175*

*Agency did not meet the 10-visit therapy threshold to qualify for therapy add-on adjustment.

Episode Two

Cost of 3 therapy visits =	$300
Episode payment =	$300*
Agency profit/loss for episode one =	$0

*Agency only provided 3 visits in episode two making it a LUPA episode.

improve the provision of these services. However, if the patient was not in need of therapy service until late in the episode, there is no inefficiency in the agency's process of care, and there is nothing the agency can do to recover this lost revenue.

The financial implications of providing ten therapy visits and not being able to claim a therapy add-on can be huge. In the example noted above, the provision of seven visits in the first episode will cost the agency an additional $700 (assuming the cost of a therapy visit is $100), and no additional revenue will be provided to the agency to help cover this additional cost.

In the example depicted in Figure 8-20, the agency made a small profit in episode one and broke even in the second episode (LUPA episode). If the agency managed to provide all 10 visits in the first episode, its financial outcomes would have been much better. Figure 8-21 provides an example for comparison.

It is not difficult to recognize the positive impact of meeting the 10-visit therapy threshold. Place yourself in a management position in your agency and think about how much time you might spend making sure that therapy plans of treatment are implemented timely and efficiently.

Principle Seven: Outlier Payments

The seventh and final principle of PPS is the outlier payment. Although the PPS payment structure provides adequate reimbursement for most Medicare beneficiaries, there is an entire contingent of patients who require such an intensive level of service that even with the therapy add-on the agency will lose a significant amount of money providing their care.

The outlier payment is an additional payment above the episode payment, which is intended to reduce the losses the agency experiences, not eliminate them altogether. In other words, catastrophic cases which are eligible for an outlier payment will remain losing cases for the agency, but the additional payment will make the loss smaller.

As stated at the beginning of this chapter, the PPS is based on averages and the assumption that the agency will have more profitable episodes than losing episodes; therefore, the financial losses asso-

FIGURE 8-21: FINANCIAL IMPLICATIONS ASSOCIATED WITH PROVIDING 10 THERAPY VISITS IN A SINGLE EPISODE

Episode One

Cost of 10 nursing visits =	$1,000
Cost of 10 therapy visits =	$1,000
Cost of 9 home healthcare aide visits =	$225
Total cost of episode one =	$1,925
Episode payment =	$4,100
Agency profit/loss for episode one =	$2,175*

*Agency met the 10-visit therapy threshold to qualify for an approximate $2,000 therapy add-on adjustment.

ciated with a catastrophic case should be offset by other cases that are profitable.

FEE-FOR-SERVICE

Unlike the PPS system, the fee-for-service payment mechanism generally pays the home health agency for every authorized visit the agency makes to a beneficiary. In this system, the number of visits provided to the patient are usually controlled by an insurance company or a case management system.

Agencies are usually required to make one home visit to assess the patient's needs in the home environment and then establish a plan of treatment that includes the type and frequency of service necessary to return the patient to their optimal level of functioning. This information is then communicated to a case reviewer who then authorizes a finite number of visits that must occur within a specified amount of time, i.e. skilled nursing two times a week for two. At the end of the two-week period, the agency has to obtain additional authorization to continue services. To make a decision to authorize additional visits and ongoing services, the case reviewer is dependent on the clinical documentation.

In this system, the home care agency and its staff are contracted by an insurance company to provide skilled home visits and not necessarily provide case management services. The agency is expected to communicate to the case reviewer barriers limiting the patient from achieving goals and preventing their return to independence. For example, the home healthcare nurse might find that a congestive heart failure patient does not own a bathroom scale. Recognizing that identification of subtle changes in a patient's weight might prevent a very expensive hospitalization, the insurance company may provide the patient with a bathroom scale if the patient does not have one or cannot afford to purchase one.

In essence, the home healthcare nurse becomes the eyes and ears of the insurance company, and all patient-related decisions must include input from the case reviewer. The agency is paid for every authorized visit made to the patient. Any unauthorized visits may not be reimbursed; therefore, the home health agency must diligently track both visits and authorizations to assure reimbursement for services rendered to the patient.

SUMMARY

As noted earlier, in most other settings, the organization's fiscal soundness is not directly related to every nursing assessment and plan of care. The price for the autonomous practice of nursing in home health is accountability. The nurse's decision to provide unnecessary visits to patients can quickly add up to real financial losses for the agency.

EXAM QUESTIONS

CHAPTER 8

Questions 86-98

86. Case mix management requires that

    a. agencies avoid patients that will result in financial losses.

    b. agencies to understand exactly what type of patients are referred and how much service they typically require.

    c. minimized services are provided to the patient regardless of the patient's needs.

    d. not-for-profit agencies do not have to pay close attention to their case mix.

87. Agencies can legitimately maximize their profits under the Medicare prospective payment system by

    a. providing expert and efficient management of the patient's plan of care.

    b. only accepting patients that are profitable.

    c. providing a minimum of services regardless of the patient's documented need.

    d. increasing the per visit charge to Medicare.

88. Extra and unnecessary visits provided to a Medicare beneficiary will likely

    a. improve the patient's satisfaction with the agency's services.

    b. maintain referral source satisfaction.

    c. result in improved patient outcomes.

    d. negatively impact the agency's financial condition.

89. The individual patient's Medicare episodic payment is based on the

    a. patient's clinical and functional status.

    b. combination of the patient's clinical status, functions status and the service utilization indicators.

    c. geographic location of the agency.

    d. number of visits the patient requires.

90. Regardless of the patient's discharge disposition, the agency will receive a full episode payment whenever the patient receives

    a. one visit.

    b. at least two visits.

    c. six visits.

    d. a phone call from the agency to arrange services.

91. Which of the following will result in a low utilization payment adjustment?

    a. a patient who receives 3 nursing and 1 physical therapy visit

    b. a patient who receives one physical therapy, two social work visits, one nursing visit for IV therapy, and one nursing visit for wound care

    c. four home health aide visits and one nursing visit which occur before the patients discharged

    d. one Medical Social Worker visit, one occupational therapy visit, and three nursing visit in the first five days of the episode which result in the patient being transferred to a long-term care facility

92. The Mrs. Spooner case presented in this chapter demonstrates which type of episode payment?

    a. partial episode payment (PEP)

    b. full episode payment

    c. unavoidable LUPA episode

    d. avoidable LUPA episode

93. For an agency to claim a significant change in condition payment adjustment (SCIC), which of the following conditions must be satisfied?

    a. There must be an unanticipated change in the patient's condition, a physician order that reflects a change in the plan of treatment and documentation that the patient is agreeable to the SCIC designation.

    b. The agency must obtain a physician's order that reflects a change in the plan of treatment, and the patient must be agreeable to the SCIC designation.

    c. A SCIC OASIS must be completed, that change must be unanticipated and a physician order is obtained to change the plan of treatment accordingly.

    d. The agency only needs to document that the patient is agreeable to the SCIC designation.

94. The revenue associated with a SCIC payment adjustment

    a. may be positive or negative depending on the proportion of days left in the episode after the change has been identified.

    b. always results in increased revenue for the agency.

    c. always results in decreased revenue for the agency.

    d. does not impact the agency's reimbursement.

95 The bundling provision of PPS reimbursement

    a. only requires the agency to be financially responsible for outpatient therapy services that the patient receives.

    b. requires the agency to provide all of the medical supplies that the patient requires.

    c. requires the agency to only provide supplies that are directly related to the physician certified plan of treatment.

    d. only requires the agency to provide catheter and ostomy supplies.

96. In an attempt to manage the cost of medical supplies, agencies

    a. should refuse to care for patients who are known to have high supply costs.

    b. should request that the patient sign a waiver of liability and take the responsibility for the cost of supplies.

    c. have implemented strict supply management systems.

    d. billed patients for the non-covered portion of their supply expenses.

97. To maximize the reimbursement associated with the therapy add-on, agencies should

    a. closely monitor the provision of therapy service and strive to have therapy services begin as soon as the need is identified.

    b. require the therapists to establish plans of care that result in 10 visits, regardless of the patient's documented need.

    c. teach the therapists nursing skills and substitute nursing visits with therapy visits.

    d. have the patient receive a visit from each of the therapy disciplines to uncover any unidentified needs, thereby increasing the likelihood that the 10 visit threshold will be met.

98. Outlier payments

    a. are lucrative enough to change a financially losing episode to one that is profitable.

    b. are only available to not-for-profit agencies.

    c. are intended to reduce the agency's financial losses but not eliminate them altogether.

    d. require the completion of an additional OASIS document.

CHAPTER 9

THE MEDICARE HOME HEALTH NURSING BENEFIT

CHAPTER OBJECTIVE:

At the completion of this chapter, the reader will be able to recall the rules that govern the provision of Medicare home healthcare services.

LEARNING OBJECTIVE:

After studying this chapter, the reader will be able to

1. identify services that meet the skilled nursing standards.

2. recognize the characteristics of a homebound patient.

INTRODUCTION

Medicare is a federally funded health insurance program that generally provides coverage to all Americans who are age 65 or older. The Medicare Trust Fund is administered by the Center for Medicare and Medicaid Services (CMS). In addition to providing healthcare coverage, CMS also provides regulation and oversight to the majority of healthcare providers in the United States.

Like all health insurance providers, Medicare has an explicit set of criteria that must be met before the patient can qualify for services. Once a beneficiary meets the criteria for services, the home healthcare agency must assure that all of the services billed to Medicare are actually covered by the Medicare home health benefit. Virtually every nurse who works in an agency that cares for Medicare beneficiaries must have a working knowledge of the guidelines that will be discussed in this chapter.

THE HEALTH INSURANCE MANUAL (HIM-11)

The HIM-11 requires an agency to assure that the patient is entitled to receive Medicare benefits. It is incumbent on the agency to assure that the patient is eligible for Medicare covered home healthcare services before services are provided. To assure compliance with this condition, the nurse conducting the admission visit is usually responsible to verify, to the best of their ability, the patient's eligibility (Home Health Agency Manual, 2002).

An agency's intake process usually requires the referral source to provide information about who will be paying for the patient's services. If the patient is a Medicare beneficiary, the agency will document the patient's Medicare number and forward it to the nurse who will be making the home visit for verification. This is simply accomplished by matching the numbers provided by the Intake Department to the numbers on the patient's Medicare card. Discrepancies are usually reported back to the agency, and further investigations are conducted.

All agencies providing services to Medicare beneficiaries are required to be certified to participate in the Medicare program (Home Health Agency Manual, 2002). This concept was discussed in-depth in Chapter 5 and will not be reiterated here, other than to say that an attempt to receive reimbursement from Medicare without being a certified provider is considered illegal and will more than likely result in accusations of Medicare fraud.

During the admission process, the nurse must be sure that the services to be provided are covered under the Medicare benefit. Section 204 in the HIM-11 provides a detailed description of the conditions that the patient must meet to qualify for Medicare home healthcare services (Home Health Agency Manual, 2002). Qualifications include the expectation that the services are provided to a beneficiary who is confined to their home and under the care of a physician. Medicare only covers services that are established under a physician certified plan of care and are provided on an intermittent basis (Home Health Agency Manual, 2002). The details of these conditions will be covered later in this chapter.

In addition to the conditions outlined above, the agency is responsible to assure that the care provided to the Medicare beneficiary is reasonable and necessary (Home Health Agency Manual, 2002). Although physician certification of the plan of care provides support in determinations of reasonable and necessary care, not all care ordered by the physician is reasonable or necessary. Consider the case of Mrs. Obenchain.

Mrs. Obenchain

Mrs. Obenchain is an 82-year-old patient admitted to home healthcare. Her physician ordered plan requires the nurse to evaluate Mrs. Obenchain's diabetes status three times a week. During the admission process, the nurse has a physician order to check a fasting blood sugar; to

evaluate Mrs. Obenchain's compliance with her diabetic diet; to teach Mrs. Obenchain the proper techniques to prepare and administer her insulin; and to teach Mrs. Obenchain the proper disposal of her used syringes.

Mrs. Obenchain tells the nurse that she has been a diabetic for over 20 years, and she is confident in her ability to manage her diabetes. When the nurse asks Mrs. Obenchain about why she thinks a home healthcare referral was made, she tells the nurse, "I have been cheating quite a lot over the holidays, and my blood sugars have been running high."

Her fasting blood sugar is 117. She demonstrates her ability to fill her syringe with the proper dose of mixed insulin. She easily and skillfully administers the insulin and then shows you that she disposes of all of her used syringes in a hard plastic bottle that she keeps under her sink. She states, "When it is half full, I close the cover and tape it real tight before I throw it away. I wouldn't want somebody to get stuck with my needle… that would be a terrible thing."

Mrs. Obenchain shows the nurse her glucose diary and is able to recall her diet for the last day and a half. All of her choices seem appropriate, yet the nurse reviews the agency's diet teaching instruction sheet. She states, "I know all of this honey, I could be teaching you."

At the completion of this visit, should the nurse determine that Mrs. Obenchain needs home healthcare services to teach her to manage her diabetes? Would the services be reasonable and necessary? As an experienced home healthcare nurse, the nurse has been "duped" by patients in the past and feels that a few visits should be provided to Mrs. Obenchain "just to make sure she is as proficient as she seems." Would these services be reasonable and necessary?

When a Medicare reviewer evaluates the medical record to determine if the services provided were reasonable and necessary, they look at the entire case, not just one or two visit notes. The HIM-11 requires the reviewer to make coverage determinations that take into account the individualized and unique needs of the patient (Home Health Agency Manual, 2002). In addition to evaluating the nurse's notes, the reviewer assesses the supporting documentation found in the patient's medical record, such as the physician certified plan of treatment/485 and the OASIS.

PATIENT CONDITIONS

There are four basic conditions that the patient must satisfy to qualify for the Medicare home healthcare benefit. The patient must:

- Be homebound;

- Require skilled services;

- Have his/her plan of care established and certified by a physician; and

- Require care on an intermittent basis.

When establishing a home health plan of care, it is the agency's responsibility to assure that the patient meets the above qualifications. Failure to be in compliance with these conditions for every beneficiary could be construed as fraud or abuse.

Although it would seem that determining a patient's homebound status would be an easy process, the language that guides the home healthcare nurse to make this determination is vague at best. The issue of homebound status is an ongoing point of contention between the home healthcare industry and Medicare. As a result, Medicare has attempted to clarify this language.

In July of 2002, Medicare released a "clarification" of the language related to homebound. It states that a patient can leave their home for the purposes of receiving healthcare, treatment or services without jeopardizing their homebound status. Regular absences from the home to attend outpatient reha-

bilitation, dialysis or adult day care are considered therapeutic in nature and would not disqualify the patient from receiving Medicare home healthcare services (Home Health Agency Manual, 2002).

For many years, agencies considered a patient that was able to drive not homebound and would disqualify the patient from receiving Medicare benefits. However, the July 2002 clarification prohibits agencies from using the ability to drive as the only factor that determines the patient's homebound status. In fact, as long as the patient's absence from their home is infrequent or relatively short in duration or requires a taxing effort, the patient is to be considered homebound (Home Health Agency Manual, 2002).

A patient will not jeopardize their homebound status if they attend a religious service or have an occasional absence for other non-medical purposes such as "an occasional trip to the barber, a walk around the block, a drive, attendance at a family reunion, funeral, graduation, or other infrequent or unique event" (Home Health Agency Manual, 2002, p. 14).

If the patient leaves home, they will be able to access Medicare home healthcare benefits as long as leaving requires a considerable and taxing effort, or the assistance of a person or device, or supervision of the patient while they are outside of the home. The following examples demonstrate patients who meet these criteria and would not be disqualified from accessing Medicare home healthcare services.

- A patient who is bed bound and requires the use of a Hoyer lift to transfer to a wheelchair;

- A patient with severe dementia who can not leave the home without close supervision and assistance for safety;

- A patient with a hip replacement who has stairs leading outside of their home and requires a walker for safe ambulation;

- A patient with COPD who requires continuous oxygen therapy and exhibits dyspnea on exertion of less than 20 feet; or

- A patient with severe peripheral vascular disease and venous stasis ulcers on their lower extremities whose physician restricts activity by requiring the patient to minimize their ambulation and to keep their legs elevated.

On occasion, the patient's place of residence might create some confusion about whether the patient is entitled to receive Medicare home healthcare services. The HIM-11 defines the patient's residence as anywhere the patient lives, i.e. private home, apartment or rooming house (Home Health Agency Manual, 2002). A patient is not entitled to receive Medicare home healthcare services if their residence is part of an institution or facility. Certainly, a patient who lives in a nursing home would not be eligible to receive home healthcare services; however, if the patient lives in an assisted living facility, they might be eligible (Home Health Agency Manual, 2002).

The second condition the patient must meet is to be under the care of a physician who will take responsibility for the certification of the home healthcare plan of care. The plan of care must include information such as the patient's medical diagnoses, medications, functional limitations, activities permitted, and safety measures. Appendix A provides an example of the home health plan of treatment/485 that is used to communicate this information to the physician.

Box 21 on the 485 found in Appendix A is the place where the nurse is to document complete and specific treatment orders. For the purposes of home healthcare, a complete physician order includes the discipline, frequency, duration and service. The following are examples of complete physician orders.

- Skilled nursing bid x 5 days to administer Lovenox® injections as ordered;

- Skilled nursing 2 x week x 1 week, then

TABLE 9-1: MEDICARE DEFINITIONS

Discipline - includes but is not limited to nursing, home health aide, physical, speech and occupation therapy.

Frequency - the number of times per day, week or month the agency will be providing the service.

Duration - the period of time which the service will be provided.

Service or Treatment - specifically which procedure will be performed i.e. assessment, teaching or intervention.

Source: Home Health Agency Manual. (2002). *Home Health Agency Manual Chapter II Coverage of Services.* [Available online: http://cms.hhs.gov/manuals/11_hha/hh200.asp]. Accessed February 9, 2002.

---

every other week x 8 to assess patient's cardiopulmonary status and evaluate medication compliance; and

- Skilled nursing 1 x month to administer vitamin B12 as ordered. Home healthcare aide 2 x week to assist patient with shower and personal care needs.

In addition to establishing a plan of treatment at the patient's start of care, the agency is required to recertify the plan of care every 60 days for as long as the patient continues to need home healthcare services. Since the status of a home healthcare patient can, and often does change frequently, the home healthcare nurse is required to prepare a comprehensive up-to-date 485 that will be sent to the physician for signature.

Examples of changes in the patient's status include, but are not limited to, adjustments to the patient's medication plan, additional or discontinued services, or treatment changes based on an improvement or deterioration. The HIM-11 requires the nurse to obtain a physician signed interim order whenever the patient's plan of care needs to be amended (Home Health Agency Manual, 2002).

The recertification of a home health plan of care/485 requires the nurse to assure that the medications, diagnosis, orders etc. are all up-to-date and reflect the patient's current status. Fortunately, most agencies have a computer system that makes amendments to the plan of care as they occur. When the nurse has to send the recertification plan of care to the physician, all the nurse has to do is verify that the computer generated 485 is correct. Once the physician receives the 485, they are required to sign and date in Box 27 (Appendix A). The physician signature is intended to: "Certify/recertify that this patient is confined to his/her home and needs intermittent skilled nursing care, physical therapy and /or speech therapy or continues to need occupational therapy. The patient is under my care, and I have authorized the services on this plan of care and will periodically review the plan (CMS form 485, 1994, p. 1)."

In addition to meeting the conditions and criteria discussed above, Section 205 requires the patient to demonstrate the need for skilled nursing, physical or speech therapy on an intermittent basis or a continuing need for occupational therapy (Home Health Agency Manual, 2002). For the purposes of Medicare coverage, skilled nursing is classified as:

- Observation and assessment of the patient's status when the skills of a professional nurse are required to identify a change in the patient's status;

- Management and evaluation of the patient's plan of care;

- Teaching and training activities;

- Administration of medications, medical gases, or tube feedings;

- Maintenance of the patient's airway or catheter;

- Wound care or ostomy care; or

- Rehabilitation nursing procedures and heat treatments.

There are endless examples that can be provided to illustrate the home healthcare services cov-

ered by Medicare. In fact, just about every case discussed in this course exemplified Medicare covered services. At this point, it is more appropriate to illustrate the services that are not covered.

The first and most obvious is daily skilled services that do not have an end point in sight. Medicare only provides for intermittent skilled care. For example, if a patient has an extensive wound that, despite daily dressing changes, does not show any sign of improvement, Medicare will not pay for service to go on ad infinitum. If the nurse anticipates that the wound will show signs of healing in 2 or 3 months, daily visits will be covered.

Medicare does not pay for a skilled nurse to prefill patient's medications. It will pay for the administration of oral, subcutaneous, intravenous, intramuscular and other methods of medication administration. Medicare will pay for a nurse to administer a daily insulin injection to a patient, but it will not pay for the nurse to prefill the syringes and leave them for the patient to self-administer. The nurse can provide medication prefill services as long as they are not the sole reason that they are visiting the patient. Once the patient no longer has a skilled need, the nurse cannot continue to visit the patient to prefill medications and charge Medicare for the visits.

For these reasons, many agencies prefer to identify a caregiver who can be taught to prefill the patient's medication. Since teaching is a Medicare covered skill, teaching a patient or a caregiver to prefill a medication box or take all medications as part of the physician certified plan of care are skilled, they are also covered by the patient's Medicare benefit.

For the most part, Medicare will not reimburse for the nurse to reinforce teaching that has already been accomplished. It will provide short-term benefits for the nurse to assess compliance with material that was taught or to evaluate the comprehension of the patient. For example, if a patient was discharged from the hospital independent in the administration of insulin and could verbalize an understanding of their dietary restriction, Medicare will not pay for the home healthcare nurse to re-teach this information to the patient unless the nurse assesses that the patient does not demonstrate the same level of independence when they returned home. Although these two examples might induce more questions than answers, it is unlikely that anyone can master the intricacies of the HIM-11 until they have the opportunity to apply them to real life patient scenarios.

SUMMARY

Some agencies require all staff to read the HIM-11 and provide a copy as part of an orientation program. Until a nurse has the opportunity to apply these regulations to the actual nuances of real live patient care, the nurse cannot begin to recognize the ambiguities and the unanswered questions that remain. For some, the regulations might not make sense or seem contradictory when applied to patient situations, but the HIM-11 is the proverbial "bible" of Medicare eligibility, and it is in the best interest of the patient that the nurse and the agency follow these regulations stringently.

EXAM QUESTIONS

CHAPTER 9
Questions 99-100

99. A patient who is able to drive a car

    a. is disqualified from receiving Medicare home health benefits.

    b. is qualified to receive Medicare home health benefits regardless of their home-bound status.

    c. may be eligible to receive a prorated portion of Medicare home health benefits.

    d. may be eligible to receive Medicare home health benefits if it requires a taxing effort to leave home and if the patient only does so for periods of infrequent and short duration.

100. Daily nursing visits for the administration of insulin injections to a blind diabetic who has no caregiver and visits three times a week to teach a patient to take their oral medications correctly are examples of

    a. services that exceed the reasonable and necessary standard.

    b. care that is too costly to be provided by Medicare certified agencies.

    c. services that are considered non-skilled and disqualify the patient from receiving Medicare home health benefits.

    d. skilled services.

   This concludes the final examination. An answer key will be sent with your certificate so that you can determine which of your answers were correct and incorrect.

SUMMARY

The intent of this course was to provide the home healthcare nurse with an overview of the clinical practice realities. For some, home healthcare is considered the area where a nurse can go and "take a break" from the demands of practice. The home healthcare nurse is often thought of as one who visits with elderly patients and takes a blood pressure or changes a dressing. Certainly both of those tasks are completed every day by thousands of home healthcare nurses across the country. However, practicing in home healthcare provides the nurse with challenges that can not be conceived by nurses who have never ventured into community-based nursing.

The most successful home healthcare nurses are those who are comfortable functioning in an autonomous practice environment. Although there are surely other autonomous practice settings, for some patients, the skills and competencies of the home healthcare nurse can mean the difference between dependence or independence, life or death.

Unlike facility-based practice, home healthcare does not have a second or third shift that can act as a safety net for something missed. If the home healthcare nurse does not complete a comprehensive and thorough assessment of the patient on every visit, subtle symptoms or problems could be missed. When the patient complains of being "tired today" or states, "I slept in the chair last night," the home healthcare must investigate the implications of these comments. Every patient interaction provides clues to the patient's physical and emotional well-being. The presence of a monitor that will "beep" when the patient is becoming unstable is almost unheard of. Every patient's home represents a new set of issues, barriers, and hurdles to be overcome.

Control is the patient's. Flexibility, creativity, empathy and patience are mandatory nursing skills.

By in large, the majority of home healthcare is the delivery of nursing care. Agencies are structured by nurses to support the provision of nursing care. Nurses at all levels have an opportunity to not only connect with patients to assist them with achieving their desired outcomes, but also to collaborate with other disciplines and participate in the development of new nursing knowledge.

Reductions in reimbursement; the aging of the population; implementation of new technologies, such as telemedicine; and the diversity of American culture will continue to provide the nurses who choose home healthcare with opportunities for ongoing growth and development of their professional skills. The question is, are you up to the challenge?

RESOURCES

ASSOCIATIONS/ ORGANIZATIONS

American Nurses Association
600 Maryland Avenue, SW
Suite 100 West
Washington, DC 20024
Tel: 202-651-7000
     1-800-274-4ANA (4262)
Fax: 202-651-7001
www.ana.org

Home Healthcare Nurses Association
228 7th Street, SE,
Washington, DC 20003
Tel: 202-546-4756
www.hhna.org

National Association for Home Care
228 Seventh Street, SE,
Washington, DC 20003
Tel: 202-547-7424
Fax: 202-547-3540
www.nahc.org

Visiting Nurse Associations of America
99 Summer Street, Suite 1700
Boston, MA 02110
Tel: 617-737-3200
Fax: 617-737-1144
www.vnaa.org

PUBLICATIONS

Home Healthcare Nurse
The Journal for the Home Care and Hospice Professional
16522 Hunters Green Parkway
Hagerstown, MD 21740-2116
Tel: 1-800-638-3030
Fax: 301-223-2400
Lippincott Williams & Wilkins
ISBN 0884-741X
www.lww.com

Remington Report
30100 Town Center Drive Suite 0-421
Laguna Niguel, CA 92677
Tel: 1-800-247-4781
Fax: 1-949-715-1797
www.remingtonreport.com

APPENDIX A

HOME HEALTH CERTIFICATION AND PLAN OF CARE

Department of Health and Human Services
Centers for Medicare & Medicaid Services

Form Approved
OMB No. 0938-0357

HOME HEALTH CERTIFICATION AND PLAN OF CARE

1. Patient's HI Claim No.	2. Start of Care Date	3. Certification Period From: To:	4. Medical Record No.	Provider No.

6. Patient's Name and Address	7. Provider's Name, Address and Telephone Number

8. Date of Birth	9. Sex M F	10. Medications: Dose/Frequency/Route (N) new (C) Changed

11. ICD-9-CM	Principal Diagnosis	Date
12. ICD-9-CM	Surgical Procedure	Date
13. ICD-9-CM	Other Pertinent Diagnoses	Date

14. DME and Supplies	15. Safety Measures
16. Nutrition Req.	17. Allergies

18.A. Functional Limitations

1. Amputation	5. Paralysis	9. Legally Blind	
2. Bowel/Bladder(incontinence)	6. Endurance	A Dyspnea With	
3. Contracture	7. Ambulation	Minimal Exertion	
4. Hearing	8. Speech	B Other (Specify)	

18.B. Activities Permitted

1. Complete Bedrest	6. Partial Weight Bearing	A Wheelchair
2. Bedrest BRP	7. Independent At Home	B Walker
3. Up As Tolerated	8. Crutches	C No Restrictions
4. Transfer Bed/Chair	9. Cane	D Other (Specify)
5. Exercises Prescribed		

19. Mental Status:	1. Oriented	3. Forgetful	5. Disoriented	7. Agitated
	2. Comatose	4. Depressed	6. Lethargic	8. Other

20. Prognosis	1. Poor	2. Guarded	3. Fair	4. Good	5. Excellent

21. Orders for Discipline and Treatments (Specify Amount/Frequency/Duration)

22. Goals/Rehabilitation Potential/Discharge Plans

23. Nurse's Signature and Date of Verbal SOC Where Applicable	25. Date HHA Received Signed POT
24. Physician's Name and Address	26. I certify/recertify that this patient is confined to his/her home and needs intermitted skilled nursing care, physical therapy and/or speech therapy or continues to need occupational therapy. The patient is under my care, and I have authorized the services on this plan of care will periodically review the plan.
27. Attending Physician's Signature and Date Signed	required for payment of Federal funds may be subject to fine, imprisonment, or civil penalty under applicable Federal laws.

Form CMS-485 (C-3) (02-94) Formerly HCFA-485) (Print Aligned)

APPENDIX B

Outcome and Assessment Information Set (OASIS-B1)

START OF CARE VERSION
(also used for Resumption of Care Following Inpatient Stay)

Items to be Used at this Time Point	M0080-M0825

CLINICAL RECORD ITEMS

(M0080) Discipline of Person Completing Assessment:

☐ 1-RN   ☐ 2-PT   ☐ 3-SLP/ST   ☐ 4-OT

(M0090) Date Assessment Completed: __ __ / __ __ / __ __ __ __
　　　　　　　　　　　　　　　　　month day　　year

(M0100) This Assessment is Currently Being Completed for the Following Reason:

Start/Resumption of Care
☐　1 – Start of care—further visits planned
☐　3 – Resumption of care (after inpatient stay)

DEMOGRAPHICS AND PATIENT HISTORY

(M0175) From which of the following Inpatient Facilities was the patient discharged during the past 14 days? (Mark all that apply.)

☐　1 - Hospital
☐　2 - Rehabilitation facility
☐　3 - Skilled nursing facility
☐　4 - Other nursing home
☐　5 - Other (specify) _____
☐ NA - Patient was not discharged from an inpatient facility [If NA, go to M0200]

(M0180) Inpatient Discharge Date (most recent):

　　__ __ / __ __ / __ __ __ __
　　month day　　year

☐ UK - Unknown

(M0190) Inpatient Diagnoses and ICD-9-CM code categories (three digits required; five digits optional) for only those conditions treated during an inpatient facility stay within the last 14 days (no surgical or V-codes):

Inpatient Facility Diagnosis	ICD-9-CM
a. _____	(__ __ __ . __ __)
b. _____	(__ __ __ . __ __)

Effective 10/1/2003
List each Inpatient Diagnosis and ICD-9-CM code at the level of highest specificity for only those conditions treated during an inpatient stay within the last 14 days (no surgical, E-codes, or V-codes):

2

Inpatient Facility Diagnosis	ICD-9-CM
a. _____	(__ __ __ . __ __)
b. _____	(__ __ __ . __ __)

(M0200) Medical or Treatment Regimen Change Within Past 14 Days: Has this patient experienced a change in medical or treatment regimen (e.g., medication, treatment, or service change due to new or additional diagnosis, etc.) within the last 14 days?

☐ 0 - No [If No, go to M0220]
☐ 1 - Yes

(M0210) List the patient's Medical Diagnoses and ICD-9-CM code categories (three digits required; five digits optional) <u>for those conditions requiring changed medical or treatment regimen</u> (no surgical or V-codes):

Changed Medical Regimen Diagnosis	ICD-9-CM
a. _____	(__ __ __ . __ __)
b. _____	(__ __ __ . __ __)
c. _____	(__ __ __ . __ __)
d. _____	(__ __ __ . __ __)

Effective 10/1/2003

List the patient's Medical Diagnoses and ICD-9-CM codes at the level of highest specificity for those conditions requiring changed medical or treatment regimen (no surgical, E-codes, or V-codes):

Changed Medical Regimen Diagnosis	ICD-9-CM
a. _____	(__ __ __ . __ __)
b. _____	(__ __ __ . __ __)
c. _____	(__ __ __ . __ __)
d. _____	(__ __ __ . __ __)

(M0220) Conditions Prior to Medical or Treatment Regimen Change or Inpatient Stay Within Past 14 Days: If this patient experienced an inpatient facility discharge or change in medical or treatment regimen within the past 14 days, indicate any conditions which existed <u>prior to</u> the inpatient stay or change in medical or treatment regimen. (Mark all that apply.)

☐ 1 - Urinary incontinence
☐ 2 - Indwelling/suprapubic catheter
☐ 3 - Intractable pain
☐ 4 - Impaired decision-making
☐ 5 - Disruptive or socially inappropriate behavior
☐ 6 - Memory loss to the extent that supervision required
☐ 7 - None of the above
☐ NA - No inpatient facility discharge <u>and</u> no change in medical or treatment regimen in past 14 days
☐ UK - Unknown

(M0230/M0240) Diagnoses and Severity Index: List each medical diagnosis or problem for which the patient is receiving home care and ICD-9-CM code category (three digits required; five digits optional – no surgical or V-codes) and rate them using the following severity index. (Choose one value that represents the most severe rating appropriate for each diagnosis.) ICD-9-CM sequencing requirements must be followed if multiple coding is indicated for any diagnoses.

Effective 10/1/2003

List each diagnosis and ICD-9-CM code at the level of highest specificity (no surgical codes) for which the patient is receiving home care. Rate each condition using the following severity index. (Choose one value that represents the most severe rating appropriate for each diagnosis.) E-codes (for M0240 only) or V-codes (for M0230 or M0240) may be used. ICD-9-CM sequencing requirements must be followed if multiple coding is indicated for any diagnoses. If a V-code is reported in place of a case mix diagnosis, then M0245 Payment Diagnosis should be completed. Case mix diagnosis is a primary or first secondary diagnosis that determines the Medicare PPS case mix group.

Severity Rating

    0 - Asymptomatic, no treatment needed at this time
    1 - Symptoms well controlled with current therapy
    2 - Symptoms controlled with difficulty, affecting daily functioning; patient needs ongoing
        monitoring
    3 - Symptoms poorly controlled, patient needs frequent adjustment in treatment and dose
        monitoring
    4 - Symptoms poorly controlled, history of rehospitalizations

(M0230) Primary Diagnosis	ICD-9-CM	Severity Rating
a. _____	(_ _ _ . _ _)	☐ 0　☐ 1　☐ 2　☐ 3　☐ 4

(M0240) Other Diagnoses	ICD-9-CM	Severity Rating
b. _____	(_ _ _ _ . _ _)	☐ 0　☐ 1　☐ 2　☐ 3　☐ 4
c. _____	(_ _ _ _ . _ _)	☐ 0　☐ 1　☐ 2　☐ 3　☐ 4
d. _____	(_ _ _ _ . _ _)	☐ 0　☐ 1　☐ 2　☐ 3　☐ 4
e. _____	(_ _ _ _ . _ _)	☐ 0　☐ 1　☐ 2　☐ 3　☐ 4
f. _____	(_ _ _ _ . _ _)	☐ 0　☐ 1　☐ 2　☐ 3　☐ 4

Effective 10/1/2003

(M0245)　Payment Diagnosis (optional): If a V-code was reported in M0230 in place of a case mix diagnosis, list the primary diagnosis and ICD-9-CM code, determined in accordance with OASIS requirements in effect before October 1, 2003--no V-codes, E-codes, or surgical codes allowed. ICD-9-CM sequencing requirements must be followed. Complete both lines (a) and (b) if the case mix diagnosis is a manifestation code or in other situations where multiple coding is indicated for the primary diagnosis; otherwise, complete line (a) only.

(M0245) Primary Diagnosis	ICD-9-CM
a. _____	(_ _ _ . _ _)

(M0245) First Secondary Diagnosis	ICD-9-CM
b. _____	(_ _ _ . _ _)

(M0250)　Therapies the patient receives <u>at home</u>: (Mark all that apply.)

    ☐　1 - Intravenous or infusion therapy (excludes TPN)
    ☐　2 - Parenteral nutrition (TPN or lipids)
    ☐　3 - Enteral nutrition (nasogastric, gastrostomy, jejunostomy, or any other artificial entry into
           the alimentary canal)
    ☐　4 - None of the above

4

(M0260) Overall Prognosis: BEST description of patient's overall prognosis for <u>recovery from this episode of illness</u>.

    ☐   0 -   Poor: little or no recovery is expected and/or further decline is imminent
    ☐   1 -   Good/Fair: partial to full recovery is expected
    ☐   UK -   Unknown

(M0270) Rehabilitative Prognosis: BEST description of patient's prognosis for   <u>functional status</u>.

    ☐   0 -   Guarded: minimal improvement in functional status is expected; decline is possible
    ☐   1 -   Good: marked improvement in functional status is expected
    ☐   UK -   Unknown

(M0280) Life Expectancy: (Physician documentation is not required.)

    ☐   0 -   Life expectancy is greater than 6 months
    ☐   1 -   Life expectancy is 6 months or fewer

(M0290) High Risk Factors   characterizing this patient: (Mark all that apply.)

    ☐   1 -   Heavy smoking
    ☐   2 -   Obesity
    ☐   3 -   Alcohol dependency
    ☐   4 -   Drug dependency
    ☐   5 -   None of the above
    ☐   UK -   Unknown

LIVING ARRANGEMENTS

(M0300) Current Residence:

    ☐   1 -   Patient's owned or rented residence (house, apartment, or mobile home owned or rented by patient/couple/significant other)
    ☐   2 -   Family member's residence
    ☐   3 -   Boarding home or rented room
    ☐   4 -   Board and care or assisted living facility
    ☐   5 -   Other (specify) _____

(M0340) Patient Lives With: (Mark all that apply.)

    ☐   1 -   Lives alone
    ☐   2 -   With spouse or significant other
    ☐   3 -   With other family member
    ☐   4 -   With a friend
    ☐   5 -   With paid help (other than home care agency staff)
    ☐   6 -   With other than above

SUPPORTIVE ASSISTANCE

(M0350) Assisting Person(s) Other than Home Care Agency Staff: (Mark all that apply.)

    ☐   1 -   Relatives, friends, or neighbors living outside the home
    ☐   2 -   Person residing in the home (EXCLUDING paid help)
    ☐   3 -   Paid help
    ☐   4 -   None of the above [If None of the above, go to M0390]
    ☐   UK -   Unknown [If Unknown, go to M0390]

5

(M0360) Primary Caregiver   taking <u>lead</u> responsibility for providing or managing the patient's care, providing the most frequent assistance, etc. (other than home care agency staff):

- ☐   0 -   No one person [If No one person, go to   M0390]
- ☐   1 -   Spouse or significant other
- ☐   2 -   Daughter or son
- ☐   3 -   Other family member
- ☐   4 -   Friend or neighbor or community or church member
- ☐   5 -   Paid help
- ☐ UK -   Unknown [If Unknown, go to M0390]

(M0370) How often does the patient receive assistance from the primary caregiver?

- ☐   1 -   Several times during day and night
- ☐   2 -   Several times during day
- ☐   3 -   Once daily
- ☐   4 -   Three or more times per week
- ☐   5 -   One to two times per week
- ☐   6 -   Less often than weekly
- ☐ UK -   Unknown

(M0380) Type of Primary Caregiver Assistance: (Mark all that apply.)

- ☐   1 -   ADL assistance (e.g., bathing, dressing, toileting, bowel/bladder, eating/feeding)
- ☐   2 -   IADL assistance (e.g., meds, meals, housekeeping, laundry, telephone, shopping, finances)
- ☐   3 -   Environmental support (housing, home maintenance)
- ☐   4 -   Psychosocial support (socialization, companionship, recreation)
- ☐   5 -   Advocates or facilitates patient's participation in appropriate medical care
- ☐   6 -   Financial agent, power of attorney, or conservator of finance
- ☐   7 -   Health care agent, conservator of person, or medical power of attorney
- ☐ UK -   Unknown

SENSORY STATUS

(M0390) Vision with corrective lenses if the patient usually wears them:

- ☐   0 -   Normal vision: sees adequately in most situations; can see medication labels, newsprint.
- ☐   1 -   Partially impaired: cannot see medication labels or newsprint, but <u>can</u> see obstacles in path, and the surrounding layout; can count fingers at arm's length.
- ☐   2 -   Severely impaired: cannot locate objects without hearing or touching them <u>or</u> patient nonresponsive.

(M0400) Hearing and Ability to Understand Spoken Language in patient's own language (with hearing aids if the patient usually uses them):

- ☐   0 -   No observable impairment. Able to hear and understand complex or detailed instructions and extended or abstract conversation.
- ☐   1 -   With minimal difficulty, able to hear and understand most multi-step instructions and ordinary conversation. May need occasional repetition, extra time, or louder voice.
- ☐   2 -   Has moderate difficulty hearing and understanding simple, one-step instructions and brief conversation; needs frequent prompting or assistance.
- ☐   3 -   Has severe difficulty hearing and understanding simple greetings and short comments. Requires multiple repetitions, restatements, demonstrations, additional time.
- ☐   4 -   <u>Unable</u> to hear and understand familiar words or common expressions consistently, <u>or</u> patient nonresponsive.

6

(M0410) Speech and Oral (Verbal) Expression of Language (in patient's own language):

☐   0 -   Expresses complex ideas, feelings, and needs clearly, completely, and easily in all situations with no observable impairment.

☐   1 -   Minimal difficulty in expressing ideas and needs (may take extra time; makes occasional errors in word choice, grammar or speech intelligibility; needs minimal prompting or assistance).

☐   2 -   Expresses simple ideas or needs with moderate difficulty (needs prompting or assistance, errors in word choice, organization or speech intelligibility). Speaks in phrases or short sentences.

☐   3 -   Has severe difficulty expressing basic ideas or needs and requires maximal assistance or guessing by listener. Speech limited to single words or short phrases.

☐   4 -   Unable to express basic needs even with maximal prompting or assistance but is not comatose or unresponsive (e.g., speech is nonsensical or unintelligible).

☐   5 -   Patient nonresponsive or unable to speak.

(M0420) Frequency of Pain interfering with patient's activity or movement:

☐   0 -   Patient has no pain or pain does not interfere with activity or movement

☐   1 -   Less often than daily

☐   2 -   Daily, but not constantly

☐   3 -   All of the time

(M0430) Intractable Pain: Is the patient experiencing pain that is not easily relieved, occurs at least daily, and affects the patient's sleep, appetite, physical or emotional energy, concentration, personal relationships, emotions, or ability or desire to perform physical activity?

☐   0 -   No

☐   1 -   Yes

INTEGUMENTARY STATUS

(M0440) Does this patient have a Skin Lesion or an Open Wound? This excludes "OSTOMIES."

☐   0 -   No [If No, go to M0490]

☐   1 -   Yes

(M0445) Does this patient have a Pressure Ulcer?

☐   0 -   No [If No, go to M0468]

☐   1 -   Yes

7

(M0450)   Current Number   of Pressure Ulcers at Each Stage: (Circle one response for each stage.)

Pressure Ulcer Stages		Number of Pressure Ulcers				
a)	Stage 1: Nonblanchable erythema of intact skin; the heralding of skin ulceration. In darker-pigmented skin, warmth, edema, hardness, or discolored skin may be indicators.	0	1	2	3	4 or more
b)	Stage 2: Partial thickness skin loss involving epidermis and/or dermis. The ulcer is superficial and presents clinically as an abrasion, blister, or shallow crater.	0	1	2	3	4 or more
c)	Stage 3: Full-thickness skin loss involving damage or necrosis of subcutaneous tissue which may extend down to, but not through, underlying fascia. The ulcer presents clinically as a deep crater with or without undermining of adjacent tissue.	0	1	2	3	4 or more
d)	Stage 4: Full-thickness skin loss with extensive destruction, tissue necrosis, or damage to muscle, bone, or supporting structures (e.g., tendon, joint capsule, etc.)	0	1	2	3	4 or more
e)	In addition to the above, is there at least one pressure ulcer that cannot be observed due to the presence of eschar or a nonremovable dressing, including casts? ☐ 0 - No ☐ 1 - Yes						

(M0460)   Stage of Most Problematic (Observable) Pressure Ulcer:

☐   1 -   Stage 1
☐   2 -   Stage 2
☐   3 -   Stage 3
☐   4 -   Stage 4
☐ NA -   No observable pressure ulcer

(M0464)   Status of Most Problematic (Observable) Pressure Ulcer:

☐   1 -   Fully granulating
☐   2 -   Early/partial granulation
☐   3 -   Not healing
☐ NA -   No observable pressure ulcer

(M0468)   Does this patient have a Stasis Ulcer ?

☐   0 -   No [If No, go to M0482]
☐   1 -   Yes

(M0470)   Current Number of Observable Stasis Ulcer(s):

☐   0 -   Zero
☐   1 -   One
☐   2 -   Two
☐   3 -   Three
☐   4 -   Four or more

(M0474)   Does this patient have at least one Stasis Ulcer that Cannot be Observed due to the presence of a nonremovable dressing?

☐   0 -   No
☐   1 -   Yes

8

(M0476) Status of Most Problematic (Observable) Stasis Ulcer:

- ☐ 1 - Fully granulating
- ☐ 2 - Early/partial granulation
- ☐ 3 - Not healing
- ☐ NA - No observable stasis ulcer

(M0482) Does this patient have a Surgical Wound?

- ☐ 0 - No [If No, go to M0490]
- ☐ 1 - Yes

(M0484) Current Number of (Observable) Surgical Wounds: (If a wound is partially closed but has <u>more</u> than one opening, consider each opening as a separate wound.)

- ☐ 0 - Zero
- ☐ 1 - One
- ☐ 2 - Two
- ☐ 3 - Three
- ☐ 4 - Four or more

(M0486) Does this patient have at least one Surgical Wound that Cannot be Observed   due to the presence of a nonremovable dressing?

- ☐ 0 - No
- ☐ 1 - Yes

(M0488) Status of Most Problematic (Observable) Surgical Wound:

- ☐ 1 - Fully granulating
- ☐ 2 - Early/partial granulation
- ☐ 3 - Not healing
- ☐ NA - No observable surgical wound

RESPIRATORY STATUS

(M0490) When is the patient dyspneic or noticeably Short of Breath?

- ☐ 0 - Never, patient is not short of breath
- ☐ 1 - When walking more than 20 feet, climbing stairs
- ☐ 2 - With moderate exertion (e.g., while dressing, using commode or bedpan, walking distances less than 20 feet)
- ☐ 3 - With minimal exertion (e.g., while eating, talking, or performing other ADLs) or with agitation
- ☐ 4 - At rest (during day or night)

(M0500) Respiratory Treatments utilized at home: (Mark all that apply.)

- ☐ 1 - Oxygen (intermittent or continuous)
- ☐ 2 - Ventilator (continually or at night)
- ☐ 3 - Continuous positive airway pressure
- ☐ 4 - None of the above

ELIMINATION STATUS

(M0510) Has this patient been treated for a Urinary Tract Infection   in the past 14 days?

- ☐ 0 - No
- ☐ 1 - Yes
- ☐ NA - Patient on prophylactic treatment
- ☐ UK - Unknown

9

(M0520) Urinary Incontinence or Urinary Catheter Presence:

    ☐ 0 - No incontinence or catheter (includes anuria or ostomy for urinary drainage) [If No, go to M0540]

    ☐ 1 - Patient is incontinent

    ☐ 2 - Patient requires a urinary catheter (i.e., external, indwelling, intermittent, suprapubic) [Go to M0540]

(M0530) When does Urinary Incontinence occur?

    ☐ 0 - Timed-voiding defers incontinence

    ☐ 1 - During the night only

    ☐ 2 - During the day and night

(M0540) Bowel Incontinence Frequency:

    ☐ 0 - Very rarely or never has bowel incontinence

    ☐ 1 - Less than once weekly

    ☐ 2 - One to three times weekly

    ☐ 3 - Four to six times weekly

    ☐ 4 - On a daily basis

    ☐ 5 - More often than once daily

    ☐ NA - Patient has ostomy for bowel elimination

    ☐ UK - Unknown

(M0550) Ostomy for Bowel Elimination: Does this patient have an ostomy for bowel elimination that (within the last 14 days): a) was related to an inpatient facility stay, or b) necessitated a change in medical or treatment regimen?

    ☐ 0 - Patient does not have an ostomy for bowel elimination.

    ☐ 1 - Patient's ostomy was not related to an inpatient stay and did not necessitate change in medical or treatment regimen.

    ☐ 2 - The ostomy was related to an inpatient stay or did necessitate change in medical or treatment regimen.

NEURO/EMOTIONAL/BEHAVIORAL STATUS

(M0560) Cognitive Functioning: (Patient's current level of alertness, orientation, comprehension, concentration, and immediate memory for simple commands.)

    ☐ 0 - Alert/oriented, able to focus and shift attention, comprehends and recalls task directions independently.

    ☐ 1 - Requires prompting (cuing, repetition, reminders) only under stressful or unfamiliar conditions.

    ☐ 2 - Requires assistance and some direction in specific situations (e.g., on all tasks involving shifting of attention), or consistently requires low stimulus environment due to distractibility.

    ☐ 3 - Requires considerable assistance in routine situations. Is not alert and oriented or is unable to shift attention and recall directions more than half the time.

    ☐ 4 - Totally dependent due to disturbances such as constant disorientation, coma, persistent vegetative state, or delirium.

(M0570) When Confused (Reported or Observed):

    ☐ 0 - Never

    ☐ 1 - In new or complex situations only

    ☐ 2 - On awakening or at night only

    ☐ 3 - During the day and evening, but not constantly

    ☐ 4 - Constantly

    ☐ NA - Patient nonresponsive

(M0580) When Anxious (Reported or Observed):

     ☐   0 -   None of the time
     ☐   1 -   Less often than daily
     ☐   2 -   Daily, but not constantly
     ☐   3 -   All of the time
     ☐   NA -   Patient nonresponsive

(M0590) Depressive Feelings Reported or Observed in Patient: (Mark all that apply.)

     ☐   1 -   Depressed mood (e.g., feeling sad, tearful)
     ☐   2 -   Sense of failure or self reproach
     ☐   3 -   Hopelessness
     ☐   4 -   Recurrent thoughts of death
     ☐   5 -   Thoughts of suicide
     ☐   6 -   None of the above feelings observed or reported

(M0610) Behaviors Demonstrated at <u>Least Once a Week (R</u>eported or Observed):   (Mark all that apply.)

     ☐   1 -   Memory deficit: failure to recognize familiar persons/places, inability to recall events of past 24 hours, significant memory loss so that supervision is required
     ☐   2 -   Impaired decision-making: failure to perform usual ADLs or IADLs, inability to appropriately stop activities, jeopardizes safety through actions
     ☐   3 -   Verbal disruption: yelling, threatening, excessive profanity, sexual references, etc.
     ☐   4 -   Physical aggression: aggressive or combative to self and others (e.g., hits self, throws objects, punches, dangerous maneuvers with wheelchair or other objects)
     ☐   5 -   Disruptive, infantile, or socially inappropriate behavior (excludes verbal actions)
     ☐   6 -   Delusional, hallucinatory, or paranoid behavior
     ☐   7 -   None of the above behaviors demonstrated

(M0620) Frequency of Behavior Problems (Reported or Observed) (e.g., wandering episodes, self abuse, verbal disruption, physical aggression, etc.):

     ☐   0 -   Never
     ☐   1 -   Less than once a month
     ☐   2 -   Once a month
     ☐   3 -   Several times each month
     ☐   4 -   Several times a week
     ☐   5 -   At least daily

(M0630) Is this patient receiving Psychiatric Nursing Services at home provided by a qualified psychiatric nurse?

     ☐   0 -   No
     ☐   1 -   Yes

11

ADL/IADLs

> For M0640-M0800, complete the "Current" column for all patients. For these same items, complete the "Prior" column only at start of care and at resumption of care; mark the level that corresponds to the patient's condition 14 days prior to start of care date (M0030) or resumption of care date (M0032). In all cases, record what the patient is   able to do .

(M0640) Grooming: Ability to tend to personal hygiene needs (i.e., washing face and hands, hair care, shaving or make up, teeth or denture care, fingernail care).

Prior Current
☐ ☐ 0 - Able to groom self unaided, with or without the use of assistive devices or adapted methods.
☐ ☐ 1 - Grooming utensils must be placed within reach before able to complete grooming activities.
☐ ☐ 2 - Someone must assist the patient to groom self.
☐ ☐ 3 - Patient depends entirely upon someone else for grooming needs.
☐   UK - Unknown

(M0650) Ability to Dress Upper Body (with or without dressing aids) including undergarments, pullovers, front-opening shirts and blouses, managing zippers, buttons, and snaps:

Prior Current
☐ ☐ 0 - Able to get clothes out of closets and drawers, put them on and remove them from the upper body without assistance.
☐ ☐ 1 - Able to dress upper body without assistance if clothing is laid out or handed to the patient.
☐ ☐ 2 - Someone must help the patient put on upper body clothing.
☐ ☐ 3 - Patient depends entirely upon another person to dress the upper body.
☐   UK - Unknown

(M0660) Ability to Dress Lower Body (with or without dressing aids) including undergarments, slacks, socks or nylons, shoes:

Prior Current
☐ ☐ 0 - Able to obtain, put on, and remove clothing and shoes without assistance.
☐ ☐ 1 - Able to dress lower body without assistance if clothing and shoes are laid out or handed to the patient.
☐ ☐ 2 - Someone must help the patient put on undergarments, slacks, socks or nylons, and shoes.
☐ ☐ 3 - Patient depends entirely upon another person to dress lower body.
☐   UK - Unknown

(M0670) Bathing: Ability to wash entire body. Excludes grooming (washing face and hands only).

Prior Current
☐ ☐ 0 - Able to bathe self in shower or tub independently.
☐ ☐ 1 - With the use of devices, is able to bathe self in shower or tub independently.
☐ ☐ 2 - Able to bathe in shower or tub with the assistance of another person:
         (a) for intermittent supervision or encouragement or reminders, OR
         (b) to get in and out of the shower or tub, OR
         (c) for washing difficult to reach areas.
☐ ☐ 3 - Participates in bathing self in shower or tub, but requires presence of another person throughout the bath for assistance or supervision.
☐ ☐ 4 - Unable to use the shower or tub and is bathed in bed or bedside chair.
☐ ☐ 5 - Unable to effectively participate in bathing and is totally bathed by another person.
☐   UK - Unknown

12

(M0680) Toileting: Ability to get to and from the toilet or bedside commode.

Prior Current
☐ ☐ 0 - Able to get to and from the toilet independently with or without a device.
☐ ☐ 1 - When reminded, assisted, or supervised by another person, able to get to and from the toilet.
☐ ☐ 2 - Unable to get to and from the toilet but is able to use a bedside commode (with or without assistance).
☐ ☐ 3 - Unable to get to and from the toilet or bedside commode but is able to use a bedpan/urinal independently.
☐ ☐ 4 - Is totally dependent in toileting.
☐   UK - Unknown

(M0690) Transferring: Ability to move from bed to chair, on and off toilet or commode, into and out of tub or shower, and ability to turn and position self in bed if patient is bedfast.

Prior Current
☐ ☐ 0 - Able to independently transfer.
☐ ☐ 1 - Transfers with minimal human assistance or with use of an assistive device.
☐ ☐ 2 - Unable to transfer self but is able to bear weight and pivot during the transfer process.
☐ ☐ 3 - Unable to transfer self and is unable to bear weight or pivot when transferred by another person.
☐ ☐ 4 - Bedfast, unable to transfer but is able to turn and position self in bed.
☐ ☐ 5 - Bedfast, unable to transfer and is unable to turn and position self.
☐   UK - Unknown

(M0700) Ambulation/Locomotion: Ability to SAFELY walk, once in a standing position, or use a wheelchair, once in a seated position, on a variety of surfaces.

Prior Current
☐ ☐ 0 - Able to independently walk on even and uneven surfaces and climb stairs with or without railings (i.e., needs no human assistance or assistive device).
☐ ☐ 1 - Requires use of a device (e.g., cane, walker) to walk alone or requires human supervision or assistance to negotiate stairs or steps or uneven surfaces.
☐ ☐ 2 - Able to walk only with the supervision or assistance of another person at all times.
☐ ☐ 3 - Chairfast, unable to ambulate but is able to wheel self independently.
☐ ☐ 4 - Chairfast, unable to ambulate and is unable to wheel self.
☐ ☐ 5 - Bedfast, unable to ambulate or be up in a chair.
☐   UK - Unknown

(M0710) Feeding or Eating: Ability to feed self meals and snacks. Note: This refers only to the process of eating , chewing , and swallowing , not preparing the food to be eaten.

Prior Current
☐ ☐ 0 - Able to independently feed self.
☐ ☐ 1 - Able to feed self independently but requires:
           (a) meal set-up; OR
           (b) intermittent assistance or supervision from another person; OR
           (c) a liquid, pureed or ground meat diet.
☐ ☐ 2 - Unable to feed self and must be assisted or supervised throughout the meal/snack.
☐ ☐ 3 - Able to take in nutrients orally and receives supplemental nutrients through a nasogastric tube or gastrostomy.
☐ ☐ 4 - Unable to take in nutrients orally and is fed nutrients through a nasogastric tube or gastrostomy.
☐ ☐ 5 - Unable to take in nutrients orally or by tube feeding.
☐   UK - Unknown

13

(M0720) Planning and Preparing Light Meals (e.g., cereal, sandwich) or reheat delivered meals:

<u>Prior</u> <u>Current</u>
☐　☐　0　-　(a) Able to independently plan and prepare all light meals for self or reheat delivered meals; <u>OR</u>
　　　　　　(b) Is physically, cognitively, and mentally able to prepare light meals on a regular basis but has not routinely performed light meal preparation in the past (i.e., prior to this home care admission).
☐　☐　1　-　<u>Unable</u> to prepare light meals on a regular basis due to physical, cognitive, or mental limitations.
☐　☐　2　-　Unable to prepare any light meals or reheat any delivered meals.
☐　　　UK　-　Unknown

(M0730) Transportation: Physical and mental ability to <u>safely</u> use a car, taxi, or public transportation (bus, train, subway).

<u>Prior</u> <u>Current</u>
☐　☐　0　-　Able to independently drive a regular or adapted car; <u>OR</u> uses a regular or handicap-accessible public bus.
☐　☐　1　-　Able to ride in a car only when driven by another person; <u>OR</u> able to use a bus or handicap van only when assisted or accompanied by another person.
☐　☐　2　-　<u>Unable</u> to ride in a car, taxi, bus, or van, and requires transportation by ambulance.
☐　　　UK　-　Unknown

(M0740) Laundry: Ability to do own laundry -- to carry laundry to and from washing machine, to use washer and dryer, to wash small items by hand.

<u>Prior</u> <u>Current</u>
☐　☐　0　-　(a) Able to independently take care of all laundry tasks; <u>OR</u>
　　　　　　(b) Physically, cognitively, and mentally able to do laundry and access facilities, <u>but</u> has not routinely performed laundry tasks in the past (i.e., prior to this home care admission).
☐　☐　1　-　Able to do only light laundry, such as minor hand wash or light washer loads. Due to physical, cognitive, or mental limitations, needs assistance with heavy laundry such as carrying large loads of laundry.
☐　☐　2　-　<u>Unable</u> to do any laundry due to physical limitation or needs continual supervision and assistance due to cognitive or mental limitation.
☐　　　UK　-　Unknown

(M0750) Housekeeping: Ability to safely and effectively perform light housekeeping and heavier cleaning tasks.

<u>Prior</u> <u>Current</u>
☐　☐　0　-　(a) Able to independently perform all housekeeping tasks; <u>OR</u>
　　　　　　(b) Physically, cognitively, and mentally able to perform <u>all</u> housekeeping tasks but has not routinely participated in housekeeping tasks in the past (i.e., prior to this home care admission).
☐　☐　1　-　Able to perform only <u>light</u> housekeeping (e.g., dusting, wiping kitchen counters) tasks independently.
☐　☐　2　-　Able to perform housekeeping tasks with intermittent assistance or supervision from another person.
☐　☐　3　-　<u>Unable</u> to consistently perform any housekeeping tasks unless assisted by another person throughout the process.
☐　☐　4　-　Unable to effectively participate in any housekeeping tasks.
☐　　　UK　-　Unknown

14

(M0760)   Shopping: Ability to plan for, select, and purchase items in a store and to carry them home or arrange delivery.

Prior   Current
☐   ☐   0 -
- (a) Able to plan for shopping needs and independently perform shopping tasks, including carrying packages; <u>OR</u>
- (b) Physically, cognitively, and mentally able to take care of shopping, but has not done shopping in the past (i.e., prior to this home care admission).

☐   ☐   1 -   Able to go shopping, but needs some assistance:
- (a) By self is able to do only light shopping and carry small packages, but needs someone to do occasional major shopping; <u>OR</u>
- (b) <u>Unable</u> to go shopping alone, but can go with someone to assist.

☐   ☐   2 -   <u>Unable</u> to go shopping, but is able to identify items needed, place orders, and arrange home delivery.

☐   ☐   3 -   Needs someone to do all shopping and errands.

☐   UK -   Unknown

(M0770)   Ability to Use Telephone: Ability to answer the phone, dial numbers, and <u>effectively</u> use the telephone to communicate.

Prior   Current
☐   ☐   0 -   Able to dial numbers and answer calls appropriately and as desired.

☐   ☐   1 -   Able to use a specially adapted telephone (i.e., large numbers on the dial, teletype phone for the deaf) and call essential numbers.

☐   ☐   2 -   Able to answer the telephone and carry on a normal conversation but has difficulty with placing calls.

☐   ☐   3 -   Able to answer the telephone only some of the time or is able to carry on only a limited conversation.

☐   ☐   4 -   <u>Unable</u> to answer the telephone at all but can listen if assisted with equipment.

☐   ☐   5 -   Totally unable to use the telephone.

☐   ☐   NA -   Patient does not have a telephone.

☐   UK -   Unknown

MEDICATIONS

(M0780)   Management of Oral Medications: <u>Patient's ability</u> to prepare and take <u>all</u> prescribed oral medications reliably and safely, including administration of the correct dosage at the appropriate times/intervals. <u>Excludes</u> injectable and IV medications. (NOTE: This refers to ability, not compliance or willingness.)

Prior   Current
☐   ☐   0 -   Able to independently take the correct oral medication(s) and proper dosage(s) at the correct times.

☐   ☐   1 -   Able to take medication(s) at the correct times if:
- (a) individual dosages are prepared in advance by another person; <u>OR</u>
- (b) given daily reminders; <u>OR</u>
- (c) someone develops a drug diary or chart.

☐   ☐   2 -   <u>Unable</u> to take medication unless administered by someone else.

☐   ☐   NA -   No oral medications prescribed.

☐   UK -   Unknown

15

(M0790)   Management of Inhalant/Mist Medications: <u>Patient's ability</u> to prepare and take <u>all</u> prescribed inhalant/mist medications (nebulizers, metered dose devices) reliably and safely, including administration of the correct dosage at the appropriate times/intervals. <u>Excludes </u>all other forms of medication (oral tablets, injectable and IV medications).

<u>Prior</u> <u>Current</u>
☐ ☐ 0 - Able to independently take the correct medication and proper dosage at the correct times.
☐ ☐ 1 - Able to take medication at the correct times if:
(a) individual dosages are prepared in advance by another person, <u>OR</u>
(b) given daily reminders.
☐ ☐ 2 - <u>Unable</u> to take medication unless administered by someone else.
☐ ☐ NA - No inhalant/mist medications prescribed.
☐   UK - Unknown

(M0800)   Management of Injectable Medications: <u>Patient's ability</u> to prepare and take <u>all</u> prescribed injectable medications reliably and safely, including administration of correct dosage at the appropriate times/intervals. <u>Excludes </u>IV medications.

<u>Prior</u> <u>Current</u>
☐ ☐ 0 - Able to independently take the correct medication and proper dosage at the correct times.
☐ ☐ 1 - Able to take injectable medication at correct times if:
(a) individual syringes are prepared in advance by another person, <u>OR</u>
(b) given daily reminders.
☐ ☐ 2 - <u>Unable</u> to take injectable medications unless administered by someone else.
☐ ☐ NA - No injectable medications prescribed.
☐   UK - Unknown

EQUIPMENT MANAGEMENT

(M0810)   Patient Management of Equipment (includes ONLY___ oxygen, IV/infusion therapy, enteral/ parenteral nutrition equipment or supplies):   <u>Patient's ability</u> to set up, monitor and change equipment reliably and safely, add appropriate fluids or medication, clean/store/dispose of equipment or supplies using proper technique. (NOTE: This refers to ability, not compliance or willingness.)

☐ 0 - Patient manages all tasks related to equipment completely independently.
☐ 1 - If someone else sets up equipment (i.e., fills portable oxygen tank, provides patient with prepared solutions), patient is able to manage all other aspects of equipment.
☐ 2 - Patient requires considerable assistance from another person to manage equipment, but independently completes portions of the task.
☐ 3 - Patient is only able to monitor equipment (e.g., liter flow, fluid in bag) and must call someone else to manage the equipment.
☐ 4 - Patient is completely dependent on someone else to manage all equipment.
☐ NA - No equipment of this type used in care [If NA, go to M0825]

(M0820)   Caregiver Management of Equipment (includes   ONLY oxygen, IV/infusion equipment, enteral/ parenteral nutrition, ventilator therapy equipment or supplies):   <u>Caregiver's ability</u> to set up, monitor, and change equipment reliably and safely, add appropriate fluids or medication, clean/store/dispose of equipment or supplies using proper technique. (NOTE: This refers to ability, not compliance or willingness.)

☐ 0 - Caregiver manages all tasks related to equipment completely independently.
☐ 1 - If someone else sets up equipment, caregiver is able to manage all other aspects.
☐ 2 - Caregiver requires considerable assistance from another person to manage equipment, but independently completes significant portions of task.
☐ 3 - Caregiver is only able to complete small portions of task (e.g., administer nebulizer treatment, clean/store/dispose of equipment or supplies).
☐ 4 - Caregiver is completely dependent on someone else to manage all equipment.
☐ NA - No caregiver
☐ UK - Unknown

The Outcome and Assessment Information Set (OASIS) is the intellectual property of the Center for Health Services and Policy Research, Denver, Colorado. It is used with permission.

16

THERAPY NEED

(M0825) Therapy Need: Does the care plan of the Medicare payment period for which this assessment
will define a case mix group indicate a need for therapy (physical, occupational, or speech
therapy) that meets the threshold for a Medicare high-therapy case mix group?

☐   0 - No
☐   1 - Yes
☐ NA   -

APPENDIX C

Outcome and Assessment Information Set (OASIS-B1)

TRANSFER VERSION
(used for Transfer to an Inpatient Facility)

Items to be Used at this Time Point ------------------------- M0080-M0100, M0830-M0855, M0890-M0906

CLINICAL RECORD ITEMS

(M0080) Discipline of Person Completing Assessment:

☐ 1-RN ☐ 2-PT ☐ 3-SLP/ST ☐ 4-OT

(M0090) Date Assessment Completed: __ __ / __ __ / __ __ __ __
month day year

(M0100) This Assessment is Currently Being Completed for the Following Reason:

Transfer to an Inpatient Facility
☐ 6 – Transferred to an inpatient facility—patient not discharged from agency
☐ 7 – Transferred to an inpatient facility—patient discharged from agency

EMERGENT CARE

(M0830) Emergent Care: Since the last time OASIS data were collected, has the patient utilized any of the following services for emergent care (other than home care agency services)? (Mark all that apply.)

☐ 0 - No emergent care services [If no emergent care, go to M0855]
☐ 1 - Hospital emergency room (includes 23-hour holding)
☐ 2 - Doctor's office emergency visit/house call
☐ 3 - Outpatient department/clinic emergency (includes urgicenter sites)
☐ UK - Unknown [If UK, go to M0855]

(M0840) Emergent Care Reason: For what reason(s) did the patient/family seek emergent care? (Mark all that apply.)

☐ 1 - Improper medication administration, medication side effects, toxicity, anaphylaxis
☐ 2 - Nausea, dehydration, malnutrition, constipation, impaction
☐ 3 - Injury caused by fall or accident at home
☐ 4 - Respiratory problems (e.g., shortness of breath, respiratory infection, tracheobronchial obstruction)
☐ 5 - Wound infection, deteriorating wound status, new lesion/ulcer
☐ 6 - Cardiac problems (e.g., fluid overload, exacerbation of CHF, chest pain)
☐ 7 - Hypo/Hyperglycemia, diabetes out of control
☐ 8 - GI bleeding, obstruction
☐ 9 - Other than above reasons
☐ UK - Reason unknown

2

DATA ITEMS COLLECTED AT INPATIENT FACILITY ADMISSION ONLY

(M0855) To which Inpatient Facility has the patient been admitted?

     ☐   1 -   Hospital [Go to M0890]
     ☐   2 -   Rehabilitation facility [Go to M0903]
     ☐   3 -   Nursing home [Go to M0900]
     ☐   4 -   Hospice [Go to M0903]
     ☐   NA -   No inpatient facility admission

(M0890) If the patient was admitted to an acute care Hospital , for what Reason was he/she admitted?

     ☐   1 -   Hospitalization for <u>emergent</u> (unscheduled) care
     ☐   2 -   Hospitalization for <u>urgent</u> (scheduled within 24 hours of admission) care
     ☐   3 -   Hospitalization for <u>elective</u> (scheduled more than 24 hours before admission) care
     ☐   UK -   Unknown

(M0895) Reason for Hospitalization: (Mark all that apply.)

     ☐   1 -   Improper medication administration, medication side effects, toxicity, anaphylaxis
     ☐   2 -   Injury caused by fall or accident at home
     ☐   3 -   Respiratory problems (SOB, infection, obstruction)
     ☐   4 -   Wound or tube site infection, deteriorating wound status, new lesion/ulcer
     ☐   5 -   Hypo/Hyperglycemia, diabetes out of control
     ☐   6 -   GI bleeding, obstruction
     ☐   7 -   Exacerbation of CHF, fluid overload, heart failure
     ☐   8 -   Myocardial infarction, stroke
     ☐   9 -   Chemotherapy
     ☐   10 -   Scheduled surgical procedure
     ☐   11 -   Urinary tract infection
     ☐   12 -   IV catheter-related infection
     ☐   13 -   Deep vein thrombosis, pulmonary embolus
     ☐   14 -   Uncontrolled pain
     ☐   15 -   Psychotic episode
     ☐   16 -   Other than above reasons
        | Go to M0903 |

(M0900) For what Reason(s) was the patient Admitted to a Nursing Home ? (Mark all that apply.)

     ☐   1 -   Therapy services
     ☐   2 -   Respite care
     ☐   3 -   Hospice care
     ☐   4 -   Permanent placement
     ☐   5 -   Unsafe for care at home
     ☐   6 -   Other
     ☐   UK -   Unknown

(M0903) Date of Last (Most Recent) Home Visit:

        __ __ / __ __ / __ __ __ __
        month   day   year

(M0906) Discharge/Transfer/Death Date: Enter the date of the discharge, transfer, or death (at home) of the patient.

        __ __ / __ __ / __ __ __ __
        month   day   year

APPENDIX D

Outcome and Assessment Information Set (OASIS-B1)

FOLLOW-UP VERSION

Items to be Used at this Time Point ----------- M0080-M0100, M0175, M0230-M0250, M0390, M0420, M0440, M0450, M0460, M0476, M0488, M0490, M0530-M0550, M0610, M0650-M0700, M0825

CLINICAL RECORD ITEMS

(M0080) Discipline of Person Completing Assessment:

☐ 1-RN   ☐ 2-PT   ☐ 3-SLP/ST   ☐ 4-OT

(M0090) Date Assessment Completed: __ __ / __ __ / __ __ __ __
                                      month day   year

(M0100) This Assessment is Currently Being Completed for the Following Reason:

Follow-Up
☐   4 – Recertification (follow-up) reassessment [Go to M0175]
☐   5 – Other follow-up [Go to M0175]

DEMOGRAPHICS AND PATIENT HISTORY

(M0175) From which of the following Inpatient Facilities   was the patient discharged during the past 14 days? (Mark all that apply.)

☐ 1 - Hospital
☐ 2 - Rehabilitation facility
☐ 3 - Skilled nursing facility
☐ 4 - Other nursing home
☐ 5 - Other (specify) _____
☐ NA - Patient was not discharged from an inpatient facility

(M0230/M0240)   Diagnoses and Severity Index: List each medical diagnosis or problem for which the patient is receiving home care and ICD-9-CM code category (three digits required; five digits optional – no surgical or V-codes) and rate them using the following severity index. (Choose one value that represents the most severe rating appropriate for each diagnosis.) ICD-9-CM sequencing requirements must be followed if multiple coding is indicated for any diagnoses.

> Effective 10/1/2003
>
> List each diagnosis and ICD-9-CM code at the level of highest specificity (no surgical codes) for which the patient is receiving home care. Rate each condition using the following severity index. (Choose one value that represents the most severe rating appropriate for each diagnosis.) E-codes (for M0240 only) or V-codes (for M0230 or M0240) may be used. ICD-9-CM sequencing requirements must be followed if multiple coding is indicated for any diagnoses. If a V-code is reported in place of a case mix diagnosis, then M0245 Payment Diagnosis should be completed. Case mix diagnosis is a primary or first secondary diagnosis that determines the Medicare PPS case mix group.

The Outcome and Assessment Information Set (OASIS) is the intellectual property of the Center for Health Services and Policy Research, Denver, Colorado. It is used with permission.

2

Severity Rating
0 - Asymptomatic, no treatment needed at this time
1 - Symptoms well controlled with current therapy
2 - Symptoms controlled with difficulty, affecting daily functioning; patient needs ongoing
    monitoring
3 - Symptoms poorly controlled, patient needs frequent adjustment in treatment and dose
    monitoring
4 - Symptoms poorly controlled, history of rehospitalizations

	(M0230) Primary Diagnosis	ICD-9-CM	Severity Rating				
a.	_____	(__ __ __ . __ __)	☐ 0	☐ 1	☐ 2	☐ 3	☐ 4
	(M0240) Other Diagnoses	ICD-9-CM	Severity Rating				
b.	_____	(__ __ __ __ . __ __)	☐ 0	☐ 1	☐ 2	☐ 3	☐ 4
c.	_____	(__ __ __ __ . __ __)	☐ 0	☐ 1	☐ 2	☐ 3	☐ 4
d.	_____	(__ __ __ __ . __ __)	☐ 0	☐ 1	☐ 2	☐ 3	☐ 4
e.	_____	(__ __ __ __ . __ __)	☐ 0	☐ 1	☐ 2	☐ 3	☐ 4
f.	_____	(__ __ __ __ . __ __)	☐ 0	☐ 1	☐ 2	☐ 3	☐ 4

Effective 10/1/2003

(M0245) Payment Diagnosis (optional): If a V-code was reported in M0230 in place of a case mix diagnosis, list the primary diagnosis and ICD-9-CM code, determined in accordance with OASIS requirements in effect before October 1, 2003--no V-codes, E-codes, or surgical codes allowed. ICD-9-CM sequencing requirements must be followed. Complete both lines (a) and (b) if the case mix diagnosis is a manifestation code or in other situations where multiple coding is indicated for the primary diagnosis; otherwise, complete line (a) only.

	(M0245) Primary Diagnosis	ICD-9-CM
a.	_____	(__ __ __ . __ __)
	(M0245) First Secondary Diagnosis	ICD-9-CM
b.	_____	(__ __ __ . __ __)

(M0250) Therapies the patient receives <u>at home</u>: (Mark all that apply.)

    ☐ 1 - Intravenous or infusion therapy (excludes TPN)
    ☐ 2 - Parenteral nutrition (TPN or lipids)
    ☐ 3 - Enteral nutrition (nasogastric, gastrostomy, jejunostomy, or any other artificial entry into
        the alimentary canal)
    ☐ 4 - None of the above

SENSORY STATUS

(M0390) Vision with corrective lenses if the patient usually wears them:

    ☐ 0 - Normal vision: sees adequately in most situations; can see medication labels, newsprint.
    ☐ 1 - Partially impaired: cannot see medication labels or newsprint, but <u>can</u> see obstacles in
        path, and the surrounding layout; can count fingers at arm's length.
    ☐ 2 - Severely impaired: cannot locate objects without hearing or touching them <u>or</u> patient
        nonresponsive.

3

(M0420) Frequency of Pain interfering with patient's activity or movement:

- ☐ 0 - Patient has no pain or pain does not interfere with activity or movement
- ☐ 1 - Less often than daily
- ☐ 2 - Daily, but not constantly
- ☐ 3 - All of the time

INTEGUMENTARY STATUS

(M0440) Does this patient have a Skin Lesion or an Open Wound? This excludes "OSTOMIES."

- ☐ 0 - No [If No, go to M0490]
- ☐ 1 - Yes

(M0450) Current Number of Pressure Ulcers at Each Stage: (Circle one response for each stage.)

	Pressure Ulcer Stages	Number of Pressure Ulcers				
a)	Stage 1: Nonblanchable erythema of intact skin; the heralding of skin ulceration. In darker-pigmented skin, warmth, edema, hardness, or discolored skin may be indicators.	0	1	2	3	4 or more
b)	Stage 2: Partial thickness skin loss involving epidermis and/or dermis. The ulcer is superficial and presents clinically as an abrasion, blister, or shallow crater.	0	1	2	3	4 or more
c)	Stage 3: Full-thickness skin loss involving damage or necrosis of subcutaneous tissue which may extend down to, but not through, underlying fascia. The ulcer presents clinically as a deep crater with or without undermining of adjacent tissue.	0	1	2	3	4 or more
d)	Stage 4: Full-thickness skin loss with extensive destruction, tissue necrosis, or damage to muscle, bone, or supporting structures (e.g., tendon, joint capsule, etc.)	0	1	2	3	4 or more
e)	In addition to the above, is there at least one pressure ulcer that cannot be observed due to the presence of eschar or a nonremovable dressing, including casts? ☐ 0 - No ☐ 1 - Yes					

(M0460) [Skip this item if patient has no pressure ulcers]

Stage of Most Problematic (Observable) Pressure Ulcer:

- ☐ 1 - Stage 1
- ☐ 2 - Stage 2
- ☐ 3 - Stage 3
- ☐ 4 - Stage 4
- ☐ NA - No observable pressure ulcer

(M0476) [Skip this item if patient has no stasis ulcers]

Status of Most Problematic (Observable) Stasis Ulcer:

- ☐ 1 - Fully granulating
- ☐ 2 - Early/partial granulation
- ☐ 3 - Not healing
- ☐ NA - No observable stasis ulcer

The Outcome and Assessment Information Set (OASIS) is the intellectual property of the Center for Health Services and Policy Research, Denver, Colorado. It is used with permission.

4

(M0488)   [Skip this item if patient has no surgical wounds]

Status of Most Problematic (Observable) Surgical Wound:

- ☐   1   -   Fully granulating
- ☐   2   -   Early/partial granulation
- ☐   3   -   Not healing
- ☐   NA   -   No observable surgical wound

RESPIRATORY STATUS

(M0490)   When is the patient dyspneic or noticeably Short of Breath?

- ☐   0   -   Never, patient is not short of breath
- ☐   1   -   When walking more than 20 feet, climbing stairs
- ☐   2   -   With moderate exertion (e.g., while dressing, using commode or bedpan, walking distances less than 20 feet)
- ☐   3   -   With minimal exertion (e.g., while eating, talking, or performing other ADLs) or with agitation
- ☐   4   -   At rest (during day or night)

ELIMINATION STATUS

(M0530)   [Skip this item if patient has no urinary incontinence or does have a urinary catheter]

When does Urinary Incontinence occur?

- ☐   0   -   Timed-voiding defers incontinence
- ☐   1   -   During the night only
- ☐   2   -   During the day and night

(M0540)   Bowel Incontinence Frequency:

- ☐   0   -   Very rarely or never has bowel incontinence
- ☐   1   -   Less than once weekly
- ☐   2   -   One to three times weekly
- ☐   3   -   Four to six times weekly
- ☐   4   -   On a daily basis
- ☐   5   -   More often than once daily
- ☐   NA   -   Patient has ostomy for bowel elimination

(M0550)   Ostomy for Bowel Elimination: Does this patient have an ostomy for bowel elimination that (within the last 14 days): a) was related to an inpatient facility stay, <u>or</u> b) necessitated a change in medical or treatment regimen?

- ☐   0   -   Patient does <u>not</u> have an ostomy for bowel elimination.
- ☐   1   -   Patient's ostomy was <u>not</u> related to an inpatient stay and did <u>not</u> necessitate change in medical or treatment regimen.
- ☐   2   -   The ostomy <u>was</u> related to an inpatient stay or <u>did</u> necessitate change in medical or treatment regimen.

5

NEURO/EMOTIONAL/BEHAVIORAL STATUS

(M0610) Behaviors Demonstrated at Least Once a Week (Reported or Observed):   (Mark all that apply.)

- ☐ 1 - Memory deficit: failure to recognize familiar persons/places, inability to recall events of past 24 hours, significant memory loss so that supervision is required
- ☐ 2 - Impaired decision-making: failure to perform usual ADLs or IADLs, inability to appropriately stop activities, jeopardizes safety through actions
- ☐ 3 - Verbal disruption: yelling, threatening, excessive profanity, sexual references, etc.
- ☐ 4 - Physical aggression: aggressive or combative to self and others (e.g., hits self, throws objects, punches, dangerous maneuvers with wheelchair or other objects)
- ☐ 5 - Disruptive, infantile, or socially inappropriate behavior (excludes verbal actions)
- ☐ 6 - Delusional, hallucinatory, or paranoid behavior
- ☐ 7 - None of the above behaviors demonstrated

ADL/IADLs

(M0650) Ability to Dress Upper Body (with or without dressing aids) including undergarments, pullovers, front-opening shirts and blouses, managing zippers, buttons, and snaps:

Current
- ☐ 0 - Able to get clothes out of closets and drawers, put them on and remove them from the upper body without assistance.
- ☐ 1 - Able to dress upper body without assistance if clothing is laid out or handed to the patient.
- ☐ 2 - Someone must help the patient put on upper body clothing.
- ☐ 3 - Patient depends entirely upon another person to dress the upper body.

(M0660) Ability to Dress Lower Body (with or without dressing aids) including undergarments, slacks, socks or nylons, shoes:

Current
- ☐ 0 - Able to obtain, put on, and remove clothing and shoes without assistance.
- ☐ 1 - Able to dress lower body without assistance if clothing and shoes are laid out or handed to the patient.
- ☐ 2 - Someone must help the patient put on undergarments, slacks, socks or nylons, and shoes.
- ☐ 3 - Patient depends entirely upon another person to dress lower body.

(M0670) Bathing: Ability to wash entire body. Excludes grooming (washing face and hands only).

Current
- ☐ 0 - Able to bathe self in shower or tub independently.
- ☐ 1 - With the use of devices, is able to bathe self in shower or tub independently.
- ☐ 2 - Able to bathe in shower or tub with the assistance of another person:
  (a) for intermittent supervision or encouragement or reminders, OR
  (b) to get in and out of the shower or tub, OR
  (c) for washing difficult to reach areas.
- ☐ 3 - Participates in bathing self in shower or tub, but requires presence of another person throughout the bath for assistance or supervision.
- ☐ 4 - Unable to use the shower or tub and is bathed in bed or bedside chair.
- ☐ 5 - Unable to effectively participate in bathing and is totally bathed by another person.

6

(M0680)   Toileting: Ability to get to and from the toilet or bedside commode.

Current
- ☐   0   -   Able to get to and from the toilet independently with or without a device.
- ☐   1   -   When reminded, assisted, or supervised by another person, able to get to and from the toilet.
- ☐   2   -   <u>Unable</u> to get to and from the toilet but is able to use a bedside commode (with or without assistance).
- ☐   3   -   <u>Unable</u> to get to and from the toilet or bedside commode but is able to use a bedpan/urinal independently.
- ☐   4   -   Is totally dependent in toileting.

(M0690)   Transferring: Ability to move from bed to chair, on and off toilet or commode, into and out of tub or shower, and ability to turn and position self in bed if patient is bedfast.

Current
- ☐   0   -   Able to independently transfer.
- ☐   1   -   Transfers with minimal human assistance or with use of an assistive device.
- ☐   2   -   <u>Unable</u> to transfer self but is able to bear weight and pivot during the transfer process.
- ☐   3   -   Unable to transfer self and is <u>unable</u> to bear weight or pivot when transferred by another person.
- ☐   4   -   Bedfast, unable to transfer but is able to turn and position self in bed.
- ☐   5   -   Bedfast, unable to transfer and is <u>unable</u> to turn and position self.

(M0700)   Ambulation/Locomotion: Ability to <u>SAFELY</u> walk, once in a standing position, or use a wheelchair, once in a seated position, on a variety of surfaces.

Current
- ☐   0   -   Able to independently walk on even and uneven surfaces and climb stairs with or without railings (i.e., needs no human assistance or assistive device).
- ☐   1   -   Requires use of a device (e.g., cane, walker) to walk alone <u>or</u> requires human supervision or assistance to negotiate stairs or steps or uneven surfaces.
- ☐   2   -   Able to walk only with the supervision or assistance of another person at all times.
- ☐   3   -   Chairfast, <u>unable</u> to ambulate but is able to wheel self independently.
- ☐   4   -   Chairfast, unable to ambulate and is <u>unable</u> to wheel self.
- ☐   5   -   Bedfast, unable to ambulate or be up in a chair.

THERAPY NEED

(M0825)   Therapy Need: Does the care plan of the Medicare payment period for which this assessment will define a case mix group indicate a need for therapy (physical, occupational, or speech therapy) that meets the threshold for a Medicare high-therapy case mix group?

- ☐   0   -   No
- ☐   1   -   Yes
- ☐   NA   -   Not applicable

APPENDIX E

Outcome and Assessment Information Set (OASIS-B1)

DISCHARGE VERSION
(also used for Transfer to an Inpatient Facility or Patient Death at Home)

Items to be Used at Specific Time Points

Transfer to an Inpatient Facility   ----------------------------------- M0080-M0100, M0830-M0855, M0890-M0906

    Transferred to an inpatient facility—patient not discharged from an agency
    Transferred to an inpatient facility—patient discharged from agency

Discharge from Agency — Not to an Inpatient Facility

    Death at home --- M0080-M0100, M0906
    Discharge from agency-------------------------------------- M0080-M0100, M0200-M0220, M0250, M0280-M0380,
                                         M0410-M0820, M0830-M0880, M0903-M0906

CLINICAL RECORD ITEMS

(M0080)   Discipline of Person Completing Assessment:

        ☐ 1-RN   ☐ 2-PT   ☐ 3-SLP/ST   ☐ 4-OT

(M0090)   Date Assessment Completed   :   __ __ / __ __ / __ __ __ __
                                        month   day   year

(M0100)   This Assessment is Currently Being Completed for the Following Reason:

        Transfer to an Inpatient Facility
  ☐   6 –   Transferred to an inpatient facility—patient not discharged from agency [Go to M0830]
  ☐   7 –   Transferred to an inpatient facility—patient discharged from agency [Go to M0830]
        Discharge from Agency — Not to an Inpatient Facility
  ☐   8 –   Death at home [Go to M0906]
  ☐   9 –   Discharge from agency [Go to M0200]

DEMOGRAPHICS AND PATIENT HISTORY

(M0200)   Medical or Treatment Regimen Change Within Past 14 Days   : Has this patient experienced a change in
         medical or treatment regimen (e.g., medication, treatment, or service change due to new or additional
         diagnosis, etc.) within the last 14 days?

  ☐   0 -   No   [If No, go to M0250]
  ☐   1 -   Yes

(M0210)   List the patient's Medical Diagnoses and ICD-9-CM code categories (three digits required ; five digits
         optional) for those conditions requiring changed medical or treatment regimen (no surgical or V-codes):

    Changed Medical Regimen Diagnosis   ICD-9-CM
    a. _____   (__ __ __ . __ __)
    b. _____   (__ __ __ . __ __)

2

c. _____   (__ __ __ . __ __)

d. _____   (__ __ __ . __ __)

Effective 10/1/2003

List the patient's Medical Diagnoses and ICD-9-CM codes at the level of highest specificity for those conditions requiring changed medical or treatment regimen (no surgical, E-codes, or V-codes):

<u>Changed Medical Regimen Diagnosis</u>   <u>ICD-9-CM</u>

a. _____   (__ __ __ . __ __)

b. _____   (__ __ __ . __ __)

c. _____   (__ __ __ . __ __)

d. _____   (__ __ __ . __ __)

(M0220)   Conditions Prior to Medical or Treatment Regimen Change Within Past 14 Days   : If this patient experienced a change in medical or treatment regimen within the past 14 days, indicate any conditions which existed <u>prior to</u> the change in medical or treatment regimen. (Mark all that apply.)

☐   1 -   Urinary incontinence

☐   2 -   Indwelling/suprapubic catheter

☐   3 -   Intractable pain

☐   4 -   Impaired decision-making

☐   5 -   Disruptive or socially inappropriate behavior

☐   6 -   Memory loss to the extent that supervision required

☐   7 -   None of the above

(M0250)   Therapies the patient receives <u>at home</u> : (Mark all that apply.)

☐   1 -   Intravenous or infusion therapy (excludes TPN)

☐   2 -   Parenteral nutrition (TPN or lipids)

☐   3 -   Enteral nutrition (nasogastric, gastrostomy, jejunostomy, or any other artificial entry into the alimentary canal)

☐   4 -   None of the above

(M0280)   Life Expectancy: (Physician documentation is not required.)

☐   0 -   Life expectancy is greater than 6 months

☐   1 -   Life expectancy is 6 months or fewer

(M0290)   High Risk Factors   (Mark all that apply.)

☐   1 -   Heavy smoking

☐   2 -   Obesity

☐   3 -   Alcohol dependency

☐   4 -   Drug dependency

☐   5 -   None of the above

3

LIVING ARRANGEMENTS

(M0300)　Current Residence:

   ☐　1　-　Patient's owned or rented residence (house, apartment, or mobile home owned or rented by patient/couple/significant other)
   ☐　2　-　Family member's residence
   ☐　3　-　Boarding home or rented room
   ☐　4　-　Board and care or assisted living facility
   ☐　5　-　Other (specify) _____

(M0340)　Patient Lives With:　(Mark all that apply.)

   ☐　1　-　Lives alone
   ☐　2　-　With spouse or significant other
   ☐　3　-　With other family member
   ☐　4　-　With a friend
   ☐　5　-　With paid help (other than home care agency staff)
   ☐　6　-　With other than above

SUPPORTIVE ASSISTANCE

(M0350)　Assisting　Person(s) Other than Home Care Agency Staff:　　(Mark all that apply.)

   ☐　1　-　Relatives, friends, or neighbors living outside the home
   ☐　2　-　Person residing in the home (EXCLUDING paid help)
   ☐　3　-　Paid help
   ☐　4　-　None of the above　[If None of the above, go to M0410]

(M0360)　Primary Caregiver　taking <u>lead</u> responsibility for providing or managing the patient's care, providing the most frequent assistance, etc. (other than home care agency staff):

   ☐　0　-　No one person　[If No one person, go to　M0410]
   ☐　1　-　Spouse or significant other
   ☐　2　-　Daughter or son
   ☐　3　-　Other family member
   ☐　4　-　Friend or neighbor or community or church member
   ☐　5　-　Paid help

(M0370)　How Often　does the patient receive assistance from the primary caregiver?

   ☐　1　-　Several times during day and night
   ☐　2　-　Several times during day
   ☐　3　-　Once daily
   ☐　4　-　Three or more times per week
   ☐　5　-　One to two times per week
   ☐　6　-　Less often than weekly

(M0380)　Type of Primary Caregiver Assistance:　　(Mark all that apply.)

   ☐　1　-　ADL assistance (e.g., bathing, dressing, toileting, bowel/bladder, eating/feeding)
   ☐　2　-　IADL assistance (e.g., meds, meals, housekeeping, laundry, telephone, shopping, finances)
   ☐　3　-　Environmental support (housing, home maintenance)
   ☐　4　-　Psychosocial support (socialization, companionship, recreation)
   ☐　5　-　Advocates or facilitates patient's participation in appropriate medical care
   ☐　6　-　Financial agent, power of attorney, or conservator of finance
   ☐　7　-　Health care agent, conservator of person, or medical power of attorney

4

SENSORY STATUS

(M0410) Speech and Oral (Verbal) Expression of Language   (in patient's own language):

- ☐   0 - Expresses complex ideas, feelings, and needs clearly, completely, and easily in all situations with no observable impairment.
- ☐   1 - Minimal difficulty in expressing ideas and needs (may take extra time; makes occasional errors in word choice, grammar or speech intelligibility; needs minimal prompting or assistance).
- ☐   2 - Expresses simple ideas or needs with moderate difficulty (needs prompting or assistance, errors in word choice, organization or speech intelligibility). Speaks in phrases or short sentences.
- ☐   3 - Has severe difficulty expressing basic ideas or needs and requires maximal assistance or guessing by listener. Speech limited to single words or short phrases.
- ☐   4 - <u>Unable</u> to express basic needs even with maximal prompting or assistance but is not comatose or unresponsive (e.g., speech is nonsensical or unintelligible).
- ☐   5 - Patient nonresponsive or unable to speak.

(M0420) Frequency of Pain   interfering with patient's activity or movement:

- ☐   0 - Patient has no pain or pain does not interfere with activity or movement
- ☐   1 - Less often than daily
- ☐   2 - Daily, but not constantly
- ☐   3 - All of the time

(M0430) Intrac table Pain : Is the patient experiencing pain that is <u>not easily relieved</u>, occurs at least daily, and affects the patient's sleep, appetite, physical or emotional energy, concentration, personal relationships, emotions, or ability or desire to perform physical activity?

- ☐   0 - No
- ☐   1 - Yes

INTEGUMENTARY STATUS

(M0440) Does this patient have a Skin Lesion or an Open Wound? This excludes "OSTOMIES."

- ☐   0 - No [If No, go to M0490]
- ☐   1 - Yes

(M0445) Does this patient have a Pressure Ulcer?

- ☐   0 - No [If No, go to M0468]
- ☐   1 - Yes

5

(M0450)   Current Number of Pressure Ulcers at Each Stage: (Circle one response for each stage.)

	Pressure Ulcer Stages	Number of Pressure Ulcers				
a)	Stage 1: Nonblanchable erythema of intact skin; the heralding of skin ulceration. In darker-pigmented skin, warmth, edema, hardness, or discolored skin may be indicators.	0	1	2	3	4 or more
b)	Stage 2: Partial thickness skin loss involving epidermis and/or dermis. The ulcer is superficial and presents clinically as an abrasion, blister, or shallow crater.	0	1	2	3	4 or more
c)	Stage 3: Full-thickness skin loss involving damage or necrosis of subcutaneous tissue which may extend down to, but not through, underlying fascia. The ulcer presents clinically as a deep crater with or without undermining of adjacent tissue.	0	1	2	3	4 or more
d)	Stage 4: Full-thickness skin loss with extensive destruction, tissue necrosis, or damage to muscle, bone, or supporting structures (e.g., tendon, joint capsule, etc.)	0	1	2	3	4 or more
e)	In addition to the above, is there at least one pressure ulcer that cannot be observed due to the presence of eschar or a nonremovable dressing, including casts? ☐ 0 - No ☐ 1 - Yes					

(M0460)   Stage of Most Problematic (Observable) Pressure Ulcer:

    ☐ 1 -   Stage 1
    ☐ 2 -   Stage 2
    ☐ 3 -   Stage 3
    ☐ 4 -   Stage 4
    ☐ NA -   No observable pressure ulcer

(M0464)   Status of Most Problematic (Observable) Pressure Ulcer:

    ☐ 1 -   Fully granulating
    ☐ 2 -   Early/partial granulation
    ☐ 3 -   Not healing
    ☐ NA -   No observable pressure ulcer

(M0468)   Does this patient have a Stasis Ulcer ?

    ☐ 0 -   No [If No, go to M0482]
    ☐ 1 -   Yes

(M0470)   Current Number of Observable Stasis Ulcer(s):

    ☐ 0 -   Zero
    ☐ 1 -   One
    ☐ 2 -   Two
    ☐ 3 -   Three
    ☐ 4 -   Four or more

(M0474)   Does this patient have at least one Stasis Ulcer that Cannot be Observed   due to the presence of a nonremovable dressing?

    ☐ 0 -   No
    ☐ 1 -   Yes

6

(M0476)   Status of Most Problematic (Ob   servable) Stasis Ulcer:

☐   1   -   Fully granulating
☐   2   -   Early/partial granulation
☐   3   -   Not healing
☐   NA   -   No observable stasis ulcer

(M0482)   Does this patient have a Surgical Wound?

☐   0   -   No [If No, go to M0490]
☐   1   -   Yes

(M0484)   Current Number of (Observable) Surgical Wounds: <u>more</u>

☐   0   -   Zero
☐   1   -   One
☐   2   -   Two
☐   3   -   Three
☐   4   -   Four or more

(M0486)   Does this patient have at least one Surgical Wound that   Cannot be Observed   due to the presence of a nonremovable dressing?

☐   0   -   No
☐   1   -   Yes

(M0488)   Status of Most Problematic (Observable) Surgical Wound:

☐   1   -   Fully granulating
☐   2   -   Early/partial granulation
☐   3   -   Not healing
☐   NA   -   No observable surgical wound

RESPIRATORY STATUS

(M0490)   When is the patient dyspneic or noticeably Short of Breath?

☐   0   -   Never, patient is not short of breath
☐   1   -   When walking more than 20 feet, climbing stairs
☐   2   -   With moderate exertion (e.g., while dressing, using commode or bedpan, walking distances less than 20 feet)
☐   3   -   With minimal exertion (e.g., while eating, talking, or performing other ADLs) or with agitation
☐   4   -   At rest (during day or night)

(M0500)   Respiratory Treatments utilized at home: (Mark all that apply.)

☐   1   -   Oxygen (intermittent or continuous)
☐   2   -   Ventilator (continually or at night)
☐   3   -   Continuous positive airway pressure
☐   4   -   None of the above

7

ELIMINATION STATUS

(M0510) Has this patient been treated for a Urinary Tract Infection   in the past 14 days?

- ☐ 0 - No
- ☐ 1 - Yes
- ☐ NA - Patient on prophylactic treatment

(M0520) Urinary Incontinence or Urinary Catheter Presence:

- ☐ 0 - No incontinence or catheter (includes anuria or ostomy for urinary drainage) [If No, go to M0540]
- ☐ 1 - Patient is incontinent
- ☐ 2 - Patient requires a urinary catheter (i.e., external, indwelling, intermittent, suprapubic) [Go to M0540]

(M0530) When does Urinary Incontinence occur?

- ☐ 0 -
- ☐ 1 - During the night only
- ☐ 2 - During the day and night

(M0540) Bowel Incontinence Frequency:

- ☐ 0 - Very rarely or never has bowel incontinence
- ☐ 1 - Less than once weekly
- ☐ 2 - One to three times weekly
- ☐ 3 - Four to six times weekly
- ☐ 4 - On a daily basis
- ☐ 5 - More often than once daily
- ☐ NA - Patient has ostomy for bowel elimination

(M0550) Ostomy for Bowel Elimination: Does this patient have an ostomy for bowel elimination that (within the last 14 days) necessitated a change in medical or treatment regimen?

- ☐ 0 - Patient does not have an ostomy for bowel elimination.
- ☐ 1 - Patient's ostomy did not necessitate change in medical or treatment regimen.
- ☐ 2 - The ostomy did necessitate change in medical or treatment regimen.

NEURO/EMOTIONAL/BEHAVIORAL STATUS

(M0560) Cognitive Functioning: (Patient's current level of alertness, orientation, comprehension, concentration, and immediate memory for simple commands.)

- ☐ 0 - Alert/oriented, able to focus and shift attention, comprehends and recalls task directions independently.
- ☐ 1 - Requires prompting (cuing, repetition, reminders) only under stressful or unfamiliar conditions.
- ☐ 2 - Requires assistance and some direction in specific situations (e.g., on all tasks involving shifting of attention), or consistently requires low stimulus environment due to distractibility.
- ☐ 3 - Requires considerable assistance in routine situations. Is not alert and oriented or is unable to shift attention and recall directions more than half the time.
- ☐ 4 - Totally dependent due to disturbances such as constant disorientation, coma, persistent vegetative state, or delirium.

8

(M0570)   When Confused (Reported or Observed):

☐   0   -   Never
☐   1   -   In new or complex situations only
☐   2   -   On awakening or at night only
☐   3   -   During the day and evening, but not constantly
☐   4   -   Constantly
☐   NA -   Patient nonresponsive

(M0580)   When Anxious (Reported or Observed):

☐   0   -   None of the time
☐   1   -   Less often than daily
☐   2   -   Daily, but not constantly
☐   3   -   All of the time
☐   NA -   Patient nonresponsive

(M0590)   Depressive Feelings Reported or Observed in Patient: (Mark all that apply.)

☐   1   -   Depressed mood (e.g., feeling sad, tearful)
☐   2   -   Sense of failure or self reproach
☐   3   -   Hopelessness
☐   4   -   Recurrent thoughts of death
☐   5   -   Thoughts of suicide
☐   6   -   None of the above feelings observed or reported

(M0610)   Behaviors Demonstrated at Least Once a Week (Reported or Observed):   (Mark all that apply.)

☐   1   -   Memory deficit: failure to recognize familiar persons/places, inability to recall events of past 24 hours, significant memory loss so that supervision is required
☐   2   -   Impaired decision-making: failure to perform usual ADLs or IADLs, inability to appropriately stop activities, jeopardizes safety through actions
☐   3   -   Verbal disruption: yelling, threatening, excessive profanity, sexual references, etc.
☐   4   -   Physical aggression: aggressive or combative to self and others (e.g., hits self, throws objects, punches, dangerous maneuvers with wheelchair or other objects)
☐   5   -   Disruptive, infantile, or socially inappropriate behavior (excludes verbal actions)
☐   6   -   Delusional, hallucinatory, or paranoid behavior
☐   7   -   None of the above behaviors demonstrated

(M0620)   Frequency of Behavior Problems (Reported or Observed)   (e.g., wandering episodes, self abuse, verbal disruption, physical aggression, etc.):

☐   0   -   Never
☐   1   -   Less than once a month
☐   2   -   Once a month
☐   3   -   Several times each month
☐   4   -   Several times a week
☐   5   -   At least daily

(M0630)   Is this patient receiving Psychiatric Nursing Services at home provided by a qualified psychiatric nurse?

☐   0   -   No
☐   1   -   Yes

9

ADL/IADLs

(M0640)　Grooming: Ability to tend to personal hygiene needs (i.e., washing face and hands, hair care, shaving or make up, teeth or denture care, fingernail care).

Current

- ☐　0　-　Able to groom self unaided, with or without the use of assistive devices or adapted methods.
- ☐　1　-　Grooming utensils must be placed within reach before able to complete grooming activities.
- ☐　2　-　Someone must assist the patient to groom self.
- ☐　3　-　Patient depends entirely upon someone else for grooming needs.

(M0650)　Ability to Dress <u>Upper</u> Body (with or without dressing aids) including undergarments, pullovers, front-opening shirts and blouses, managing zippers, buttons, and snaps:

Current

- ☐　0　-　Able to get clothes out of closets and drawers, put them on and remove them from the upper body without assistance.
- ☐　1　-　Able to dress upper body without assistance if clothing is laid out or handed to the patient.
- ☐　2　-　Someone must help the patient put on upper body clothing.
- ☐　3　-　Patient depends entirely upon another person to dress the upper body.

(M0660)　Ability to Dress <u>Lower</u> Body (with or without dressing aids) including undergarments, slacks, socks or nylons, shoes:

Current

- ☐　0　-　Able to obtain, put on, and remove clothing and shoes without assistance.
- ☐　1　-　Able to dress lower body without assistance if clothing and shoes are laid out or handed to the patient.
- ☐　2　-　Someone must help the patient put on undergarments, slacks, socks or nylons, and shoes.
- ☐　3　-　Patient depends entirely upon another person to dress lower body.

(M0670)　Bathing: Ability to wash entire body. <u>Excludes </u>grooming (washing face and hands only).

Current

- ☐　0　-　Able to bathe self in <u>shower or tub</u> independently.
- ☐　1　-　With the use of devices, is able to bathe self in shower or tub independently.
- ☐　2　-　Able to bathe in shower or tub with the assistance of another person:
  (a) for intermittent supervision or encouragement or reminders, <u>OR</u>
  (b) to get in and out of the shower or tub, <u>OR</u>
  (c) for washing difficult to reach areas.
- ☐　3　-　Participates in bathing self in shower or tub, <u>but</u> requires presence of another person throughout the bath for assistance or supervision.
- ☐　4　-　<u>Unable</u> to use the shower or tub and is bathed in <u>bed or bedside chair</u>.
- ☐　5　-　Unable to effectively participate in bathing and is totally bathed by another person.

(M0680)　Toileting: Ability to get to and from the toilet or bedside commode.

Current

- ☐　0　-　Able to get to and from the toilet independently with or without a device.
- ☐　1　-　When reminded, assisted, or supervised by another person, able to get to and from the toilet.
- ☐　2　-　<u>Unable</u> to get to and from the toilet but is able to use a bedside commode (with or without assistance).
- ☐　3　-　<u>Unable</u> to get to and from the toilet or bedside commode but is able to use a bedpan/urinal independently.
- ☐　4　-　Is totally dependent in toileting.

10

(M0690) Transferring: Ability to move from bed to chair, on and off toilet or commode, into and out of tub or shower, and ability to turn and position self in bed if patient is bedfast.

Current
☐   0 -   Able to independently transfer.
☐   1 -   Transfers with minimal human assistance or with use of an assistive device.
☐   2 -   Unable to transfer self but is able to bear weight and pivot during the transfer process.
☐   3 -   Unable to transfer self and is unable to bear weight or pivot when transferred by another person.
☐   4 -   Bedfast, unable to transfer but is able to turn and position self in bed.
☐   5 -   Bedfast, unable to transfer and is unable to turn and position self.

(M0700) Ambulation/Locomotion: Ability to   SAFELY walk, once in a standing position, or use a wheelchair, once in a seated position, on a variety of surfaces.

Current
☐   0 -   Able to independently walk on even and uneven surfaces and climb stairs with or without railings (i.e., needs no human assistance or assistive device).
☐   1 -   Requires use of a device (e.g., cane, walker) to walk alone or requires human supervision or assistance to negotiate stairs or steps or uneven surfaces.
☐   2 -   Able to walk only with the supervision or assistance of another person at all times.
☐   3 -   Chairfast, unable to ambulate but is able to wheel self independently.
☐   4 -   Chairfast, unable to ambulate and is unable to wheel self.
☐   5 -   Bedfast, unable to ambulate or be up in a chair.

(M0710) Feeding or Eating: Ability to feed self meals and snacks.   Note: This refers only to the process of eating , chewing , and swallowing , not preparing the food to be eaten.

Current
☐   0 -   Able to independently feed self.
☐   1 -   Able to feed self independently but requires:
          (a) meal set-up; OR
          (b) intermittent assistance or supervision from another person; OR
          (c)
☐   2 -   Unable to feed self and must be assisted or supervised throughout the meal/snack.
☐   3 -   Able to take in nutrients orally and receives supplemental nutrients through a nasogastric tube or gastrostomy.
☐   4 -   Unable to take in nutrients orally and is fed nutrients through a nasogastric tube or gastrostomy.
☐   5 -   Unable to take in nutrients orally or by tube feeding.

(M0720) Planning and Preparing Light Meals (e.g., cereal, sandwich) or reheat delivered meals:

Current
☐   0 -   (a) Able to independently plan and prepare all light meals for self or reheat delivered meals; OR
          (b) Is physically, cognitively, and mentally able to prepare light meals on a regular basis but has not routinely performed light meal preparation in the past (i.e., prior to this home care admission).
☐   1 -   Unable to prepare light meals on a regular basis due to physical, cognitive, or mental limitations.
☐   2 -   Unable to prepare any light meals or reheat any delivered meals.

11

(M0730) Transportation: Physical and mental ability to <u>safely</u> use a car, taxi, or public transportation (bus, train, subway).

Current
- ☐ 0 - Able to independently drive a regular or adapted car; <u>OR</u> uses a regular or handicap-accessible public bus.
- ☐ 1 - Able to ride in a car only when driven by another person; <u>OR</u> able to use a bus or handicap van only when assisted or accompanied by another person.
- ☐ 2 - <u>Unable</u> to ride in a car, taxi, bus, or van, and requires transportation by ambulance.

(M0740) Laundry: Ability to do own laundry -- to carry laundry to and from washing machine, to use washer and dryer, to wash small items by hand.

Current
- ☐ 0 - (a) Able to independently take care of all laundry tasks; <u>OR</u>
           (b) Physically, cognitively, and mentally able to do laundry and access facilities, <u>but</u> has not routinely performed laundry tasks in the past (i.e., prior to this home care admission).
- ☐ 1 - Able to do only light laundry, such as minor hand wash or light washer loads. Due to physical, cognitive, or mental limitations, needs assistance with heavy laundry such as carrying large loads of laundry.
- ☐ 2 - <u>Unable</u> to do any laundry due to physical limitation or needs continual supervision and assistance due to cognitive or mental limitation.

(M0750) Housekeeping: Ability to safely and effectively perform light housekeeping and heavier cleaning tasks.

Current
- ☐ 0 - (a) Able to independently perform all housekeeping tasks; <u>OR</u>
           (b) Physically, cognitively, and mentally able to perform <u>all</u> housekeeping tasks but has not routinely participated in housekeeping tasks in the past (i.e., prior to this home care admission).
- ☐ 1 - Able to perform only <u>light</u> housekeeping (e.g., dusting, wiping kitchen counters) tasks independently.
- ☐ 2 - Able to perform housekeeping tasks with intermittent assistance or supervision from another person.
- ☐ 3 - <u>Unable</u> to consistently perform any housekeeping tasks unless assisted by another person throughout the process.
- ☐ 4 - Unable to effectively participate in any housekeeping tasks.

(M0760) Shopping: Ability to plan for, select, and purchase items in a store and to carry them home or arrange delivery.

Current
- ☐ 0 - (a) Able to plan for shopping needs and independently perform shopping tasks, including carrying packages; <u>OR</u>
           (b) Physically, cognitively, and mentally able to take care of shopping, but has not done shopping in the past (i.e., prior to this home care admission).
- ☐ 1 - Able to go shopping, but needs some assistance:
           (a) By self is able to do only light shopping and carry small packages, but needs someone to do occasional major shopping; <u>OR</u>
           (b) <u>Unable</u> to go shopping alone, but can go with someone to assist.
- ☐ 2 - <u>Unable</u> to go shopping, but is able to identify items needed, place orders, and arrange home delivery.
- ☐ 3 - Needs someone to do all shopping and errands.

12

(M0770) Ability to Use Telephone : Ability to answer the phone, dial numbers, and <u>effectively</u> use the telephone to communicate.

<u>Current</u>
- ☐ 0 - Able to dial numbers and answer calls appropriately and as desired.
- ☐ 1 - Able to use a specially adapted telephone (i.e., large numbers on the dial, teletype phone for the deaf) and call essential numbers.
- ☐ 2 - Able to answer the telephone and carry on a normal conversation but has difficulty with placing calls.
- ☐ 3 - Able to answer the telephone only some of the time or is able to carry on only a limited conversation.
- ☐ 4 - <u>Unable</u> to answer the telephone at all but can listen if assisted with equipment.
- ☐ 5 - Totally unable to use the telephone.
- ☐ NA - Patient does not have a telephone.

MEDICATIONS

(M0780) Management of Oral Medications : <u>Patient's ability</u> to prepare and take <u>all</u> prescribed oral medications reliably and safely, including administration of the correct dosage at the appropriate times/intervals. <u>Excludes</u> injectable and IV medications. (NOTE: This refers to ability, not compliance or willingness.)

<u>Current</u>
- ☐ 0 - Able to independently take the correct oral medication(s) and proper dosage(s) at the correct times.
- ☐ 1 - Able to take medication(s) at the correct times if:
  (a) individual dosages are prepared in advance by another person; <u>OR</u>
  (b) given daily reminders; <u>OR</u>
  (c) someone develops a drug diary or chart.
- ☐ 2 - <u>Unable</u> to take medication unless administered by someone else.
- ☐ NA - No oral medications prescribed.

(M0790) Management of Inhalant/Mist Medications : <u>Patient's ability</u> to prepare and take <u>all</u> prescribed inhalant/mist medications (nebulizers, metered dose devices) reliably and safely, including administration of the correct dosage at the appropriate times/intervals. <u>Excludes</u> all other forms of medication (oral tablets, injectable and IV medications).

<u>Current</u>
- ☐ 0 - Able to independently take the correct medication and proper dosage at the correct times.
- ☐ 1 - Able to take medication at the correct times if:
  (a) individual dosages are prepared in advance by another person, <u>OR</u>
  (b) given daily reminders.
- ☐ 2 - <u>Unable</u> to take medication unless administered by someone else.
- ☐ NA - No inhalant/mist medications prescribed.

(M0800) Management of Injectable Medications : <u>Patient's ability</u> to prepare and take <u>all</u> prescribed injectable medications reliably and safely, including administration of correct dosage at the appropriate times/intervals. <u>Excludes</u> IV medications.

<u>Current</u>
- ☐ 0 - Able to independently take the correct medication and proper dosage at the correct times.
- ☐ 1 - Able to take injectable medication at correct times if:
  (a) individual syringes are prepared in advance by another person, <u>OR</u>
  (b) given daily reminders.
- ☐ 2 - <u>Unable</u> to take injectable medications unless administered by someone else.
- ☐ NA - No injectable medications prescribed.

13

EQUIPMENT MANAGEMENT

(M0810) Patient Management of Equipment (includes ONLY___ oxygen, IV/infusion therapy,   enteral/ parenteral nutrition equipment or supplies):   Patient's ability to set up, monitor and change equipment reliably and safely, add appropriate fluids or medication, clean/store/dispose of equipment or supplies using proper technique. (NOTE: This refers to ability, not compliance or willingness.)

☐　0　-　Patient manages all tasks related to equipment completely independently.

☐　1　-　If someone else sets up equipment (i.e., fills portable oxygen tank, provides patient with prepared solutions), patient is able to manage all other aspects of equipment.

☐　2　-　Patient requires considerable assistance from another person to manage equipment, but independently completes portions of the task.

☐　3　-　Patient is only able to monitor equipment (e.g., liter flow, fluid in bag) and must call someone else to manage the equipment.

☐　4　-　Patient is completely dependent on someone else to manage all equipment.

☐　NA　-　No equipment of this type used in care [If NA, go to M0830]

(M0820) Caregiver Management of Equipment (includes   ONLY oxygen, IV/infusion equipment, enteral/ parenteral nutrition, ventilator therapy equipment or supplies)   : Caregiver's ability to set up,

clean/store/dispose of equipment or supplies using proper technique. (NOTE: This refers to ability, not compliance or willingness.)

☐　0　-　Caregiver manages all tasks related to equipment completely independently.

☐　1　-　If someone else sets up equipment, caregiver is able to manage all other aspects.

☐　2　-　Caregiver requires considerable assistance from another person to manage equipment, but independently completes significant portions of task.

☐　3　-　Caregiver is only able to complete small portions of task (e.g., administer nebulizer treatment, clean/store/dispose of equipment or supplies).

☐　4　-　Caregiver is completely dependent on someone else to manage all equipment.

☐　NA　-　No caregiver

EMERGENT CARE

(M0830) Emergent Care: Since the last time OASIS data were collected, has the patient utilized any of the following services for emergent care (other than home care agency services)? (Mark all that apply.)

☐　0　-　No emergent care services [If no emergent care, go to M0855]

☐　1　-　Hospital emergency room (includes 23-hour holding)

☐　2　-　Doctor's office emergency visit/house call

☐　3　-　Outpatient department/clinic emergency (includes urgicenter sites)

☐　UK　-　Unknown [If UK, go to M0855]

14

(M0840) Emergent Care Reason: For what reason(s) did the patient/family seek emergent care? (Mark all that apply.)

- ☐ 1 - Improper medication administration, medication side effects, toxicity, anaphylaxis
- ☐ 2 - Nausea, dehydration, malnutrition, constipation, impaction
- ☐ 3 - Injury caused by fall or accident at home
- ☐ 4 - Respiratory problems (e.g., shortness of breath, respiratory infection, tracheobronchial obstruction)
- ☐ 5 - Wound infection, deteriorating wound status, new lesion/ulcer
- ☐ 6 - Cardiac problems (e.g., fluid overload, exacerbation of CHF, chest pain)
- ☐ 7 - Hypo/Hyperglycemia, diabetes out of control
- ☐ 8 - GI bleeding, obstruction
- ☐ 9 - Other than above reasons
- ☐ UK - Reason unknown

DATA ITEMS COLLECTED AT INPATIENT FACILITY ADMISSION OR AGENCY DISCHARGE ONLY

(M0855) To which Inpatient Facility has the patient been admitted?

- ☐ 1 - Hospital [Go to M0890]
- ☐ 2 - Rehabilitation facility [Go to M0903]
- ☐ 3 - Nursing home [Go to M0900]
- ☐ 4 - Hospice [Go to M0903]
- ☐ NA - No inpatient facility admission

(M0870) Discharge Disposition : Where is the patient after discharge from your agency? (Choose only one answer.)

- ☐ 1 - Patient remained in the community (not in hospital, nursing home, or rehab facility)
- ☐ 2 - Patient transferred to a noninstitutional hospice [Go to M0903]
- ☐ 3 - Unknown because patient moved to a geographic location not served by this agency [Go to M0903]
- ☐ UK - Other unknown [Go to M0903]

(M0880) After discharge, does the patient receive health, personal, or support Services or Assistance? (Mark all that apply.)

- ☐ 1 - No assistance or services received
- ☐ 2 - Yes, assistance or services provided by family or friends
- ☐ 3 - Yes, assistance or services provided by other community resources (e.g., meals-on-wheels, home health services, homemaker assistance, transportation assistance, assisted living, board and care)

> Go to M0903

(M0890) If the patient was admitted to an acute care Hospital , for what Reason was he/she admitted?

- ☐ 1 - Hospitalization for <u>emergent</u> (unscheduled) care
- ☐ 2 - Hospitalization for <u>urgent</u> (scheduled within 24 hours of admission) care
- ☐ 3 - Hospitalization for <u>elective</u> (scheduled more than 24 hours before admission) care
- ☐ UK - Unknown

15

(M0895) Reason fo r Hospitalization: (Mark all that apply.)

    ☐   1 -   Improper medication administration, medication side effects, toxicity, anaphylaxis
    ☐   2 -   Injury caused by fall or accident at home
    ☐   3 -   Respiratory problems (SOB, infection, obstruction)
    ☐   4 -   Wound or tube site infection, deteriorating wound status, new lesion/ulcer
    ☐   5 -   Hypo/Hyperglycemia, diabetes out of control
    ☐   6 -   GI bleeding, obstruction
    ☐   7 -   Exacerbation of CHF, fluid overload, heart failure
    ☐   8 -   Myocardial infarction, stroke
    ☐   9 -   Chemotherapy
    ☐ 10 -   Scheduled surgical procedure
    ☐ 11 -   Urinary tract infection
    ☐ 12 -   IV catheter-related infection
    ☐ 13 -   Deep vein thrombosis, pulmonary embolus
    ☐ 14 -   Uncontrolled pain
    ☐ 15 -   Psychotic episode
    ☐ 16 -   Other than above reasons

       | Go to M0903 |

(M0900) For what Reason(s) was the patient Admitted to a Nursing Home ? (Mark all that apply.)

    ☐   1 -   Therapy services
    ☐   2 -   Respite care
    ☐   3 -   Hospice care
    ☐   4 -   Permanent placement
    ☐   5 -   Unsafe for care at home
    ☐   6 -   Other
    ☐ UK -   Unknown

(M0903) Date of Last (Most Recent) Home Visit:

      __ __ / __ __ / __ __ __ __
      month day   year

(M0906) Discharge/Transfer/Death Date : Enter the date of the discharge, transfer, or death (at home) of the patient.

      __ __ / __ __ / __ __ __ __
      month day   year

APPENDIX F

PRIVACY ACT STATEMENT - HEALTH CARE RECORDS

THIS STATEMENT GIVES YOU ADVICE REQUIRED BY LAW (the Privacy Act of 1974).
THIS STATEMENT IS NOT A CONSENT FORM. IT WILL NOT BE USED TO RELEASE OR TO USE YOUR HEALTH CARE INFORMATION.

I. AUTHORITY FOR COLLECTION OF YOUR INFORMATION, INCLUDING YOUR SOCIAL SECURITY NUMBER, AND WHETHER OR NOT YOU ARE REQUIRED TO PROVIDE INFORMATION FOR THIS ASSESSMENT. Sections 1102(a), 1154, 1861(o), 1861(z), 1863, 1864, 1865, 1866, 1871, 1891(b) of the Social Security Act.

Medicare and Medicaid participating home health agencies must do a complete assessment that accurately reflects your current health and includes information that can be used to show your progress toward your health goals. The home health agency must use the "Outcome and Assessment Information Set" (OASIS) when evaluating your health. To do this- the agency must get information form every patient. This information is used by the Center for Medicare and Medicaid Service (CMS, the federal Medicare and Medicaid Agency) to be sure the home health agency meets quality standards and gives appropriate health care to it's patients. You have the right to refuse to provide information for the assessment to the home health agency. If your information is included in an assessment, it is protected under the federal Privacy Act of 1974 and the "Home Health Agency Outcome and Assessment Information Set" (HHA OASIS) System of Records. You have the right to see, copy, review, and request correction of your information in the HHA OASIS System of Records.

II. PRINCIPAL PURPOSES FOR WHICH YOUR INFORMATION IS INTENDED TO BE USED

The information collected will be entered into the Home Health Agency Outcome and Assessment Information Set (HHA OASIS) System No. 09-70-9002. Your health care information in the HHA OASIS System of Records will be used for the following purposes:

- support litigation involving the Centers for Medicare & Medicaid Services;
- support regulatory, reimbursement, and policy functions performed within the Centers for Medicare & Medicaid Services or by a contractor or consultant;
- study the effectiveness and quality of care provided by those home health agencies;
- survey and certification of Medicare and Medicaid home health agencies;
- provide for development, validation, and refinement of a Medicare prospective payment system;
- enable regulators to provide home health agencies with data for their internal quality improvement activities;
- support research, evaluation, or epidemiological projects related to the prevention of disease or disability, or the restoration or maintenance of health,
- and for health care payment related projects; and A support constituent requests made to a Congressional representative.

III. ROUTINE USES

These " routine uses " specify the circumstances when the Centers for Medicare & Medicaid Services may release your information from the HHA OASIS System of Records without your consent. Each prospective recipient must agree in writing to ensure the continuing confidentiality and security of your information.
Disclosures of the information may be to:

1. The federal Department of Justice for litigation involving the Center for Medicare and Medicaid Services;
2. contractors or consultants working for the Centers for Medicare & Medicaid Services to assist in the performance of a service related to this system of records and who need to access these records to perform the activity;
3. an agency of a State government for purposes of determining, evaluating, and/or assessing cost, effectiveness, and/or quality of health care services provided in the State; for developing and operating Medicaid reimbursement systems; or for the administration of Federal/State home health agency programs within the State;
4. another Federal or State agency to contribute to the accuracy of the Centers for Medicare & Medicaid Services' health insurance operations (payment, treatment and coverage) and/or to support State agencies in the evaluations and monitoring of care provided by HHAs;
5. Quality improvement organizations, to perform Title XI or Title XVIII functions relating to assessing and improving home health agency quality of care;
6. an individual or organization for a research, evaluation, or epidemiological project related to the prevention of disease or disability, the restoration or maintenance of health, or payment related projects;
7. a congressional office in response to a constituent inquiry made at the written request of the constituent about whom the record is maintained.

IV. EFFECT ON YOU, IF YOU DO NOT PROVIDE INFORMATION

The home health agency needs the information contained in the Outcome and Assessment Information Set in order to give you quality care. It is important that the information be correct. Incorrect information could result in payment errors. Incorrect information also could make it hard to be sure that the agency is giving you quality services. If you choose not to provide information, there is no federal requirement for the home health agency to refuse you services.

> **NOTE:** This statement may be included in the admission packet for all new home health agency admissions. Home health agencies may **request** you or your representative to sign this statement to document that this statement was given to you. **Your signature is NOT required.** If you or your representative sign the statement, the signature merely indicates that you received this statement. You or your representative must be supplied with a copy of this statement.

CONTACT INFORMATION

If you want to ask the Center for Medicare and Medicaid Services to see, review, copy, or correct your personal health information that the Federal agency maintains in its HHA OASIS System of Records: Call 1-800-MEDICARE, toll free, for assistance in contacting the HHA OASIS System Manager. TTY for the hearing and speech impaired: 1-877-486-2048.

APPENDIX G

Rights and Responsibilities for Medical Supplies
And Rehabilitative Services

Patient Name:_____   ___ID#_____

Dear Patient:

Effective October 1, 2000, Medicare regulations require that all billable medical supplies and rehabilitative services (physical therapy, occupational therapy, and speech therapy) be provided as part of your Medicare home health benefit while you are receiving home health services from our agency.

If you are using medical supplies other than those provided by our staff, please discuss with your nurse or therapist how you can obtain supplies through our agency while you are a patient of My Town Visiting Nurse Association. IF you choose to obtain those supplies from your own vender; you may be responsible to pay for them. Diabetic and incontinence supplies are examples of exceptions to this change and remain the responsibility of the patient.

If you are receiving rehabilitative services in an outpatient center, please inform your nurse or therapist so that arrangements can be made for you to receive your therapy from our agency if at all possible.

I understand my rights and responsibilities regarding medical supplies and rehabilitative services.

_____   _____
Patient Signature   Date

_____   _____
Clinician Signature/Credentials   Date

GLOSSARY

Adverse Event Outcome Report: A computer-generated report derived from the analysis of an agency's OASIS data. The report provides the agency with its incidence for each of the 13 adverse event outcomes. This report also provides a comparison of the agency's incidence rate to the incidence rate of the reference group.

benchmarking: The process by which the performance of one agency is compared to all others that have contributed data during the same time period. Agencies use the process of benchmarking to establish realistic goals for performance improvement activities.

Case Mix Report: Provides the agency with a summary of OASIS data for all patients who appear on the agency's End Result Outcome Report.

Center for Medicare and Medicaid Services (CMS): (Formerly known, as the HCFA) A part of the Federal Department of Health and Human Services. CMS is responsible for regulating and administering the Medicare benefit.

Conditions of Participation: The Federal guidelines that provide healthcare providers with a detailed and extensive explanation of the minimum requirements to obtain and maintain Medicare certification.

End Result Outcome Report: Provides the agency with an aggregate level summary that details the agency's performance on each of the 41 patient outcomes measured. This report is the result of analysis of the agency's OASIS data by the Center for Medicare and Medicaid Services.

End Result Outcomes: Measure the change in a patient's clinical and functional status between two points in time. The change in the patient's status can be positive (improved), negative (declined), or null (unchanged).

Episode of care: A 60-day period, all episodes are discrete and cannot overlap in any way.

Level of significance: A statistical value which identifies the probability the difference between an agency's performance and national reference is due to chance.

Low Utilization Payment Adjustment (LUPA): An adjustment to the Medicare PPS episode payment that is applied when a home health beneficiary receives less than 5 home visits.

negative outcomes: Achieved when the patient declines from a more functional to a less functional status.

null outcomes: Occur when the patient's status neither improves or declines. The patient's condition remains stable when compared at two points in time.

Partial Episode Payment (PEP): A proportional adjustment to the Medicare PPS episode payment that is applied when the patient does not complete an episode of care as a result of a transfer to another agency.

positive outcomes: Achieved when the patient improves from a less functional to a more functional status.

Prospective payment system (PPS): The Medicare home healthcare reimbursement system whereby CMS provides the agency with an episodic payment which is based on the patient's OASIS assessment.

Risk adjustment: A statistical application that minimizes the influence of patient related factors such as age, or functional ability that might adversely impact the agency's outcomes.

Significant change in condition (SCIC): An adjustment to the Medicare PPS episode payment that is applied when the patient experiences an unanticipated change in their status which results in a change in the agency's physician ordered plan of treatment.

BIBLIOGRAPHY

3M National Expert Design Project. (2000). [Available online: http://www.fazzi.com]. Accessed October 15, 2002.

American Association of Respiratory Care. (2003). *What is a respiratory therapist?* [Available online: http://www.aarc.org/patient-education/]. Accessed October 13, 2002.

American Association of Speech-Language-Hearing Association. (1997-2002). *Swallowing problems in adults.* [Available online: http://www.asha.org/speech/swallowing/]. Accessed October 13, 2002.

American Nurses' Association. (1985). *Code for nurses with interpretive statements.* Kansas City, MO: Author.

American Nurses' Association. (1986). *Standards of home health nursing practice.* Kansas City, MO: Author.

American Nurses' Association. (1999). *Scope and standards of home health nursing practice.* Washington, DC: Author.

American Nurses' Association. (2001). *Code of ethics for nurses with interpretive statements.* Washington, DC: Author.

American Occupational Therapy Association. (1999-2003). *Consumer information.* [Available online: http://www.aota.org/featured/area6/index.asp]. Accessed October 13, 2002.

American Red Cross Nursing. (2000). [Available online: http://www.redcross.org/services/nursing/history]. Accessed July 28, 2002.

Association for Computing Machinery (ACM) *Code of ethics and professional conduct.* (1997). [Available online: http://www.acm.org/constitution/code.html]. Accessed August 18, 2002.

Basic statistics about home care 2001. (2001). [Available online: http://www.nahc.org/Consumers/hestats.html]. Accessed September 19, 2003.

Benchmark of the Week #38. (2002). Home health line, XXVIII (13).

Benchmark of the Week #75. (2003). Home health line, XXVIII (3).

Cardoza, C., President and CEO, Visiting Nurse Association of Southeastern Massachusetts, Inc. (November 18, 2002.) Personal communication.

CMS form 485. (1994). [Available online: http://cms.hhs.gov/forms/cms485.pdf]. Accessed February 9, 2003.

Dietetics and nutrition. (2002). [Available online: http://www.pilotyourcareer.com]. Accessed October 13, 2002.

Doty, P. (1919). A retrospective of the influenza epidemic. *The Public Health Nurse, 11*(12), 949-957.

Guccione, A. (1999). What is a physical therapist? *PT Magazine, October 1999.* [Available online: http://internet.apta.org/pt-magazine/oct99/closer.html]. Accessed October 13, 2002.

Health Care Financing Administration, Department of Health and Human Services. (1999). *Conditions of participation.* [Available online: http://www.access.gpo.gov/nara/cfr/waisidx_99/42cfr484_99.html]. Accessed January 15, 2003.

Health insurance is a family matter. (2002). [Available online: http://www4.national academies.org/news.nsf/isbn/009085187]. Accessed September 28, 2002.

Helping and healing people. (2002). [Available online: http://www.metlife.com/Applications/Corporate/html]. Accessed July 28, 2002.

History of nursing. (1996). [Available online: http://www.virtualnurse.com/nana/Historyof Nursing.html]. Accessed July 24, 2002.

Home health agency manual, chapter II coverage of services. (2002). [Available online: http://cms.hhs.gov/manuals/11_hha/hh200.asp]. Accessed February 9, 2002.

Home health agencies PPS. (2002). Update. *Federal Register, 67*(125), 43616-43629

Humphrey, C. (November 18, 2002.) Personal communication.

Joint Commisssion on Accreditation of Health Care Organizations (JCAHO). (2001). *Comprehensive accreditation manual for home care, 2001-2002.* Oakbrook Terrace, IL: Author.

Medicare home health care: Payments to home health agencies are considerably higher than costs. (May, 2002). (Government Accounting Office, GAO-02-663). Washington, DC: U.S. Government Printing Office.

Medical social worker. (2002). *What kind of training is required?* [Available online: http://www-med.stanford.edu/school/smysp/nojava/explore/careers/career32.html]. Accessed November 9, 2002.

Medicare Payment Advisory Commission (Medpac). *A Data Book: Healthcare Spending and the Medicare Program,* June 2003. [Available online: http://www.medpac.gov/publications/congressional_reports/Jun03Data BookSec5.pdf]. Accessed September, 2003.

Nurses' learning network. (2001). *Scope of chemical dependency in nursing.* [Available online: http://www.nurseslearning.com/syllabus]. Accessed September 3, 2002.

Office of Inspector General. List by exclusion type. [Available online: http://eclusions.oig.hhs.gov/bystype2.html]. Accessed January 22, 2003.

On reforming Medicare home health benefit: Hearing before the subcommittee on health and environment. (March 5, 1997). [Available online: http://www.hcfa.gov/testimony/1997/homeh.htm]. Accessed July 28, 2002.

Outcome assessment information set user's manual. (1999). *Implementing OASIS at a home health agency to improve patient outcomes.* Washington, DC: U.S. Government Printing Office.

Personal health care expenditures, by funds: Calendar years 1994-2001. (2001). [Available online: http://cms.hhs.gov/statistics/nhe/historical/t9.asp]. Accessed September 19, 2003.

Profiles in caring: Lillian D. Wald. (1996-2003). [Available online: http://www.nahc.org/NAHC/Val/Columns.html]. Accessed July 28, 2002.

Prospective payment system for home health agencies; Final rule. (July 3, 2000). *Federal Register,* 41128-41214.

Reichley, M. (1999). Advances in home care: Then, now and into the future. *Success in Home Care, 3*(6), 10, 12-18.

The American Experience: Influenza 1918. (1997-2002). [Available on-line: http://www.pbs.org/wgbh/amex/influenza/tguide/index/html]. Accessed August, 2002.

The American heritage dictionary of the English language, (4th ed.). (2000). Boston: Houghton Mifflin Company

The Boston dispensary. (1955). [Available on-line: http://www.simmons.edu/libraries/archives.htm]. Accessed August 26, 2002.

The Florence Nightingale story. (1999). [Available on-line: http://www.florence-nightingale.co.uk/flo2.htm]. Accessed July 27, 2003.

The Nightingale pledge. (2001). [Available on-line: http://www.contryjoe.com/nightingale/pledge.htm]. Accessed September 2, 2002.

INDEX

PRETEST KEY

Home Health Nursing: A Comprehensive Review of Practical and Professional Issues

Question	Answer	Chapter
1	D	1
2	B	1
3	C	2
4	B	2
5	C	2
6	C	3
7	D	4
8	C	4
9	B	4
10	D	4
11	A	5
12	C	6
13	B	6
14	D	6
15	C	7
16	B	7
17	C	8
18	C	8
19	D	9
20	C	9

Notes

Notes

Notes

Notes

Western Schools® offers over 1,400 hours to suit all your interests – and requirements!

Visit us online at **westernschools.com** for all our latest CE offerings!
For a free catalog call **1-800-438-8888**

REV. 3/22/06